form and image
in the fiction of
   HENRY
MILLER

Jane A. Nelson
Bradford Junior College

*form and image
in the fiction of*
*HENRY
MILLER*

WAYNE STATE UNIVERSITY PRESS, DETROIT, 1970

Published simultaneously in Canada
by The Copp Clark Publishing Company
517 Wellington Street, West
Toronto 2B, Canada.

Library of Congress Catalog Card Number: 69-10515
Standard Book Number: 8143-1400-7

contents

5

Contents

acknowledgments

To Professor James Gindin of the University
of Michigan, department of English, I am indebted for numerous helpful suggestions and criticisms. Without his encourage-
ment this study might have dared less. To Professor Joe Lee
Davis of the same department, who encouraged my first interest in Henry Miller, I owe a special debt many years overdue.
I would also like to thank Professors Edwin A. Engel and Lyall
H. Powers of the department of English and Professor Robert
J. Niess of the department of Romance languages and literature,
University of Michigan, for their generous assistance and comments. Professor Marvin Felheim's thoughtful criticisms of
the manuscript led to a number of final revisions. Others have
contributed substantially to this book: Professors John Virtue
and Thomas Dume of the department of English, Eastern
Michigan University, drew a number of bibliographical items
to my attention; Mr. W. B. Rea, University of Michigan, aided
my search for financial assistance; Professor Glenn Wright,
a former colleague in the department of American thought
and language at Michigan State University, read and proofread
early stages of the manuscript; Dr. Ann Ridgeway criticized a
late draft and saw to numerous details connected with pre-

paring it for publication; Mrs. Mary K. Hervol patiently typed from a difficult copy; Charles Nelson cheerfully ran numerous errands and suffered considerable domestic inconvenience during its writing. I wish also to remember those friends abroad who sent me copies of Miller's books unavailable at that time in this country and thank the Wolgamot Society of Ann Arbor for finding others. I hope I have made suitable acknowledgment in my text to the scholars and critics whose thought I have found most stimulating in recent years. They cannot be considered responsible, however, for any distortions of their ideas nor for the uses to which I put them. In addition, I wish to thank Mrs. Elizabeth Pass, of Wayne State University Press, for her painstaking work with my manuscript.

I am grateful to the publishers and individuals listed below for their generous cooperation in granting permission to reprint the extensive quotations in this book. Such inclusions were necessary because of the relative unfamiliarity of many of the sources I used. It was also desirable to have important passages from Miller's fiction available on the page for close analysis.

Beacon Press: Simon O. Lesser, *Fiction and the Unconscious* (© 1957).

H. H. Brinton, *The Mystic Will* (© 1930; published by The Macmillan Co.).

Cornell University Press: Angus Fletcher, *Allegory: The Theory of a Symbolic Mode* (© 1964 by Cornell University. Used by permission of Cornell University Press).

Grove Press, Inc.: The following works by Henry Miller: *Tropic of Cancer* (© 1961); *Tropic of Capricorn* (© 1961); *Black Spring* (© 1963); *The Rosy Crucifixion* (© 1965).

Harcourt, Brace & World, Inc.: C. G. Jung, *Modern Man in Search of a Soul*, trans. W. S. Dell and Cary F. Baynes (© 1933).

The Hogarth Press Ltd., Mrs. Katharine Jones, and Liveright Publishing Corporation: Ernest Jones, *On the Nightmare* (© 1951).

Indiana University Press and Oxford University Press: Wolfgang Kayser, *The Grotesque in Art and Literature*, trans. Ulrich Weisstein (© 1963).

The Julian Press, Inc.: Thomas Wright, *Sexual Symbolism: A History of Phallic Worship*, Vol. 2: *The Worship of the Generative Powers during the Middle Ages of Western Europe* (© 1957).

The Macmillan Company and Chatto and Windus Ltd.: J. B. Beer, *Coleridge the Visionary* (© 1959).

New Directions Publishing Corp. and Laurence Pollinger Limited: The following works by Henry Miller: *The Books in My Life* (all rights reserved); *Sunday after the War* (© 1944 by H. M.); *The Wisdom of the Heart* (© 1941 by New Directions)—reprinted by permission of New Directions.

Princeton University Press: Northrop Frye, *Anatomy of Criticism* (© 1957).

Princeton University Press and the Bollingen Foundation and Routledge & Kegan Paul Ltd.: Mircea Eliade, *The Myth of the Eternal Return*, trans. Willard R. Trask, Bollingen Series XLVI (© 1954); Erich Neumann, *The Origin and History of Consciousness*, trans. R. F. C. Hull, Bollingen Series XLII (© 1954) and *The Great Mother*, trans. Ralph Manheim, Bollingen Series XLVII (© 1955); *The Collected Works of C. G. Jung*, eds. G. Adler, M. Fordham, and H. Read, trans. R. F. C. Hull, Bollingen Series XX, Vol. 5: *Symbols of Transformation* (© 1956), Vol. 7: *Two Essays on Analytical Psychology* (© 1953), Vol. 8: *The Structure and Dynamics of the Psyche* (© 1960), Vol. 9, Pt. 1: *The Archetypes and the Collective Unconscious* and Vol. 9, Pt. 2: *Aion: Researches into the Phenomenology of the Self* (© 1959), Vol. 11: *Psychology and Religion: West and East* (© 1958), Vol. 12: *Psychology and Alchemy* (© 1953), Vol. 14: *Mysterium Coniunctionis* (© 1963); C. G. Jung and Carl Kerényi, *Essays on a Science of Mythology: The Myth of the Divine Child and the Mysteries of Eleusis*, trans. R. F. C. Hull, Bollingen Series XXII (© 1949).

Stein and Day, Inc. and Jonathan Cape Ltd.: Leslie A. Fiedler, *Waiting for the End* (© 1964 by L. A. F.).

Twayne Publishers, Inc.: Kingsley Widmer, *Henry Miller* (© 1963).

introduction

More than thirty years after the publication of his first major work, Henry Miller's literary reputation remains uncertain and insecure. Those who acknowledged his ability early did so cautiously,[1] recognizing that his work defied precise definition and description. To what extent was he writing autobiography? Or novel? Was his Paris world a Bohemian underground or an inner landscape to which the psychoanalyst rather than the literary critic had greater access? Even sympathetic critics found the word *literature* unsatisfactory when it was used to describe Miller's work.[2]

His importance was more readily acknowledged in France, where, after all, his books were available. In 1947 one French study of modern American literature included a chapter on Henry Miller, prophesying that America would eventually recognize and accept him as an important writer. The same critic also realized that Miller's offensive realism should be explained by the anagogic pattern: his search for the absolute requires that he must first loathe and denounce before he acquires the power to move toward God or the absolute.[3] His is the traditional path of the visionary and mystic, whatever apparently strange roads he insists on traveling.

Such recognition of Miller's importance and thematic concerns does not appear in American literary histories, however. If his work is mentioned at all, it is with an uneasy reluctance to accept him as a significant contributor to American literature. Critics often find it difficult to separate his work from his life, moreover, and both from an "offensive irrelevance" to the times through which he lived, despite his recent and flourishing popularity. Although Leslie Fiedler finds it astonishing that Miller could turn his back on human misery during the period of the Great Depression, he does find in his work a significant relevance to the present: "Miller is the laureate or, better, the prophet of the new personalism, and hence the first important self-consciously anti-tragic writer in America." [4] Fiedler still sees Miller's fiction, however, as autobiographical in a narrow sense, and the precise nature of Miller's prophecy goes unexamined.

The first difficulty one has in evaluating Henry Miller is recognizing the nature of his vision. Tolerant readers can identify the street-corner prophet immediately and acknowledge his insistence that our civilization is a nightmare to be denounced. Yet he says nothing that is new or surprising on this subject. Those who recognize the religious intensity and consistency of his prophetic proclamations about the self, however, are often unwilling to acknowledge that such visions are substantial and universal. Like Kingsley Widmer, they see only adolescent posturing, although they recognize the vitality and sincerity that emerge from what they call formlessness and bad taste.[5] In reviews of Miller's works helpless paradoxes emerge: Miller is a "basement" transcendentalist who writes "wearisome surrealism," "acres of plain careless" prose, and yet is our greatest existentialist and the "presiding genius at the *Götterdämmerung* of American transcendentalism." [6]

Certainly before we praise or condemn Miller, we must clearly recognize the nature of his vision. The extreme and contradictory responses to his work suggest that this recognition has not yet occurred. The present study will develop one approach to Miller that may help to describe his vision and to identify the allegorical structure of the fiction that represents it. The analysis should serve to place him more securely among writers of literary confessions and not among novelists. Such classification is also necessary before we evaluate his achievement.

Miller belongs properly among those writers whose work Jung characterizes as *visionary*. Jung distinguishes between two modes of artistic creation, the *visionary* and the *psychological*. *Psychological* works of literature are those in which the writer's fictional world is easily recognized by what we call "consciousness," even though the reader may be forced to become fully aware of what he does not wish to confront. But the nature of a *visionary* work is different, and Jung's description of it reminds us of Miller's fiction:

> It arises from timeless depths; it is foreign and cold, many-sided, demonic and grotesque. A grimly ridiculous sample of the eternal chaos—a *crimen laesae majestatis humanae*, to use Nietzsche's words—it bursts asunder our human standards of value and of aesthetic form. The disturbing vision of monstrous and meaningless happenings that in every way exceed the grasp of human feeling and comprehension makes quite other demands upon the powers of the artist than do the experiences of the foreground of life. . . . But the primordial experiences rend from top to bottom the curtain upon which is painted the picture of an ordered world, and allow a glimpse into the unfathomed abyss of what has not yet become.[7]

Jung goes on to describe the usual reaction provoked by such visionary works:

> We are astonished, taken aback, confused, put on our guard or even disgusted—and we demand commentaries and explanations. We are reminded in nothing in everyday, human life, but rather of dreams, night-time fears and the dark recesses of the mind that we sometimes see with misgiving. The reading public for the most part repudiates this kind of writing—unless, indeed, it is coarsely sensational—and even the literary critic feels embarrassed by it.[8]

Such visions may lead us to conclude that a highly personal experience lies behind the literary form, reducing the work itself to a problem in pathology. Jung argues, however, that the work of the visionary artist should be considered "the symbolic expression" of something imperfectly known. It is the world that seers, prophets, and enlighteners have been acquainted with throughout man's history, and it should be studied in its own right.

Visionary art lends itself successfully to archetypal criticism. A close scrutiny of the images in Henry Miller's fiction, for example, will reveal unmistakably the outlines and forms of these archetypes. In fact, those very episodes in which the images seem especially incongruous and the symbols hopelessly obscure, actually reveal the symbolic action central to the significance of Miller's early fiction.

One is able to discern not only the archetypal images but certain processes or patterns which define the self Miller is exploring and the nature of the struggle in which his narrative *I* is engaged. Behind what is apparently an account of amorous adventures—ludicrous, monstrous, and grotesque—is a struggle of the *I* as consciousness seeking to establish its independence from the unconscious, symbolized by the Archetypal Feminine and manifested in the female figures of Miller's world as well as in myriad non-human forms.[9]

These images of the Archetypal Feminine are among the most significant of those which fill the pages Miller writes. His prose is characteristically highly textured in the sense that few passages appear in which there is not a proliferation of images. Jung has pointed out that the archetype itself can never be described, since it is a "form" of the unconscious, but that the images which fill out this form are the means by which the archetype "appears" to consciousness and is experienced by it. This process, which Jung designates a "symbolic process," is an "experience in images and of images." [10] The images of the Archetypal Feminine which the *I* experiences in Miller represent only one aspect of the transpersonal unconscious Jung postulates. Yet, because the unconscious is frequently experienced as feminine, it is as a manifestation of the feminine that Miller's narrator usually encounters the unconscious as something threatening or promising, the source both of creative power and castrating dominance.

The first part of this study explores the extent to which a Jungian analysis of the archetypal processes and images provides the reader with sufficient insight into the nature of

Miller's vision for the traditional outlines of this vision to be recognized. In the second part, the archetypal symbols of the self are identified, and their relationship to the larger concerns of the theoretical arguments that appear in Miller are explained. In the last part, I suggest the patterns into which the adventures of the *I*, which is in the process of becoming, can be organized. The nature of the *I*'s progress is examined in the structure of *Tropic of Cancer, Tropic of Capricorn,* and *The Rosy Crucifixion,* with a few comments on *Black Spring.*

These works are linked together as parts in a larger allegorical structure, for the events in the fiction yield a continuing and coherent narrative of progress in the development of the *I* from its early struggles with a numinous and threatening, yet fertile, unconscious to plateaus of integration and extended "consciousness." The traditional experiences of the vision are arranged, not formlessly and chaotically, but according to certain patterns which are revealed both in the total structure and in individual works.

The fiction is a dramatization of the process of becoming, not a record of these events in the author's life. And the forms of the individual works, I will argue, can better be described as *confession* and *anatomy,* as Northrop Frye has used these terms, than by the more familiar *novel* and *autobiography.* In part one, for the convenience of examining the relationship between the archetypes and the devices which serve to give them literary form, I have limited discussion to the Archetypal Feminine, and, especially in chapter I, to the device of *fragmentation* as it appears in *Tropic of Cancer.*

To those who argue that Jung's theories are irrelevant in literary criticism, I can answer only that they provide the most substantial insight into those passages in Miller which are most obscure. When Northrop Frye points out that Jung's book on libido symbols is an important work of literary criticism, he recognizes its usefulness for the student of literature who wishes to explore symbolic structures. In *The Mind and Art of Henry Miller,* William A. Gordon has acknowledged the Jungian "spirit" of Miller's imagery, but not the extent to which these images are central to the form of his work and create, in fact, the city worlds of Paris and New York which dominate his fiction. Moreover, because the reader of Miller may not be familiar with Jung, without adequate and extensive commentary the central mythic pattern of the action in Miller remains obscure. Not only the images, but the allegorical mode in which they appear will be explored in the following chapters.

PART ONE

the archetypal feminine

Chapter One

Fragmentation and Confession in Tropic of Cancer

The demonic, obsessive quality of the erotic experience in Henry Miller's fiction has been sufficiently recognized, as have the Medusa characteristics of his women. This recognition, however, has not led his critics to examine the formal functions these darker aspects of the erotic have in his work. Kingsley Widmer in his remarks on Miller's obsession with the Dark Lady even asserts the contrary, arguing that this important theme does not provide a significant measure of concentration in individual works.[1] Instead, in a chapter devoted to an analysis of *Tropic of Cancer*, he finds the disorder of Miller's world the only important ordering principle:

> If the discrete fragments, as in the first two chapters of *Tropic of Cancer*, seem beyond order, then the very disorder, by imitative form, gives the quality of his "anecdotal life." [2]

Probably the term *fragmentation* best describes what happens in these first two chapters of *Cancer*, but not in the sense Widmer intends when he charges that this and the following sections have no formal unity. The moments sharply and brutally created by the imagery are not as entirely discrete as Widmer finds them. Many of them are part of a constellation of images revealing the outlines of a single archetypal image. The presentation of these images may be described as an attempt to dramatize the hero's confrontation with the archetypal and primordial figures of the Terrible Mother, the negative aspect of the Great Mother archetype described by Jung and others from their studies of myth, literature, religion, and clinical phenomena. Erich Neumann's account of the psychological process of fragmentation suggests the parallel literary process in *Tropic of Cancer* through which this archetypal figure begins to emerge:

> The power of the primordial Great Mother archetype rests on the original state where everything is intermingled and undifferentiated, not to be grasped because ever in flux. Only later do images emerge from this basal unity, forming a group of related archetypes and symbols revolving about this indescribable center. The wealth of images, qualities, and symbols is essentially a product of the fragmentation effected by a consciousness which perceives, discriminates, divides, and registers from a distance. *Determinatio est negatio.* The multiplicity of images corresponds to a multiplicity of possible attitudes and possible reactions of consciousness, contrasted with the original total-reaction that seizes upon primitive man.
>
> The overpowering dynamism of the archetype is now held in check: it no longer releases paroxysms of dread, madness, ecstasy, delirium, and death. The unbearable white radiance of primordial light is broken up by the prism of consciousness into a multicolored rainbow of images and symbols. Thus from the image of the Great Mother the Good Mother is split off, recognized by consciousness, and established in the conscious world as a value. The other part, the Terrible Mother, is in our culture repressed and largely excluded from the conscious world.[3]

The archetype appears in groups of symbols, some human, some not:

> Delayed reaction and de-emotionalization run parallel to this splitting of the archetype into groups of symbols. The ego ceases to be overwhelmed as consciousness becomes

more capable of assimilating and understanding the individual symbols. The world grows clearer, orientation is more possible, and consciousness is enlarged. An anonymous and amorphous primal deity is inconceivably frightful; it is stupendous and unapproachable, incomprehensible and impossible to manipulate. The ego experiences its formlessness as something inhuman and hostile, if indeed it ever tackles the impossible task of experiencing it. So we often find an inhuman god at the beginning in the form of a beast, or some horrid anomaly and monster of miscegenation. These hideous creatures are expressions of the ego's inability to experience the featurelessness of the primal deity. The more anthropomorphic the world of gods becomes, the closer it is to the ego and the more it loses its overwhelming character. The Olympian gods are far more human and familiar than the primeval goddess of chaos.[4]

I am making extensive use of this convenient correlation between mythology and psychology for two reasons. First, Neumann's explanation of the fragmentation of the archetype describes one significant and controlling aspect of form in Henry Miller's *Tropic of Cancer:* the movement from a vaguely defined and surrealistically expressed representation of the Terrible Mother to a more sharply focused but stylized description of human figures who represent the archetype and establish the patterns by which the *I* can become aware of its relationships to these chthonic forces. Second, Neumann's description of the process by which the contents of the psyche are made available to consciousness defines and reveals precisely the nature of *confession* and *anatomy* as Miller employs these forms.

Many readers of Miller's fiction have understood that they were reading an account of the author's life, close to actual in some instances. His intimate disclosures of sexual activity are still dear to the cultist who wishes to attack American puritanism. But it is necessary to take seriously his comments on *Tropic of Cancer* in *The World of Sex:* "Liberally larded with the sexual as was that work, the concern of its author was not with sex, nor with religion, but with the problem of self-liberation." [5] To define the nature of this self-liberation is more difficult than seems immediately apparent.

The question of Miller's form, moreover, becomes important if one recognizes in his work an unmasking of the contents of the unconscious. Simon O. Lesser suggests that Miller fails as a writer because he fails to "disguise and control" his revelations. His fictional unconscious brings us too close to the real:

> In its zeal to do justice to our repressed tendencies fiction is in constant danger of overstating the case for them. Particularly if it does this too directly, with a minimum of disguise and control—we think at once of such a writer as Henry Miller—it is likely to arouse aversion rather than pleasure. But it is not always easy to say whether a work of fiction or a reader is responsible for a failure of this sort. A work which in the perspective of time may seem well balanced may cause us to recoil because it insists on telling us more of the truth, above all more of the truth about ourselves, than we are prepared to accept.[6]

The control and disguise exercised by form will not be recognized in Miller if one approaches his fiction expecting the conventions of novel and romance. Even George Orwell, whose essay on Miller remains one of the best, insists that the tempo and narrative method of *Cancer* are those of the novel. He does recognize that *Cancer* is fiction, however, not autobiography.[7]

Kingsley Widmer castigates Miller for failing as a novelist, objecting to the weakness of Miller's narrative patterns and to his lack of narrative coherence. He finds the surrealistic episodes simply escapes from reality lacking relevance in structures of individual works. He objects to characterization which does not provide sufficient "past, future, and depth" for the characters. Nor can he accept Miller's own shady moral character.[8]

For several reasons, such a response to Miller must miss or distort whatever formal elements might be available to analysis. Widmer, for example, overlooks the significance of the seasons in *Cancer*, the descent into winter and the return to spring, which serve to organize the work more than may be immediately apparent. One cannot insist on a past or a future for his characters, moreover, because many are deliberate abstractions identified by stylized analyses of their weaknesses. Others are images of archetypes. His surrealistic episodes are not an escape from the reality of a dirty Paris and the everyday monotony of Bohemian existence (a reality which is not external at all—Paris, for example, has only symbolic existence), but a movement into an inner reality in which certain images bring us close to the archetypes Jung described. Here the fragmentation described by Neumann is especially operative.

In neither *confession* nor *anatomy*, as Northrop Frye has pointed out, is narrative pattern the important means of organization; hence, to insist on sustained narrative in Miller is irrelevant. In *confession*, the coherence of the author's character and attitudes and his integration of the significant events in his life provide the fictional pattern. In *anatomy*, moreover, people are not people, but representatives of mental attitudes. To insist on realistic characterization in such a form is also irrelevant. In neither form is the actual structure of society a concern, as it is for the novelist.[9] Much more remains to be said on all these points in connection with *Cancer*. But at the beginning it is necessary to consider formal devices not usually identified with the analysis of the novel. Fragmentation is such a device.

The fragmentation of the Archetypal Feminine permits Miller to present or bring into "consciousness" the chthonic forces of the unconscious which are, according to Jung, symbolized by the feminine. Miller's *I* must come to terms with these forces before it can be liberated or integrated. In fact, it is by means of this fragmentation that the events in the "author's" life are integrated and the requirements of the confession form are met. The literary presence of the Great Mother figure is manifested not only in human forms, but in almost all congeries of images in *Cancer*, including the inorganic and animal. These elemental symbols of the Archetypal Feminine are more important in *Tropic of Cancer* than in *Capricorn*, in which a later stage in the process of the integration of the *I* is dramatized.

The central symbol of the Archetypal Feminine in *Cancer* is not a human figure but Paris itself. Miller's world is a city world. But his harlot-thronged streets and filthy alleys do not provide the reader with a tourist's guide to a Paris nether world. In passage after passage the symbolic significance of the city emerges with such insistence that a real Paris never appears. This characteristic led one of Miller's critics to complain that Miller is incapable of developing a sense of place:

> So extreme is this defect that it is often difficult to remember which of the *Tropics* deals with Paris, and which one with New York. When Miller describes a scene, he injects so many of his personal intellectual responses that the scene scarcely exists as a visual entity any longer.[10]

Frank Kermode, who recognized that Miller's Paris is pointedly symbolic, saw the city as representative of twentieth-century American and European civilization, especially (and oddly) the "puritan cultures" of the North.[11] However, his subsequent insight—the basic situation is that of the artist in a slum civilization—is too narrowly sociological. Interpretations which see Miller's nightmare city-world as symbolic of the diseased cultures of an unfortunate century do not explain why his descriptions of this city-world reproduce it almost exclusively in images and symbols that are traditional representations of the Archetypal Feminine.

Womb, cave, underworld, city, house, abyss, sea, and fountain are elemental symbols of the Archetypal Feminine. As a maternal symbol, the city is the harborer of her inhabitants. But the faithful city can also become a harlot,[12] the diseased organism that Miller describes:

> The city sprouts out like a huge organism diseased in every part, the beautiful thoroughfares only a little less repulsive because they have been drained of their pus.[13]

Miller's Paris is also a womb, the belly of the whale into which the artist must descend before he can be reborn or transformed:

> After leaving the Pension Orfila that afternoon I went to the library and there, after bathing in the Ganges and pondering over the signs of the zodiac, I began to reflect on the meaning of that inferno which Strindberg had so mercilessly depicted. And, as I ruminated, it began to grow clear to

> me, the mystery of his pilgrimage, the flight which the poet
> makes over the face of the earth, and then, as if he had been
> ordained to re-enact a lost drama, the heroic descent to the
> very bowels of the earth, the dark and fearsome sojourn in
> the belly of the whale, the bloody struggle to liberate him-
> self, to emerge clean of the past, a bright, gory sun god cast
> up on an alien shore. It was no mystery to me any longer
> why he and others (Dante, Rabelais, Van Gogh, etc., etc.)
> had made their pilgrimage to Paris. I understood then why it
> is that Paris attracts the tortured, the hallucinated, the great
> maniacs of love.[14]

The journey into the belly of the whale is fraught with danger,
for the female figure is terrible as the representative of death
for the individual. For Jung the belly of the whale is the land
of the dead where the monster Mother figure must be con-
quered before transformation or rebirth can occur.

> The Feminine is the belly-vessel as woman and also as
> earth. She is the vessel of doom, guiding the nocturnal course
> of the stars through the underworld; she is the belly of the
> "whale-dragon," which, as in the story of Jonah, swallows
> the sun hero every night in the west; she is "the destroyer at
> eventide."
>
> The Great Mother as Terrible Goddess of the earth and of
> death is herself the earth, in which things rot. The Earth
> Goddess is "the devourer of the dead bodies of mankind"
> and the "mistress and lady of the tomb." Like Gaea, the
> Greek Earth Mother, she is mistress of the vessel and at the
> same time the great underworld vessel itself, into which the
> dead souls enter, and out of which they fly up again.[15]

Such is the significance of the remainder of the passage in *Cancer* in which Miller compares his sojourn in Paris to the journey into the belly of the whale:

> One walks the streets knowing that he is mad, possessed, be-
> cause it is only too obvious that these cold, indifferent faces
> are the visages of one's keepers. Here all boundaries fade
> away and the world reveals itself for the mad slaughterhouse
> that it is. The treadmill stretches away to infinitude, the
> hatches are closed down tight, logic runs rampant, with
> bloody cleaver flashing. The air is chill and stagnant, the

language apocalyptic. Not an exit sign anywhere; no issue save death. A blind alley at the end of which is a scaffold.

> An eternal city, Paris! More eternal than Rome, more splendorous than Nineveh. The very navel of the world to which, like a blind and faltering idiot, one crawls back on hands and knees. And like a cork that has drifted finally to the dead center of the ocean, one floats here in the scum and wrack of the seas, listless, hopeless, heedless even of a passing Columbus. The cradles of civilization are the putrid sinks of the world, the charnel house to which the stinking wombs confide their bloody packages of flesh and bone.[16]

The first descriptions of the city to appear in *Cancer* are found in section one, in what may fairly be called intense, separate, and distinct moments.

But there is a substratum to be explored in these first two disorderly sections of *Cancer*. We are moving in a twilight world of semi-consciousness, and symbolic relationships among the numerous images can be mapped.

In the first two descriptions of Paris, for example, the traditional symbols of the Archetypal Feminine appear and hence the forces of the unconscious which the Feminine represents. In the first of these passages the city is realized as a watery, darkening world in which spider web and serpent figures are dimly suggested:

> Twilight hour. Indian blue, water of glass, trees glistening and liquescent. The rails fall away into the canal at Jaurès. The long caterpillar with lacquered sides dips like a roller coaster. It is not Paris. It is not Coney Island. It is a crepuscular melange of all the cities of Europe and Central America. The railroad yards below me, the tracks black, webby, not ordered by the engineer but cataclysmic in design, like those gaunt fissures in the polar ice which the camera registers in degrees of black.[17]

The theriomorphic emblem of the spider appears throughout *Cancer* associated with the female figure: ". . . I could no more think of loving Germaine than I could think of loving a spider; and if I *was* faithful, it was not to Germaine but to that bushy thing she carried between her legs." [18] Elsewhere Miller describes "the great sprawling mothers of Picasso, their breasts covered with spiders, their legend hidden deep in the labyrinth." [19] Erich Neumann discusses the symbolism of spider and web in connection with the witch characteristics of the negative Mother: "Net and noose, spider, and the octopus with its ensnaring arms are here the appropriate symbols." [20] He points out that these images appear in situations in which an individual is struggling to free himself from the Great Mother. Jung, commenting on the significance of this symbol, fixed its meaning for the passage we have been examining: "The center of the unconscious process is . . . often pictured as a spider in its web, especially when the conscious attitude is still dominated by fear of unconscious processes." [21] An example of this symbolism in Jung's text is similar to the formation of the symbol in Miller's passage; a section from the frontispiece of a collection of Brahminic sayings is reproduced, showing a web encircled by the uroboros, the figure of the snake biting its tail.[22] The parallel is not as important here as the observation that serpent, water, and spider—traditional symbols of the Archetypal Feminine—are the symbols chosen for the first impression of Paris and are symbols which appear again and again in connection with the city. Whenever the movement in *Cancer* is toward a "surreal" description of events or psychic states, these symbols and other equally important ones emerge. And they are related to the movement toward the frozen, motionless world of ice developed at great length in the episode when Miller visits Dijon, the penultimate episode of the book.

In the second passage describing Paris in the first section of *Cancer* equally significant images appear:

> Indigo sky swept clear of fleecy clouds, gaunt trees infinitely extended, their black boughs gesticulating like a sleep-walker. Somber, spectral trees, their trunks pale as cigar ash. . . . For the moment I can think of nothing—except that I am a sentient being stabbed by the miracle of these waters that reflect a forgotten world. All along the banks [of the Seine] the trees lean heavily over the tarnished mirror; when the wind rises and fills them with a rustling murmur they will shed a few tears and shiver as the water swirls by.

> I am suffocated by it. No one to whom I can communicate even a fraction of my feelings. . . .[23]

The mixed figures of speech destroy any illusion of an actual scene, and it is only in context that the river described can be identified as the Seine. The scene is experienced entirely in terms of the observer's reactions to images of sky, water, trees, and wind. These images produce a sense of isolation and of suffocation. The *I* is aware of feelings which cannot be communicated. But the symbols have important traditional values which are unmistakably involved here. Jung has identified water as "the commonest symbol of the unconscious. The lake in the valley is the unconscious, which lies, as it were, underneath consciousness, so that it is often referred to as the 'subconscious,' . . ." [24] Water is also one of the most persistent archetypal symbols of the maternal and the feminine. The Archetypal Feminine is identified by Jung with the positive forces of the unconscious: "The water that the mother, the unconscious, pours into the basin belonging to the anima is an excellent symbol for the living power of the psyche." [25] But the unconscious is also the terrifying and destructive Terrible Mother.

In the passage in which Miller walks along the Seine, he is walking along a dreadful river—a tarnished mirror, lined by somber and spectral trees, trees that shiver in the wind that rises and fills them. Jung has described the archetypal pattern of such experience as the apprehension of the autonomous nature of the spirit rushing over dark waters. The mirror at the bottom of the water is the unconscious into which consciousness must look. Jung comments on the need for this experience in the symbolically impoverished twentieth century:

> Whoever has elected for the state of spiritual poverty, the true heritage of Protestantism carried to its logical conclusion, goes the way of the soul that leads to the water. This water is no figure of speech, but a living symbol of the dark psyche.[26]

The appropriateness of these comments for Miller's quest, although their language is perhaps too religious or vaguely "mystical" for literary analysis, is confirmed by the overwhelming repetition of such experience in *Cancer*.

The city scenes of *Cancer* represent only one group of symbols which make the figure of the archetypal Terrible Mother available to the consciousness of the *I*. The process of fragmentation also produces monstrous female figures which combine animal and human features or coalesce with the streets and buildings of the city itself. The symbolic role of the city as representative of the Archetypal Feminine is verified in these figures, for the identification of the two permits them to coalesce, the parts of the female revealing the feminine significance of the city. Such almost human figures belong to the grotesque iconography of Miller's world,[27] and in their archetypal dimension are interchangeable with images of the city scene:

> Tania is a fever, too—*les voies urinaires,* Café de la Liberté, Place des Vosges, bright neckties on the Boulevard Montparnasse, dark bathrooms, Porto Sec, Abdullah cigarettes, the adagio sonata *Pathétique,* aural amplificators, anecdotal seances, burnt sienna breasts, heavy garters, what time is it, golden pheasants stuffed with chestnuts, taffeta fingers, vaporish twilights turning to ilex, acromegaly, cancer and delirium, warm veils, poker chips, carpets of blood and soft thighs.[28]

The destruction of spatial barriers between entities is even more apparent in the description of Llona:

> She had a German mouth, French ears, Russian ass. Cunt international. When the flag waved it was red all the way back to the throat. You entered on the Boulevard Jules-Ferry and came out at the Porte de la Villette. You dropped your sweetbreads into the tumbrils—red tumbrils with two wheels, naturally. At the confluence of the Ourcq and Marne, where the water sluices through the dikes and lies like glass under the bridges. Llona is lying there now and the canal is full of glass and splinters; the mimosas weep, and there is a wet, foggy fart on the windowpanes.[29]

Several of these visually fragmented female figures appear in the twilight consciousness of section one in *Tropic of Cancer*. By different names—Tania, Irène, Llona—they are manifestations of a devouring, castrating, chthonic Aphrodite, fascinating and deadly aspects of the Terrible Feminine. But their effect on the *I* can be positive: Tania is equated with chaos, which is destructive but also the source of the writer's inspiration. Her "Jewishness" makes her both fascinating and hateful. Irène is another deadly figure: "The trouble with Irène is that she has a valise instead of a cunt. She wants fat letters to shove in her valise." [30] The letters here are creative efforts, productions, aspects of the individual which are devoured. Of Llona:

> Men went inside her and curled up. . . . She would cut off your prick and keep it inside her forever, if you gave her permission. . . . her tongue was full of lice and tomorrows. Poor Carol, he could only curl up inside her and die. She drew a breath and he fell out—like a dead clam.[31]

The roles of these figures as wives and mistresses in the Bohemian fringe world Miller appears to inhabit are incidental to their function as symbols of the unconscious. They share this function with the city.

Like the whores and hags which throng the streets of Miller's Paris, these women are stylized by terms which insist on outlining their sexual functions. Scientific or discreet references to human anatomy could scarcely serve as effectively to underline the sexual characteristics of the human figure. Such stylization emphasizes their symbolic possibilities as efficiently for the contemporary reader as did the crude reproductions of the female exposing herself carved on the doorways of Irish churches or the ritual exhibitionism of an Etruscan goddess for those in other ages.[32] The terms used are not those of the medical textbook,[33] which would suggest a dead world of clinical abstractions. On the contrary, in certain circumstances they are quite ordinary and would pass unnoticed. Only in a literary context from which they are ordinarily excluded can they serve to effect the kind of stylization needed to render the significance of these half-realized figures. For the figures themselves are taboo.

The Gorgonesque quality of the chthonic feminine is clearly recognized in the figure of Mona, a character of even

greater significance in *Tropic of Capricorn*. She never becomes
a realistically developed character, for it is the outline of her
symbolic role that is important. In her manifestation in *Cancer*,
she belongs to the same configuration of images as the other female figures and the city. Like Aphrodite, she rises

> . . . out of a sea of faces and embraces me, embraces me pas-
> sionately—a thousand eyes, noses, fingers, legs, bottles, win-
> dows, purses, saucers all glaring at us and we in each other's
> arms oblivious. I sit down beside her and she talks—a flood
> of talk. Wild consumptive notes of hysteria, perversion, lep-
> rosy. I hear not a word because she is beautiful and I love
> her and now I am happy and willing to die.[34]

The "sea" from which she rises is itself created from a number
of non-human symbols of the Feminine. In a later passage her
Gorgonesque nature is revealed:

> I wake from a deep slumber to look at her. A pale light is
> trickling in. I look at her beautiful wild hair. I feel some-
> thing crawling down my neck. I look at her again, closely.
> Her hair is alive. I pull back the sheet—more of them. They
> are swarming over the pillow.[35]

The figure of the Gorgon is one of the most familiar representations of the Terrible Mother in ancient mythology, and
the symbolism of this figure is intimately related to the significance of the other symbols I have pointed out:

> Among the symbols of the devouring chasm we must count
> the womb in its frightening aspect, the numinous heads of
> the Gorgon and the Medusa, the woman with beard and phal-
> lus, and the male-eating spider. The open womb is the de-
> vouring symbol of the uroboric mother,[36] especially when
> connected with phallic symbols. The gnashing mouth of the
> Medusa with its boar's tusks betrays these features most
> plainly, while the protruding tongue is obviously connected
> with the phallus. The snapping—i.e., castrating—womb ap-
> pears as the jaws of hell, and the serpents writhing round the
> Medusa's head are not personalistic—pubic hairs—but
> aggressive phallic elements characterizing the fearful aspect
> of the uroboric womb. The spider can be classified among
> this group of symbols, not only because it devours the male

after coitus, but because it symbolizes the female in general, who spreads nets for the unwary male.[37]

The crawling vermin in Mona's hair, the serpents and spiders, the lice and bedbugs of the "filthy" scenes of *Tropic of Cancer* represent only a few of the important theriomorphic images in the book, but images peculiarly appropriate to the demonic world of the Terrible Feminine. Wolfgang Kayser has noted their appearance as one of the distinguishing motifs of grotesque literature:

> Certain animals are especially suitable to the grotesque— snakes, owls, toads, spiders—the nocturnal and creeping animals which inhabit realms apart from and inaccessible to man. Partly for the same reason (to which their uncertain origin is added) the same observation applies to vermin.[38]

The appropriateness of the images is clear if we remember Kayser's final definition of the grotesque as "an attempt to invoke and subdue the demonic aspects of the world." It is the power and scenery of this world that Miller's fragmentation is attempting to describe in *Tropic of Cancer*. The demonic underworld is inescapable. It is another "fragment" in which the Archetypal Feminine, the persistent symbol of the unconscious and its dangerous but fecund character, appears.

Often the filthy world in which these vermin thrive erupts, like the autonomous and powerful unconscious, into the world of cleanliness and order, as in the opening section of *Cancer*:

> I am living at the Villa Borghese. There is not a crumb of dirt anywhere, nor a chair misplaced. We are all alone here and we are dead.

> Last night Boris discovered that he was lousy. I had to shave his armpits and even then the itching did not stop. How can one get lousy in a beautiful place like this? But no matter. We might never have known each other so intimately, Boris and I, had it not been for the lice.[39]

The filthy world is necessary to the "sterile world," for without it, fertility, creation, and life are impossible. At the end of the first section, Mona and Miller leave the "filthy" Paris hotel for the Hôtel des Etats-Unis: "No more bedbugs now. The rainy season has commenced. The sheets are immaculate." [40] But encounters with the demonic world are dangerous and unpleasant. Just before an important scene in which the hero confronts the surrealistically developed figure of the Terrible Feminine, the filthy world is described in terms which register his fear and aversion:

> When I sit down to eat I always sit near the window. I am afraid to sit on the other side of the table—it is too close to the bed and the bed is crawling. I can see bloodstains on the gray sheets as I look that way, but I try not to look that way. I look out on the courtyard where they are rinsing the slop pails.[41]

The crawling vermin belong to the archetype of the Terrible Mother, clearly apparent in the serpentine hair of the Gorgonesque Mona.

Much of the animal imagery also belongs to the primordial world of the Great Mother archetype [42] and thronging animal images in *Tropic of Cancer* are one of the means by which Miller dramatizes twilight states of consciousness. Even the theriomorphic significance in the title of the book is appropriate to its thematic concerns. Cancer, the crab, is first of all a feminine sign in the zodiac. It is the sign in which the sun begins to retreat and the days grow shorter, a cold sign. Jung speaks of its significance in astrology as "feminine and watery." [43] Cancer is also the house of the moon, Luna, believed to secrete the dew or sap of life, and when all the planets are in Cancer, the end of the world by water will occur.

Not all of the animal images in *Tropic of Cancer* delineate or belong to the archetypes of the Great Mother or the Terrible Mother, however. The animal figures or images can also be the symbolic carriers of the archetype of the self, Jung's "supraordinate personality" which includes the unconscious as well as the "ego":

> Because of its unconscious component the self is so far removed from the conscious mind that it can only be *partially expressed by human figures;* the other part of it has to be expressed by *objective, abstract symbols.* The hu-

man figures are father and son, mother and daughter, king and queen, god and goddess. Theriomorphic symbols are the dragon, snake, elephant, lion, bear, and other powerful animals, or again the spider, crab, butterfly, beetle, worm, etc. Plant symbols are generally flowers (lotus and rose). These lead on to geometrical figures like the circle, the sphere, the square, the quaternity, the clock, the firmament, and so on. The indefinite extent of the unconscious component makes a comprehensive description of the human personality impossible. Accordingly, the unconscious supplements the picture with living figures ranging from the animal to the divine, as the two extremes outside man, and rounds out the animal extreme, through the addition of vegetable and inorganic abstractions, into a microcosm. These addenda have a high frequency in anthropomorphic divinities, where they appear as "attributes." [44]

However, among those which appear in section one of *Cancer*—and the list is long—many symbolize or "decorate" the world of the Archetypal Feminine. In the following passage, for example, the lion is emblematic of the forces which destroy the figure of the over-intellectualized Jew who refuses to recognize their reality:

> There are people who cannot resist the desire to get into a cage with wild beasts and be mangled. They go in even without revolver or whip. . . . [The Jew's] courage is so great that he does not even smell the dung in the corner. The spectators applaud but he does not hear. The drama, he thinks, is going on inside the cage. The cage, he thinks, is the world. Standing there alone and helpless, the door locked, he finds that the lions do not understand his language. Not one lion has ever heard of Spinoza. Spinoza? Why they can't even get their teeth into him. "Give us meat!" they roar, while he stands there petrified, his ideas frozen, his *Weltanschauung* a trapeze out of reach. A single blow of the lion's paw and his cosmogony is smashed. [45]

As a primordial image of powerful forces—forces which oppose the independence of consciousness—the lion is a primitive symbol frequently associated with the figure of the Great Mother, often in her terrible aspect as goddess of night, evil, and death. [46] To single out one image for comment, however, only draws attention to the entire complex of animal images in Miller's prose and their significance for the process of fragmentation in Miller's development of the confession.

The male figures of *Tropic of Cancer* are the subject of later discussion except that I wish to point out here that their significance in *Cancer* is not in their social roles of Jewish intellectual or Bohemian playboy but in their relationship to the chthonic feminine. Castration, dismemberment, and mutilation are the motifs which define this relationship in the descriptions of Paris and the accounts of various male "characters." The narrator draws attention to *A Man Cut in Slices*, the title of a book placed in a Paris shop window. In a dream he sees Van Norden, one of the important male figures, "about to walk away when suddenly he notices that his penis is lying on the sidewalk. It is about the size of a sawed-off broom-stick." [47] Paris streets "remind one of nothing less than a big chancrous cock laid open longitudinally." [48]

It is the relationship with a smothering, castrating, dismembering aspect of the Terrible Feminine that is important in Miller's description of Moldorf, who appears briefly in sections one and two. The archetypal nature of this relationship is underlined by the characteristics of Moldorf: Moldorf, Miller writes, is God. He is a dwarf: "Moldorf, multiform and unerring, goes through his roles—clown, juggler, contortionist, priest, lecher, mountebank." [49] His fate is to be symbolically dismembered in a fantasy scene in section two which ends when his wife Fanny consumes him: "There is something inside her, tickling, and tickling." [50] The entire scene, the figure of the dwarf himself, produces a curious melange of images and events that appear to justify one critic's characterization of Miller's fiction as an "overflowing surrealist cocktail." [51]

But reduced to its elements, the archetypal pattern emerges. The devouring destructive Feminine is represented in Moldorf's life by a domestic and conventional wife. But she shares with her whorish sisters in *Cancer* a destructive role described in almost the same terms as the others I have mentioned. Moldorf's "fate," his dwarf's stature, his designation as "God"—even perhaps Miller's choice of the sacred dung-beetle image to describe him (the Egyptian scarab was the emblem of the sun as the God who begets himself) [52]—suggest an archetypal pattern familiar in the mythology of the Great Mother. Moldorf is the companion God of the Great Mother:

> The young men whom the Mother selects for her lovers may impregnate her, they may even be fertility gods, but the fact remains that they are only phallic consorts of the Great Mother, drones serving the queen bee, who are killed off as soon as they have performed their duty of fecundation.
>
> For this reason these youthful companion gods always appear in the form of dwarfs. The pygmies who were worshiped in Cyprus, Egypt, and Phoenicia—all territories of the Great Mother—display their phallic character just like the Dioscuri, the Cabiri, and the Dactyls, including even the figure of Harpocrates.[53]

The young God-dwarf was killed or castrated as soon as he performed his function of fecundating the Great Mother:

> Death and dismemberment or castration are the fate of the phallus-bearing, youthful god. Both are clearly visible in myth and ritual, and both are associated with bloody orgies in the cult of the Great Mother.[54]

Moldorf's experience is similar to Van Norden's:

> "I tell you, when she climbs over me I can hardly get my arms around it. It blots out the whole world. She makes me feel like a little bug crawling inside her." [55]

Moldorf is the traditional homunculus,[56] belonging, as does the satyr Van Norden, to the figure of the Terrible Mother and representing one of the "human" figures in terms of which the power of the Terrible Goddess is demonstrated.

I have been speaking somewhat indiscriminately of the Great Mother and the Terrible Mother archetypes as representations of the Archetypal Feminine. Although they are related, these figures should be separated insofar as their "literary presence" is important for an analysis of the fragmentation of archetypes in *Tropic of Cancer*. For the Jungian psychoanalyst, the archetype *an sich* cannot be visually represented, and I am describing only the "perceptible, actualized representation or 'archetypal image.'"[57] The attempts to make the archetype perceptible to consciousness through a variety of images is called *fragmentation,* a term I have borrowed to describe the proliferation of "archetypal" images in Miller. The form of his fiction should not be considered a transcription of a psychic process, or a "case history," however. Such exclusive focus and concentration on certain experiences which could be called "archetypal" would seem unlikely to occur in a case history.

Yet such focus and "unity" are familiar formal characteristics of works of literature. If at the end of this study the reader is convinced that the images and experiences analyzed can be described acceptably in Jungian terms, then he may also be willing to see in the total form of Miller's work a unified allegorical structure. Miller's technical problem was one of making archetypal processes and experiences plausible to his audience. This he accomplishes in part by creating the illusion of a twentieth-century city world in which his isolated protagonist wanders on an endless "quest." The nature of this city world, however, is clearly archetypal, rendered in images which reveal the character of the Archetypal Feminine, the most inclusive term of those I have used. In *Tropic of Cancer* these images are traditionally those which have symbolized the archetype in myth, dreams, literature, and art. They appear in several strata.

The least ordered of these projections produces the archetype in elemental terms:

> The world around me is dissolving, leaving here and there spots of time. The world is a cancer eating itself away. . . . I am thinking that when the great silence descends upon all and everywhere music will at last triumph. When into the womb of time everything is again withdrawn chaos will be restored and chaos is the score upon which reality is written. You, Tania, are my chaos. It is why I sing. It is not even I, it is the world dying, shedding the skin of time. I am still alive, kicking in your womb, a reality to write upon.[58]

The symbolism of this passage is that of the Great Round, the womb of chaos; even the figure of the circular snake that bites its own tail is suggested in the cancer eating itself away and the world that sheds its skin of time.[59] Spatial entities do not exist in the "womb of time." This chaos is fertile for the self, "the score upon which reality is written."

This symbolism develops into the differentiated symbolism of the Archetypal Feminine, which has both negative and positive significance: tomb and womb, underworld and cave; symbols of containing and protection such as shield, veil, bowl, grail, earth, and water. When human forms, however monstrous, begin to emerge in the symbolic representations of the Feminine, the Terrible Mother appears in the Gorgons and other destructive goddess figures; the Good Mother appears in quite different projections.[60] All of these projections are manifestations of aspects of the transpersonal unconscious, especially the negative forces of the unconscious, which are seen as feminine antagonists to the efforts of consciousness to free itself. Moreover, these figures are alternately frightening and fascinating. From the unconscious, with its intermingling of positive and negative forces, must flow not only what is evil, but what is vital. The integration of the individual, the transformation of the artist "in the belly of the whale," the confrontation of the deadly aspects of the Feminine and the escape from them—these are the patterns into which the images of Miller's confession are arranged.

The *I* cannot escape confrontations with the deadly aspects of the Archetypal Feminine. In *Cancer*, the androgynous, Gorgonesque figure at the center of Paris, who first appears in Miller's description of the Lesbian Madame Delorme, reappears in a later surrealist episode unmistakably parallel to the first. In his encounter with Madame Delorme, he must penetrate deep into a palace in the city:

> How I ever got to Madame Delorme's, I can't imagine any more. But I got there, got inside somehow, past the butler, past the maid with her little white apron, got right inside the palace with my corduroy trousers and my hunting jacket —and not a button on my fly. Even now I can taste again the golden ambiance of that room where Madame Delorme sat

upon a throne in her mannish rig, the goldfish in the bowls, the maps of the ancient world, the beautifully bound books; I can feel again her heavy hand resting upon my shoulder, frightening me a little with her heavy Lesbian air.[61]

All the symbolic possibilities of this scene are realized in the later episode:

Standing in the courtyard with a glass eye; only half the world is intelligible. The stones are wet and mossy and in the crevices are black toads. A big door bars the entrance to the cellar; the steps are slippery and soiled with bat dung. The door bulges and sags, the hinges are falling off, but there is an enameled sign on it, in perfect condition, which says: "Be sure to close the door." Why close the door? I can't make it out. I look again at the sign but it is removed; in its place there is a pane of colored glass. I take out my artificial eye, spit on it and polish it with my handkerchief. A woman is sitting on a dais above an immense carven desk; she has a snake around her neck. The entire room is lined with books and strange fish swimming in colored globes; there are maps and charts on the wall, maps of Paris before the plague, maps of the antique world, of Knossus and Carthage, of Carthage before and after the salting. In the corner of the room I see an iron bedstead and on it a corpse is lying; the woman gets up wearily, removes the corpse from the bed and absent-mindedly throws it out the window. She returns to the huge carven desk, takes a goldfish from the bowl and swallows it. Slowly the room begins to revolve and one by one the continents slide into the sea; only the woman is left, but her body is a mass of geography.[62]

Miller's familiarity with the experiments of surrealism may have influenced his choice of images here, but the relationship with the earlier scene would argue against considering it an irrelevant literary exercise. The symbols clearly outline the archetype of the Terrible Feminine:

The terrible aspect of the Feminine always includes the uroboric snake woman, the woman with the phallus,[63] the unity of child bearing and begetting, of life and death. The Gorgon is endowed with every male attribute: the snake, the tooth, the boar's tusks, the out-thrust tongue, and sometimes even with a beard.

> In Greece the Gorgon as Artemis-Hecate is also the mistress of the night road, of fate, and of the world of the dead. As Enodia she is the guardian of crossroads and gates, and as Hecate she is the snake-entwined moon goddess of ghosts and the dead . . . .
>
> . . . As Good Mother, she is mistress of the East Gate, the gate of birth; as Terrible Mother, she is mistress of the West Gate, the gate of death, the engulfing entrance to the underworld. Gate, door, gully, ravine, abyss are the symbols of the feminine earth-womb; they are the numinous places that mark the road into the mythical darkness of the underworld.[64]

This is the enthroned, androgynous, frightening figure that Miller descends to meet symbolically in the cellar of a Paris courtyard. A mistress of the dead, deep in cave or palace, behind doors, a figure that can coalesce with continents that slide into the sea (itself one of the most persistent symbols of the Feminine)—here in many of its manifestations is the archetypal figure of the Terrible Feminine. The motif of swallowing underscores the deadliness of this figure for the *I* is symbolized by the fish [65] in its womb-like vessel. Another ancient symbol of the self, the eye,[66] appears in this passage. In the "courtyard," however, the eye is inadequate—a glass eye that sees only half the world.

Miller's ubiquitous mistress of the dead, her body a mass of geography, is a figure of fantasy; her symbolic trappings belong to the surreal world. But in the passages immediately preceding the cellar scene, the androgynous figure is suggested by the "character" Olga, apparently a part of the "real" world, the filthy Paris which both attracts and repels the *I*, filled as it is with the odors of rancid butter and halitosis, crawling with vermin and misshapen human figures. It is a Paris in which Miller sees Notre Dame rising like a tomb from the water.

The figure of Olga is unmistakably marked by masculine characteristics and even plays a masculine role in the filthy world, although the maternal, providing role of the Archetypal Feminine figure—its positive aspect—is more apparent than the destructive:

> It was just a few days ago that Olga got out of the hospital where she had her tubes burned out and lost a little excess weight. However she doesn't look as if she had gone through much suffering. She weighs almost as much as a camel-backed locomotive; she drips with perspiration, has halitosis, and still wears her Circassian wig that looks like excelsior. She has two big warts on her chin from which there sprouts a clump of little hairs; she is growing a mustache.

> The day after Olga was released from the hospital she commenced making shoes again. At six in the morning she is at her bench; she knocks out two pairs of shoes a day. . . . If Olga doesn't work there is no food.[67]

The "Madame Delorme" fantasy scene is an inner experience of the Archetypal Feminine. The external world in *Cancer* reveals a less direct (because it is projected on the outside world) but nevertheless similar relationship between the *I* and aspects of the Archetypal Feminine outlined in this analysis. The movement between this inner and outer world is part of the action of the book.

Appropriately, at the center of Paris the *I* finds an androgynous symbol of the elemental Feminine. In *Cancer*, moreover, elemental symbols dominate. In the later *Capricorn*, Mona/Mara appears in almost human form and dominates the symbolic structure. New York (the negative Feminine) is not quite as important in *Capricorn* as Paris is in *Cancer*. And the difference should be noted, for Paris, although deadly and destructive, is also a city of creation and birth. The negative and positive aspects of the Feminine lie side by side.

Although the confrontation of the negative can occur in Paris itself, Paris is contrasted with an entirely negative city in *Cancer:* Dijon. Winter is the season in which the hero of *Cancer* leaves Paris for Dijon, where he has secured a position as teacher of English. The stay in Dijon is a "descent into Hell," into a winter land where he confronts most directly the images which haunt the book. Only by such a descent and confrontation, however, can the *I* be truly integrated. Isolation drives him far into himself, where he must meet the implications of the archetypal experience:

Who am I? What am I doing here? I fall between the cold walls of human malevolence, a white figure fluttering, sinking down through the cold lake, a mountain of skulls above me. I settle down to the cold latitudes, the chalk steps washed with indigo. The earth in its dark corridors knows my step, feels a foot abroad, a wing stirring, a gasp and a shudder. I hear the learning chaffed and chuzzled, the figures mounting upward, bat slime dripping aloft and clanging with pasteboard golden wings; I hear the trains collide, the chains rattle, the locomotive chugging, snorting, sniffing, steaming and pissing. All things come to me through the clear fog with the odor of repetition, with yellow hangovers and Gadzooks and whettikins. In the dead center, far below Dijon, far below the hyperborean regions, stands God Ajax, his shoulders strapped to the mill wheel, the olives crunching, the green marsh water alive with croaking frogs.[68]

Miller finds himself in the dark corridors of the earth. The archetypal labyrinth is suggested by these dark corridors, and by the corridors through which the *I* must grope every night, seeking his room in darkness. Its image belongs to the Archetypal Feminine:

The labyrinthine way is always the first part of the night sea voyage, the descent of the male following the sun into the devouring underworld, into the deathly womb of the Terrible Mother. This labyrinthine way, which leads to the center of danger, where at the midnight hour, in the land of the dead, in the middle of the night sea voyage, the decision falls, occurs in the judgment of the dead in Egypt, in the mysteries both classical and primitive, and in the corresponding processes of psychic development in modern man. Because of its dangerous character, the labyrinth is also frequently symbolized by a net, its center as a spider.

In the rites of Malekula, the monster Le-hev-hev, as negative power of the Feminine, is also associated with the spider; with the man-devouring "mythical ogress," "the crab woman" with two immense claws; with the underworld animal, the rat; and with a giant bivalve that when opened resembles the female genital organ, and in shutting endangers man and beast.[69]

We are often in a similar world in *Cancer*. In descriptions of Paris, for example, the web of the spider appears in scenes where it is not deliberately emphasized:

> The railroad yards below me, the tracks black, webby, not ordered by the engineer but cataclysmic in design, like those gaunt fissures in the polar ice which the camera registers in degrees of black.[70]

In the Dijon episode, Ajax labors at the negative wheel of life, for the mill and loom are symbols of fate and death; this symbol has appeared before in *Cancer* when it is clearly at the center of the land of the dead:

> In the middle of the street is a wheel and in the hub of the wheel a gallows is fixed. People already dead are trying frantically to mount the gallows, but the wheel is turning too fast. . . .[71]

In Dijon Miller comes to a sterile dead world that is figuratively his "voyage to the land of the dead," the winter world into which he must descend before he can obtain the equilibrium he reaches in the last section of the book. Here he recognizes that he has to live "separate," not separate from others, but separate from the psychic pull of the unconscious, the symbol of which is the Archetypal Feminine:

> Going back in a flash over the women I've known. It's like a chain which I've forged out of my own misery. Each one bound to the other. A fear of living separate, of staying born. The door of the womb always on the latch. Dread and longing. Deep in the blood the pull of paradise. The beyond. Always the beyond. It must have all started with the navel. They cut the umbilical cord, give you a slap on the ass, and presto! you're out in the world, adrift, a ship without a rudder. You look at the stars and then you look at your navel. You grow eyes everywhere—in the armpits, between the lips, in the roots of your hair, on the soles of your feet. What is distant becomes near, what is near becomes distant. Inner-outer, a constant flux, a shedding of skins, a turning inside out. You drift around like that for years and years, until you find yourself in the dead center, and there you

slowly rot, slowly crumble to pieces, get dispersed again. Only your name remains.[72]

The eyes that he grows everywhere are symbols of the self, the inner self, the Purusha, "thousand-eyed," the Rudra with eyes on all sides, symbols of consciousness and of the creative powers of the soul,[73] hence separate from the Great Mother, which in her devouring, paradisaical aspect is deadly, and destroys the individual. The *I* finds himself in the dead-center of winter Dijon, the land of the dead. In this penultimate section of *Cancer* he has reached the bottom. With spring he returns to Paris, and finally (after an episode in which he encourages and assists his young friend to escape from a predatory French girl) he reaches the equilibrium of the final section of the confession:

> After everything had quietly sifted through my head a great peace came over me. Here, where the river gently winds through the girdle of hills, lies a soil so saturated with the past that however far back the mind roams one can never detach it from its human background. . . . So quietly flows the Seine that one hardly notices its presence. It is always there, quiet and unobtrusive, like a great artery running through the human body. In the wonderful peace that fell over me it seemed as if I had climbed to the top of a high mountain; for a little while I would be able to look around me, to take in the meaning of the landscape.
>
> Human beings make a strange fauna and flora. From a distance they appear negligible; close up they are apt to appear ugly and malicious. More than anything they need to be surrounded with sufficient space—space even more than time.
>
> The sun is setting. I feel this river flowing through me—its past, its ancient soil, the changing climate. The hills gently girdle it about: its course is fixed.[74]

Its course is fixed to the sea. One has only a brief time on the mountain. The river here seen is positive, fecundating, flowing, connecting the individual with the past, especially the human past. But the *I* has achieved a certain independence and equilibrium in this last scene in *Cancer:* a considerable transformation has occurred. The flowing of the river through his body suggests that the creative power of the unconscious is now available to him, whereas in Dijon all was frozen and dead.

The flowing imagery of *Cancer*, one of the most important of the non-human forms into which the Archetypal Feminine is fragmented, is complex and polysemous. These images belong to the water symbolism associated with the Great Mother. They are among the most primordial representations of her essential nature, and reflect the ambivalent response of man to the forms and powers of his unconscious. As "water" she is the source of life and—in dissolution—transformation and death.

Neumann has summarized the forms taken by this figure in ancient mythology and religion:

> The Great Goddess is the flowing unity of subterranean and celestial primordial water, the sea of heaven on which sail the barks of the gods of light, the circular life-generating ocean above and below the earth. To her belong all waters, streams, fountains, ponds, and springs, as well as the rain. She is the ocean of life with its life—and death—bringing seasons, and life is her child, a fish eternally swimming inside her, like the stars in the celestial ocean of the Mexican Mayauel and like men in the fishpool of Mother Church—a late manifestation of the same archetype.[75]

Such images of the Great Mother may be fearful and repellent at times, dangerous to the individual consciousness. Yet they are incestuously attractive in the promise of a womb-like release from the shocks sustained by consciousness.

The images of flowing have been noticed by most readers of *Cancer*, as have the womb symbols. But for the most part, Kingsley Widmer's comment on the meaning of these symbols is typical. They have been considered emblems of the flux of the events in life, an interpretation which can explain the river imagery but which seems inadequate if one considers the traditional meanings associated with fountain, urine, sweat, menstrual blood—in fact all flowing, fluid substances in Miller. Widmer's reading, moreover, does not explain the ambivalence of the *I* toward this imagery, and the different relationships the *I* establishes with it. His comments on the relationship between the central imagery of flowing and the events of *Cancer* illustrate my point:

> Miller seems defeated by the sordidness of the place [Dijon], the futility of teaching, the loneliness of the displaced bohemian among the pedants, and even by a childish fear of the dark and the foreign. His exuberance falters; he recognizes "a fear of living separate, of staying born." Though the message throughout *Cancer* turns on the acceptance, even embracement, of the flowing chaos of life, here the "constant flux" brings the shipwrecked sailor of the American voyage to "dead center, and there you slowly rot." Unable to accept the flux in its ordinary round of misery or to continue shouting King of the Hill from the top of the quite unmiraculous pile of everyday excrement, Miller abruptly flees Dijon and goes back to Paris where he can play the artist as burlesque and apocalyptic confidence man. The meaningless world can best be accepted in romantic and rebellious terms, as an artistic-religious vision, and not as the ordinary substance of life. Perhaps partly in spite of himself, Miller makes a striking confession in this episode which just precedes the final chapter of the book and which helps explain his culminating refusal to return to ordinary American life: the excremental absurdity of life demands that one have a rebellious role as the outsider abroad.[76]

If one considers the archetypal significance of Miller's images, he reaches quite different conclusions.

These conclusions affect the reader's recognition of Miller's form. The essential formal element of *confession*, according to Northrop Frye, is that the author's "mind" be integrated on subjects that are introverted but intellectualized in content. Hence the passages in which the "inner" meaning of the Dijon episode is examined by Miller and the relationship of the self to the images in which the archetype appears are central. Just before the Christmas holidays (again, it is in the winter of the year that the "hero" leaves for Dijon) Miller had visualized in brutal sexual imagery the obscenity of contemporary experience—paralysis, inertia, and the attempt to make the earth into an "arid plateau of health and comfort." These are obscenities because they indicate that the source (the crater—the familiar womb symbol, feminine symbol of the unconscious) is dry:

The dry, fucked-out crater is obscene. More obscene than anything is inertia. More blasphemous than the bloodiest oath is paralysis. If there is only a gaping wound left then it must gush forth though it produce nothing but toads and bats and homunculi.[77]

(Toads, bats, and homunculi are the familiars of the grotesque world, for the unconscious must have negative as well as positive aspects.) Even if the dark forces produce only the demonic, at least we are in touch with the sources of "reality." It is not the impermanence of life, filled with horror and hell as well as heaven, that dismays the hero, but the denial of its source and the loss of its vitality.

The *I* must free for himself the "flow" of the unconscious, by challenging its threat to overwhelm consciousness (the desire to return to the womb) and by confronting its negative as well as its positive character:

"I love everything that flows," said the great blind Milton of our times. I was thinking of him this morning when I awoke with a great bloody shout of joy: I was thinking of his rivers and trees and all that world of night which he is exploring. Yes, I said to myself, I too love everything that flows: rivers, sewers, lava, semen, blood, bile, words, sentences. I love the amniotic fluid when it spills out of the bag. I love the kidney with its painful gallstones, its gravel and what-not; I love the urine that pours out scalding and the clap that runs endlessly; I love the words of hysterics and the sentences that flow on like dysentery and mirror all the sick images of the soul; I love the great rivers like the Amazon and the Orinoco, where crazy men like Moravagine float on through dream and legend in an open boat and drown in the blind mouths of the river. I love everything that flows, even the menstrual flow that carries away the seed unfecund. I love scripts that flow, be they hieratic, esoteric, perverse, polymorph, or unilateral. I love everything that flows, everything that has time in it and becoming, *that brings us back to the beginning where there is never end:* the violence of the prophets, the obscenity that is ecstasy, the wisdom of the fanatic, the priest with his rubber litany, the foul words of the whore, the spittle that floats away in the gutter, the milk of the breast . . . *all that is fluid, melting, dissolute and dissolvent,* all the pus and dirt that in flowing

47

is purified, that loses its sense of origin, *that makes the great circuit toward death and dissolution. The great incestuous wish is to flow on, one with time, to merge the great image of the beyond with the here and now. A fatuous, suicidal wish that is constipated by words and paralyzed by thought.*[78]

All symbols of creative power in this passage acknowledge the fecundity of the "crater," the womb, the great Feminine Archetype of the unconscious. But the lines in italics point out the danger facing the self: the powerful, incestuous wish. The "acceptance" without differentiation of this flow and flux leads to "death," and the wish for such dissolution is primordial. Here is a clear statement of the intellectual recognition of the nature of the fecund depths of the individual, and of the necessity of avoiding the "fatuous, suicidal wish." The relationship described is elemental (certainly all the images in the passages support such an interpretation) and dangerous: the incest described suggests the uroboric incest outlined in Neumann's analysis of the elemental representations of the Great Mother archetype, along with the problem of "transformation" on the elementary level which faces the development of the individual consciousness.

> The life feeling of every ego consciousness that feels small in relation to the powers is dominated by the preponderance of the Great Round that encompasses all change. This archetype may be experienced outwardly as world or nature or inwardly as fate and the unconscious. In this phase the elementary feminine character, which still contains the transformative character within it, is "worldly"; natural existence with all its regular changes is subservient to it. The central symbol of this constellation is the unity of life amid the change of seasons and the concurrent transformation of living things. . . . the death character of the material-maternal is an expression of this archetypal domination of nature and the unconscious over life, and likewise over the undeveloped childlike, or youthfully helpless, ego consciousness. In this phase the Archetypal Feminine not only bears and directs life as a whole, and the ego in particular, but also takes everything that is born of it back into its womb of origination and death.[79]

When the narrator speaks of the incestuous wish to dissolve in the flow, he is not advocating a simple acceptance of the flow of life; he is speaking of what has been described as *uroboric incest:*

> Uroboric incest is a form of entry into the mother, of union with her, and it stands in sharp contrast to other and later forms of incest. In uroboric incest, the emphasis upon pleasure and love is in no sense active, it is more a desire to be dissolved and absorbed; passively one lets oneself be taken, sinks into the pleroma, melts away in the ocean of pleasure —a *Liebestod.*[80]

Neumann is not speaking of the personal mother:

> This incest reflects the activity of the maternal uroboros, of the Great Mother archetype, mother of life and death, whose figure is transpersonal and not reducible to the personal mother.[81]

Miller's desire to escape the Mother, a theme which pervades his fiction, is a desire to escape the dissolution of the self that surrender to the unconscious would demand.

The relationship with the "flow" that the *I* must establish if it is to become independent and escape the frozen wastes of the "dead center" requires an assertion of independence and at the same time a winning of creative energy from the unconscious. Equilibrium, or integration of the *I*, establishes just such a relationship, although it is only temporary. No real end to the glittering and deadly power of the unconscious exists, nor would such an end be desirable.

Only by experiencing the archetype through the images into which it is fragmented and arriving at conscious or intellectual recognition of "divisions" of the Archetypal Feminine is the *I* "born." And this integration and intellectualization provides the integrated pattern which identifies the confession form.

Chapter Two

The Emblems of Heaven and Hell

The female figures of Miller's New York and Paris are also emblems of the Archetypal Feminine. These figures are not characters in a mimetic fictional world, although they produce at first glance the illusion of "realism." If Miller chooses to describe the underside of city life, then hags and prostitutes are appropriate human decoration for such scenery, one might assume. Their symbolic dimension might be ignored. In the following description of the Place St. Sulpice, for example, until the last sentence or two the reader is not obliged to consider the symbolic relationships between the images which define the square and the hags and prostitutes who are the human subjects of the passage:

> Or wandering along the Seine at night, wandering and wandering, and going mad with the beauty of it, the trees leaning to, the broken images in the water, the rush of the current under the bloody lights of the bridges, the women sleeping in doorways, sleeping on newspapers, sleeping in the rain; everywhere the musty porches of the cathedrals and beggars and lice and old hags full of St. Vitus' dance; pushcarts stacked up like wine barrels in the side streets, the smell of berries in the market place and the old church sur-

rounded with vegetables and blue arc lights, the gutters slippery with garbage and women in satin pumps staggering through the filth and vermin at the end of an all-night souse. The Place St. Sulpice, so quiet and deserted, where toward midnight there came every night the woman with the busted umbrella and the crazy veil; every night she slept there on a bench under her torn umbrella, the ribs hanging down, her dress turning green, her bony fingers and the odor of decay oozing from her body; and in the morning I'd be sitting there myself, taking a quiet snooze in the sunshine, cursing the goddamned pigeons gathering up the crumbs everywhere. St. Sulpice! The fat belfries, the garish posters over the door, the candles flaming inside. The Square so beloved of Anatole France, with that drone and buzz from the altar, the splash of the fountain, the pigeons cooing, the crumbs disappearing like magic and only a dull rumbling in the hollow of the guts. Here I would sit day after day thinking of Germaine and that dirty little street near the Bastille where she lived, and that buzz-buzz going on behind the altar, the buses whizzing by, the sun beating down into the asphalt and the asphalt working into me and Germaine, into the asphalt and all Paris in the big fat belfries.[1]

The emblematic significance of the hag figure in this passage becomes more apparent when her appearance is compared with her appearance elsewhere in Miller's fictional world. Hags are found everywhere—as lavatory attendants,[2] vicious concierges, or lascivious mothers—sometimes simply as "decoration." Their symbolic role as personifications of aspects of the Great Mother, especially the negative, chthonic Terrible Mother archetype, usually is not central in the action, although as central figure in a passage from *Black Spring* the hag's inimical symbolic significance is unmistakable. In this episode from the mind's "Coney Island" she appears as the Gorgon, threatening dissolution and death:

The old hag removes her wrapper and stands before the mirror in her chemise. She has a little powder puff in her hand and with this little puff she swabs her armpits, her bosom, her thighs. All the while she weeps like an idiot. Finally she comes over to me with an atomizer and she squirts a fine spray over me. I notice that her hair is full of rats.

I watch the old hag moving about. She seems to be in a trance. Standing at the dresser she opens and closes the drawers, one after the other, mechanically. She seems to have forgotten what she remembered to go there for. Again she picks up the powder puff and with the powder puff she daubs a little powder under her armpits. On the dressing table is a little silver watch attached to a long piece of black tape. Pulling off her chemise she slings the watch around her neck; it reaches just to the pubic triangle. There comes a faint tick and then the silver turns black.

. . . .

Suddenly the old hag comes dancing in stark naked, her hands aflame. Immediately she knocks over the umbrella stand the place is in an uproar. From the upturned umbrella stand there issues a steady stream of writhing cobras traveling at lightning speed. They knot themselves around the legs of the tables, they carry away the soup tureens, they scramble into the dresser and jam the drawers, they wriggle through the pictures on the wall, through the curtain rings, through the mattresses, they coil up inside the women's hats, all the while hissing like steam boilers.

Winding a pair of cobras about my arms I go for the old hag with murder in my eyes. From her mouth, her eyes, her hair, from her vagina even, the cobras are streaming forth, always with that frightful steaming hiss as if they had been ejected fresh from a boiling crater. In the middle of the room where we are locked an immense forest opens up. We stand in a nest of cobras and our bodies come undone.[3]

"And our bodies come undone." In this fantasy Miller experiences the dissolution threatened by the Terrible Mother figure, for the images which charge this quasi-human figure with her symbolic nature are traditionally those associated with the negative elemental character of the Terrible Mother archetype. Even the forest in which this symbolic dissolution occurs is a central symbol of the Feminine—and the unconscious.[4]

Dissolution or symbolic castration is threatened by the negative Archetypal Feminine whenever it appears. Hence it is in terms of their sexual nature that the personifications of the Terrible Mother archetypes reveal themselves. The sexually aggressive accost Miller in dance halls and employment offices, subways and telephone booths. The sexually accessible are everywhere (even in "puritan" America). The puritan protests of those who resist the hero are thinly disguised sexual demands. As a result, in their relationships with his female "characters," Miller's male figures often emerge as little more than instruments of female gratification or phallic consorts. (The uncontrollable erections often described by Miller symbolize effectively the enthrallment of the male, his helplessness, his demonic possession.)

In *Tropic of Capricorn*, for example, the female figures are not realistically developed, but arranged as appearing and disappearing motifs, introducing or restating negative aspects of the Archetypal Feminine. They are all obsessively aggressive. Francie, who once attempted to seduce her brother to gratify herself, "used" the hero wherever she happened to be: "If we went dancing and she got too hot in the pants she would drag me to a telephone booth . . .";[5] Valeska, waiting with the narrator for his wife to return from an abortion, was suddenly "leaning against the table, her tongue halfway down my throat, my hand between her legs."[6] Lola, virgin and lascivious, gratifies herself vigorously:

> I was helping Lola to stoop down when suddenly she slipped, dragging me with her. She made no effort to get up; instead she caught hold of me and pressed me to her, and to my complete amazement I also felt her slip her hand in my fly. . . . and with it all she sunk her teeth into me, bruised my lips, clawed me, ripped my shirt and what the hell not. I was branded like a steer when I got home and took a look at myself in the mirror.[7]

The disappearance of these characters in the narrator's account is as casual and inevitable as the appearance of others to take their place. Francie is simply dropped for Trix and her sister. Valeska's suicide coincides with the introduction of Mara. As for Lola, her parents move to another city and the narrator never sees her again.

The aggressiveness of these women is symbolically castrating. The male, even when he is ostensibly the aggressor, is reduced to phallus:

> Every time I touched the piano I seemed to shake a cunt loose.

> If there was a party I had to bring the fucking music roll along; to me it was just like wrapping my penis in a handkerchief and slinging it under my arm.[8]

Miller's encounters with the whores of Paris and the sexually available in New York reveal almost without exception the deadliness and dangerousness of these figures as well as the nature of their fascination. As I have pointed out, even the "good" whore of Paris, Germaine (admired as "whore all the way through"), is equated with the spider symbol which is a ubiquitous symbol of the negative Feminine and the feared unconscious. She is not significant as a personality or a character or even a crude representative of the golden-hearted whore, but as another of the seemingly infinite representations of the essentially female.

The danger in the relationship with the unending personifications of the negative Feminine is underscored by the narrator's reaction to a long series of sexual adventures with his friend MacGregor in *Tropic of Capricorn:*

> On the surface it was jolly and happy-go-lucky; time passing like a sticky dream. But underneath it was fatalistic, premonitory, leaving me that next day morbid and restless.[9]

His morbidity and restlessness reveal the "sticky dream" as something other than a jolly and exhilarating jaunt through the world of sex; on the contrary, it symbolizes the enthrallment of the narrator and his dissolution. Destiny, order, meaning, identity are elsewhere, and the narrator is disturbed by his helplessness. He is vulnerable and uneasy, moreover, because he is undefined and undefinable. The self's protean nature is essentially formless at this point:

> I was really afraid of myself, of my appetite, my curiosity, my flexibility, my permeability, my malleability, my geniality, my powers of adaptation.[10]

Such vulnerability makes the hero an inevitable victim of the vigorous and myriad figures of the sexually aggressive woman. They function emblematically in Miller's obscene panorama as potent symbols of the threatening unconscious, as fragments (here rendered as partial personalities) of the Archetypal Feminine, the great "forest" where "our bodies come undone." (Death, one of the significant motifs in the structure of *Capricorn*, is the most complete dissolution of the self. For Miller dissolution is the inevitable thematic relationship between death and sex.)

The narrator in Miller's confessions moves through this world of demonic projections, of emblems charged with symbolic energy, as if possessed. Instead of an aimless drifting from adventure to adventure (which at first glance Miller's fiction seems to suggest), the hero moves toward his encounters as if compelled:

> The best thing for you to do now, Henry, is to go and get yourself a frosted chocolate and when you sit at the soda fountain keep your eyes peeled and forget about the destiny of man. . . . Instead of the frosted chocolate I keep walking and soon I'm exactly where I intended to be all the time, which is in front of the ticket window of the Roseland.[11]

The phrases "I keep walking and soon I'm exactly where I intended to be all the time" could stand as a fairly typical summary of much of the "action" of *Cancer* and *Capricorn*.

Angus Fletcher has pointed out that "the heroes of picaresque romance do not choose, they do not 'deliberate' but act on compulsion, continually demonstrating a lack of inner control."[12] Miller's narrator has suggested the picaresque hero to numerous readers, and he is certainly compelled in Fletcher's sense. The nature of this compulsion is defined by the iconographical texture of the world through which the narrator moves, especially those emblems of the Archetypal Feminine which represent the negative aspects of the Great Mother by which the hero is held in thrall. His fascination for these figures draws him through the labyrinthine streets or holds him in dramatic paralysis. His visit to Roseland dance hall is typical.

In the scene which draws his attention elemental images of
Jung's Archetypal Feminine are obvious:

> At the rail which fences off the floor I stand and watch
> them sailing around. This is no harmless recreation . . . this
> is serious business. At each end of the floor there is a sign
> reading "No Improper Dancing Allowed." Well and good.
> No harm in placing a sign at each end of the floor. In Pom-
> peii they probably hung a phallus up. This is the American
> way. . . .
>
> . . . At the outermost limit of this momentaneous nothing-
> ness my friend MacGregor arrives and is standing by my
> side and with him is the one he was talking about, the nym-
> phomaniac called Paula. She has the loose, jaunty swing and
> perch of the double-barreled sex, all her movements radiat-
> ing from the groin, always in equilibrium, always ready to
> flow, to wind and twist and clutch, the eyes going tic-toc,
> the toes twitching and twinkling, the flesh rippling like a
> lake furrowed by a breeze. This is the incarnation of the
> hallucination of sex, the sea nymph [13] squirming in the
> maniac's arms. . . . On the sea floor the oysters [14] are doing
> the St. Vitus dance, some with lockjaw, some with double-
> jointed knees. The music is sprinkled with rat poison, with
> the rattlesnake's venom, with the fetid breath of the gardenia,
> the spittle of the sacred yak. . . . Laura the nympho is
> doing the rhumba, her sex exfoliated and twisted like a
> cow's tail. . . . Laura the nympho brandishing her cunt,
> her sweet rose-petal lips toothed [15] with ballbearing
> clutches, her ass balled and socketed. . . . Laura the nym-
> pho cold as a statue, her parts eaten away, her hair musically
> enraptured. On the brink of sleep Laura stands with muted
> lips, her words falling like pollen through a fog. The Laura
> of Petrarch seated in a taxi, each word ringing through the
> cash register, then sterilized, then cauterized. Laura the bas-
> ilisk made entirely of asbestos, walking to the fiery stake
> with a mouth full of gum. Hunkydory is the word on her
> lips. The heavy fluted lips of the sea shell [16] . . . the lips of
> lost Uranian love.[17]

The dance-hall scene with its quasi-human figures of obvious emblematic significance is presented in a series of discontinuous images which nevertheless move toward a symbolic

resolution. The dissolution of these projections of the Arche-typal Feminine occurs at the end of the passage:

> All floating shadowward through the slanting fog. Last mur-muring dregs of shell-like lips slipping off the Labrador coast, oozing eastward with the mud tides, easing starward in the iodine drift. Lost Laura, last of the Petrarchs, slowly fad-ing on the brink of sleep. Not gray the world, but lackluster, the light bamboo sleep of spoon-backed innocence.
>
> And this in the black frenzied nothingness of the hollow of absence leaves a gloomy feeling of saturated despondency not unlike the topmost tip of desperation which is only the gay juvenile maggot of death's exquisite rupture with life. From this inverted cone of ecstasy life will rise again into prosaic skyscraper eminence, dragging me by the hair and teeth, lousy with howling empty joy, the animated fetus of the unborn death maggot lying in wait for rot and putrefaction.[18]

It is not surprising that the ultimate dissolution—that of death—appears. The *I* of the confession does not simply "ob-serve" the dance-hall scene. He has "engaged" symbolically with manifestations of the Terrible Feminine.

The figures of Roseland [19]—the twinkling, twitching, rip-pling, squirming Paula of the tic-toc eyes, and the Lolita-like reduction of Petrarch's Laura to a gum-chewing basilisk with "hunkydory" the word on her lips—are figures reduced to em-blems of demonic energy. Like all Miller's female figures, in-cluding even the more fully presented Mona/Mara, they have no mimetic "character." The hero establishes no "personal rela-tionships" with them, but is acted upon for good or evil or struggles to escape their fascination and domination. (Coitus with such figures is frequently described in highly symbolic terms. Often reduced to the ludicrous and grotesque or hyper-bolized into superhuman manifestations of consuming appetite, coitus becomes the symbolic engagement with a cacodemon in which the hero is reduced to phallic instrument.)

The impression of energy is produced in Miller's fictional world in several ways. Frequently it appears as the force which drives the hero through the labyrinths of his world—city street, corridor, symbolic uterus—or the magnetic force which draws him against his will into dangerous symbolic confrontations with fantasy figures or leads him toward the threat of dissolution. The consuming sexual appetites—the nymphomania, the satyriasis—the violent, aggressive, orgiastic approach to coitus: these are other ways in which demonic energy is manifested. Even the dramatic paralysis which holds the hero helpless, a victim of numinous fascination, is a manifestation of demonic power or energy.[20]

The shifting, discontinuous imagery by which the female figures are frequently described by Miller serves to create symbols of energy rather than mimetic characters who create the illusion of personalities. The hero is unable to establish human relationships with such figures:

> She is completely mine, almost slavishly so, but I do not possess her. It is I who am possessed. I am possessed by a love such as was never offered me before—an engulfing love, a total love, a love of my very toe-nails and the dirt beneath them—and yet my hands are forever fluttering, forever grasping and clutching, seizing nothing.[21]

All attempts to seize the "nothing" at the center of their being fail. The figures dissolve into synecdochic, emblematic parts. Although the impressions of their energy remain one of the constants in Miller's fiction, their "form" constantly defies mimetic reality:

> I lose the memory of words, of her name even which I pronounced like a monomaniac. I forgot what she looked like, what she felt like, what she smelt like, what she fucked like, piercing deeper and deeper into the night of the fathomless cavern. I followed her to the deepest hole of her being, to the charnel house of her soul, to the breath which had not yet expired from her lips. I sought relentlessly for her whose name was not written anywhere, I penetrated to the very altar and found—nothing. I wrapped myself around this hollow shell of nothingness like a serpent with fiery coils; I lay still for six centuries without breathing as world events sieved through to the bottom forming a slimy bed of mucus. I saw the constellations wheeling about the huge hole in the ceiling of the universe; I saw the outer planets and the black

star which was to deliver me. I saw the Dragon shaking itself free of dharma and karma, saw the new race of man stewing in the yolk of futurity. I saw through to the last sign and symbol, *but I could not read her face.* I could see only the eyes shining through, huge, fleshy-like luminous breasts, as though I were swimming behind them in the electric effluvia of her incandescent vision.

How had she come to expand thus beyond all grip of consciousness? By what monstrous law had she spread herself thus over the face of the world, revealing everything and yet concealing herself? She was hidden in the face of the sun, like the moon in eclipse; she was a mirror which had lost its quicksilver, the mirror which yields both the image and the horror. Looking into the backs of her eyes, into the pulpy translucent flesh, I saw the brain structure of all formations, all relations, all evanescence. I saw the brain within the brain, the endless machine endlessly turning, the word Hope revolving on a spit, roasting, dripping with fat, revolving ceaselessly in the cavity of the third eye. I heard her dreams mumbled in lost tongues, the stifled screams reverberating in minute crevices, the gasps, the groans, the pleasurable sighs, the swish of lashing whips. I heard her call my own name which I had not yet uttered, I heard her curse and shriek with rage. I heard everything magnified a thousand times, like a homunculus imprisoned in the belly of an organ. I caught the muffled breathing of the world, as if fixed in the very crossroads of sound.[22]

The reality of such figures is mental. The names and places and personal histories they acquire in Miller are translucent envelopes through which their symbolic significance constantly shows and from which they easily slip. It is not a Paris underworld or Bohemian underworld which Miller describes as much as an underworld of the mind in which the *I* struggles. And it is the frankly allegorical nature of Miller's imagery which insists on this interpretation. The express iconographical function of his description of female genitalia is immediately apparent, for example, in this "scene" from *Cancer:*

Suddenly I see a dark, hairy crack in front of me set in a bright, polished billiard ball; the legs are holding me like a pair of scissors. A glance at that dark, unstitched wound and

a deep fissure in my brain opens up: all the images and memories that had been laboriously or absent-mindedly assorted,
labeled, documented, filed, sealed and stamped break forth
pell-mell like ants pouring out of a crack in the sidewalk;
the world ceases to revolve, time stops, the very nexus of my
dreams is broken and dissolved and my guts spill out in a
grand schizophrenic rush, an evacuation that leaves me face
to face with the Absolute. I see again the great sprawling
mothers of Picasso, their breasts covered with spiders, their
legend hidden deep in the labyrinth. And Molly Bloom
lying on a dirty mattress for eternity. On the toilet door red
chalk cocks and the madonna uttering the diapason of woe. I
hear a wild, hysterical laugh, a room full of lockjaw, and the
body that was black glows like phosphorus. Wild, wild, utterly uncontrollable laughter, and that crack laughing at me
too, laughing through the mossy whiskers, a laugh that
creases the bright, polished surface of the billiard ball. Great
whore and mother of man with gin in her veins. Mother of
all harlots, spider rolling us in your logarithmic grave, insatiable one, fiend whose laughter rives me! I look down into
that sunken crater, world lost and without traces, and I hear
the bells chiming, two nuns at the Palace Stanislas and the
smell of rancid butter under their dresses, manifesto never
printed because it was raining, war fought to further the
cause of plastic surgery, the Prince of Wales flying around
the world decorating the graves of unknown heroes. Every
bat flying out of the belfry a lost cause, every whoopla a
groan over the radio from the private trenches of the
damned. Out of that dark, unstitched wound, that sink of
abominations, that cradle of black-thronged cities where the
music of ideas is drowned in cold fat, out of strangled Utopias is born a clown, a being divided between beauty and
ugliness, between light and chaos, a clown who when he
looks down and sidelong is Satan himself and when he looks
upward sees a buttered angel, a snail with wings.[23]

Miller's characteristic posing of the female figure with legs
outspread to display her sex destroys any titillation a suggestive
veiling of these parts or a less brutal and direct approach might
achieve. Instead, the iconographic possibilities of meaning in
such a posture are explored. In this passage the presence of the
prostitute in a shabby Paris room is incidental. The categories
of space and time dissolve. Arranged so that her genitals are ex-

posed—it is not inappropriate to call such exposure *ritual* in Miller's fictional world—she becomes the harlot representative of the Great Mother archetype and the symbol of the fecundating and deadly, creative and destructive, unconscious.

This pose has its historic counterpart in the ritual exhibitionism of primitive religious representations of the Great Mother figure. Such displays of genitals were frequently associated with orgiastic rites and grim forms of worship which acknowledge the deadly aspects of the Great Feminine as much as her fecundating and fructifying function.[24] Such exhibitionism in western civilization is "shocking" or "obscene" rather than symbolically significant, perhaps because of the rise of a patriarchal society and its influence on conventional literary patterns. Such symbolism is "dead" for Miller's audience; it has gone underground. However, as Thomas Wright's early study of *The Worship of the Generative Powers* pointed out, the significance of such figures survived into the Middle Ages with considerable vigor:

> It is a singular fact that in Ireland it was the female organ which was shown in this position of protector upon the churches, and the elaborate though rude manner in which these figures were sculptured show that they were considered as objects of great importance. They represented a female exposing herself to view in the most unequivocal manner, and are carved on a block which appears to have served as the keystone to the arch of the door-way of the church, where they were presented to the gaze of all who entered. They appear to have been found principally in the very old churches, and have been mostly taken down, so that they are only found among the ruins.[25]

Wright mentions that figurines representing the female so exposed can be found in the art of "almost every country we know," and apparently as late as the fall of the Western Empire figurines of the female with genitals exposed were found in the part of Germany occupied by the Vandals, probably representing deities worshiped by these peoples.[26] Wright's analysis of the meaning of these representations might be superseded by various psychological and anthropological interpretations today, but his early study of such figures points both to the late continuation of their appearance into the Middle Ages and to the fact that considerably before the date in which his study appeared such symbolism had long since lost its vitality and meaning in a wide social context. Its appearance in the work of a twentieth-century writer of widespread if doubtful reputation suggests less that Miller's approach to his imagery is "original" or traditional than that in the twilight zone between conscious and unconscious reality these images are still powerfully effective in their archetypal significance.

The historical and psychological significances of what has happened to the sacred harlot figure in western civilization are suggested by Erich Neumann:

> The youth struggling for self-consciousness now begins, in so far as he is an individual, to have a personal fate, and for him the Great Mother becomes the deadly and unfaithful mother. She selects one young man after another to love and destroy. In this way she becomes "the harlot." The sacred prostitute—which is what the Great Mother really is, as the vessel of fertility—takes on the negative character of the fickle jade and destroyer. With this, the great revaluation of the feminine begins, its conversion into the negative, thereafter carried to extremes in the patriarchal religions of the West. The growth of self-consciousness and the strengthening of masculinity thrust the image of the Great Mother into the background; the patriarchal society splits it up, and while only the picture of the good Mother is retained in consciousness, her terrible aspect is relegated to the unconscious.[27]

This struggle for self-consciousness is reflected in Miller's relationship with those figures which suggest the Terrible Mother in his fiction.

The formal characteristics of such episodes as the one in which the Paris whore is described might have been suggested to Miller by his familiarity with the surrealist experimenters, but these experiments themselves belong to an older tradition. Wolfgang Kayser, for example, rejects the surrealists' contention that their art "relates only the most intimate personal experiences" and in their efforts to expand the "scope of the grotesque," he identifies motifs developed and continued through centuries.[28] And in a discussion of the "isolation" of surreal images (by such devices as deformation, overemphasis of a part, discrepancies in scale), Angus Fletcher has pointed out the relationship between emblematic devices in the allegorical literature of other centuries and the discontinuous imagery of surrealism.[29] Such imagery is allegorical insofar as it forces one to recognize "the sunken understructure of thought." [30]

The emblematic nature of female genitalia, the symbolic focus of female forms in Miller's fictional world, finds its nearest systematic exegesis in Neumann's analysis of these motifs as manifestations of the Great Mother archetype. In the long section of *Tropic of Capricorn* which records the narrator's sexual adventures in the company of the satyric MacGregor, for example, one significant motif after another appears, even in those figures which apparently belong to the world of mimetic fiction. "Personality" and character and intelligence—as well as individual human histories—are irrelevant. One woman's hairiness (and the suggestion of the Gorgon) is her only significant distinguishing "characteristic":

> . . . she had wonderful long fine black hair which she arranged in ascending and descending buns on her Mongolian skull. At the nape of the neck she curled it up in a serpentine knot. . . . In the summer she wore loose sleeves and I could see the tufts of hair under her arms. The sight of it drove me wild. I imagined her as having hair all over, even in her navel. And what I wanted to do was to roll in it, bury my teeth in it.[31]

The frank sensuality of another reminds Miller of the inevitable reptile: ". . . if she had any morals they were of the reptilian order." [32] The figures are demonic, energetic representatives of the Feminine. The dark figure of Valeska (suggesting perhaps the *nigredo* symbol[33]), the reptilian tresses of the Gorgonesque figures, the exaggerated breasts and buttocks, the flourishing pubic hair, the *vagina dentata*, the labyrinthian uterus, the insatiable sexual appetite—such characteristics are rendered visually and brutally. The female figure is insistently stylized, although few readers miss the sense of energy the descriptions convey even in the "decorative" emblems of the archetype which appear casually in scene after scene, in city squares, or parks, or theatres:

> In the gallery opposite me, in the front row, sits a woman with her legs spread wide apart; she looks as though she had lockjaw, with her neck thrown back and dislocated. The woman with the red hat who is dozing over the rail—marvellous if she were to have a hemorrhage! if suddenly she spilled a bucketful on those stiff shirts below.[34]

As I observed in comments on *Cancer* in the last chapter, even Mona/Mara, the figure who most closely approaches the mimetic and the figure who is most important structurally in Miller's fiction, appears, as do these less developed figures, in those images which reveal the negative Feminine. A comparison of the passages in which she is described and the passages in which the whores of Paris are described will quickly demonstrate their similarities.

In *Cancer* and *Capricorn* especially, she appears in the same form, as part of the continuous but "separating" pattern of archetypal motifs. The similarity in form obtains from the discontinuous imagery (which forces analysis), the "dissolving" character of the imagery (which merges the human form with geography, sound, or movement), the visual absurdity, and the grotesque combinations of the human, animal, vegetable, and mineral. The effect of immense energy which is produced by these figures may well be the source of those critical judgments which proclaim that "there is no questioning his imaginative and emotional power, or the flesh and blood of the life he creates." But these women are not "flesh and blood" as we usually understand this phrase. These emblems in Miller's fiction insist on interpretation as "timeless" archetypal representations of the Great Mother, figures which break through the twentieth-century skin of his fiction repeatedly and persistently. In fact it is this repetition of emblematic motifs that enforces the symbolic significance of the female form. Their "meaning" is established by the familiar literary, mythological, and psychological significances attached traditionally to such motifs. In this way Miller's fiction establishes the nature of the psychic world he has projected.

More remains to be said about Miller's ability to reproduce this inner world in the industrial wasteland of the contemporary city. His grotesque, demonic, emblematic figures are not only monstrous combinations of human and animal forms (the serpentine tresses and the heavy fluted sea-shell lips) but often remarkably effective fusions of traditional images with those from the industrial twentieth century (the ass balled and socketed, the basilisk made entirely of asbestos, the sweet rose-petal lips toothed with ballbearing clutches). Juxtapositions of machine and fantasy worlds are not without precedent, and are the result of similar dramatic needs. Edgar Wind's analysis of the Platonic writers of Renaissance emblem books has identified the same characteristics:

> Their books of heroic devices, so rich in moral marvels and myths, are interspersed with pictures of mechanical inventions, admirable machines which harness the secret forces of nature in order to release them for a dramatic effect. Placed next to the classical columns and sirens, diamonds and laurels, salamanders, porcupines and unicorns—symbols which continue to convey their heroic lesson in the language of fable—the new waterwheels, bellows, catapults, rockets, bombards, and barbacanes seem like brutally prosaic intruders, realistic contrivances in a setting of fantasy. But to the inventors themselves—Leonardo da Vinci among them—they exemplified the magical forces of nature, forces which man carries also in his own breast.[35]

Kayser has observed that the grotesque in the twentieth century includes a fusion of organic and mechanical elements which provides the contemporary artist with a "technical" grotesque as one means of invoking the "dark forces which lurk in and behind our world."[36] In Miller such formal devices are the means of securing symbolically in this century the archetypal forms which found related symbolic expression in other ages.

The recurrent figure of Miller's burlesque queen, Cleo, for

example, is an illustration of such grotesque fusion of the organic and the mechanical. Cleo flourishes in the filthy world: "Under cover of darkness the ushers are spraying the dead and live lice and the nests of lice and the egg lice buried in the thick black curly locks of those who have no private baths. . . ." [37] In *Black Spring* she is "queen of the electric chair":

> Cleo advances out of the womb of night, her belly swollen with sewer gas. Glory! Glory! I'm climbing up the ladder. Out of the womb of night rises the old Brooklyn Bridge, a torpid dream wriggling in spume and moonfire. A drone and sizzle scraping the frets. . . . The night is cold but the queen is naked save for a jockstrap. The queen is dancing on the cold embers of the electric chair. Cleo, the darling of the Jews, is dancing on the tips of her lacquered nails; her eyes are twisted, her ears filled with blood. She is dancing through the cold night at reasonable prices. She will dance every night this week to make way for platinum bridges. . . . She stands in bare feet, her belly swollen with sewer gas, her navel rising in systolic hexameters. Cleo, the queen, purer than the purest asphalt, warmer than the warmest electricity, Cleo the queen and darling of the gods dancing on the asbestos seat of the electric chair.[38]

In *Sexus* the polysemy of her figure is increased:

> What her face was like I hardly remember any more. I have a faint recollection that her nose was *retroussé*. One would never recognize her with her clothes on, that's a cinch. You concentrated on the torso, in the center of which was a huge painted navel [39] the color of carmine. It was like a hungry mouth, this navel. Like the mouth of a fish suddenly stricken with paralysis. I'm sure her cunt wasn't half as exciting to look at. It was probably a pale bluish sliver of meat that a dog wouldn't even bother to sniff. She was alive in her midriff, in that sinuous fleshy pear which domed out from under the chest bones. The torso reminded me always of those dressmaker's models whose thighs end in a framework of umbrella ribs. As a child I used to run my hand over the umbilical swell. It was heavenly to the touch. And the fact that there were no arms or legs to the model enhanced the bulging beauty of the torso. Sometimes there was no wickerwork below—just a truncated figure with a little collar of a

neck which was always painted a shiny black. They were the intriguing ones, the lovable ones. One night in a side show I came upon a live one, just like the sewing machine models at home. She moved about on the platform with her hands, as if she were treading water. I got real close to her and engaged her in conversation. She had a head, of course, and it was a rather pretty one, something like the wax images you see in hairdressing establishments in the chic quarters of a big city. I learned that she was from Vienna; she had been born without legs. But I'm getting off the track. . . . The thing that fascinated me about her was that she had that same voluptuous swell, that pear-like ripple and bulge. I stood by her platform a long time just to survey her from all angles. It was amazing how close her legs had been pared off. Just another slice off her and she would have been minus a twat. The more I studied her the more tempted I was to push her over. I could imagine my arms around her cute little waist, imagine myself picking her up, slinging her under my arm and making off with her to ravish her in a vacant lot.[40]

The swollen belly of Cleo reminds Miller of the legless freak and the truncated dressmaker dummies throughout this section in *Sexus*. In such figures the emblematic form is clear. The imagery is "illustrative" insofar as the "normal sense world" is not imitated or created and the reader is forced to recognize intellectual relationships between disparate images.[41] From the grotesque fusion of human form and mechanical device emerges the ubiquitous symbols of the Archetypal Feminine. The truncated figure of the dressmaker dummy (as Miller describes it in this passage) with its numinous umbilical swell suggests the familiar archetypal representations of the elementary character of the Feminine in neolithic sculpture.

Jung has pointed out that when figures of the Earth Mother appear in case histories, "in form she not infrequently resembles the *neolithic ideal* of the 'Venus' of Brassempouy or that of Willendorf. . . ."[42] These are figures in which, as Neumann noted, the symbolism of a rounded vessel appears. The middle of the body is emphasized: "In the magnificent Lespugue figure, whose breasts, belly, thighs, and triangular genital zone form a single cluster, this symbolic fullness of the elementary character is still more evident. . . ." [43] Neumann has suggested that "this limitation to the zone of the belly or womb expresses the *inhuman* gruesome aspect, the radical autonomy of the belly over against the 'higher centers' of the heart, breast, and head, and enthrones it as sacred." [44]

Despite the appearance of the maternal, positive element of the Great Mother in the background of the narrator's musings, Cleo herself emerges principally as a negative, cadodemonic figure, a Gorgon:

> The spot-light focuses on the wings where at 10:23 to the dot first a hand, then an arm, then a breast will appear. The head follows after the body, as the aura follows the saint. The head is wrapped in excelsior with cabbage leaves masking the eyes; it moves like a sea urchin struggling with eels. A wireless operator is hidden in the carmined mouth of the navel: he is a ventriloquist who uses the deaf-mute code.

> Before the great spastic movements begin with a drum-like roll of the torso, Cleo circles about the stage with the hypnotic ease and lassitude of a cobra. The supple, milk-white legs are screened behind a veil of beads girdled at the waist; the pink nipples are draped with transparent gauze. She is boneless, milky, drugged: a medusa with a straw wig undulating in a lake of glass beads.[45]

Miller is perfectly aware that Cleo is a debased symbol of the alienated feminine, as his comments in the passage after this description would indicate: "The hoochie koochie dancer of the big city dances alone—a fact of staggering significance." [46] He ascribes her alienation to the puritanical code of America: "The silent law of common consent which has made of sex a furtive, nasty act to be indulged in only with the sanction of the Church." [47]

However, such an analysis of his iconography is inadequate. The "alienation" of the Archetypal Feminine, the repression of her symbolic roles in contemporary society is undoubtedly a partial explanation for the demonic expression of a power which emanates from this estranged world. (Kayser has observed that the grotesque *is* the estranged world—the world in which what is familiar or natural is revealed as strange and ominous, a world of "reality destroyed, unlikely things invented, incompatible elements juxtaposed, the existing world estranged. . . ." [48])

Hence the female figure, even when it is attractive and receptive to Miller's narrator, reveals too often the Gorgon characteristics, castrating and destructive. If the form is maternal, it is engulfing and suffocating. Death and final dissolution are threatened by such figures. But no simple acceptance of sex as "clean and healthy" can "cure" the hero and his society, or forever destroy the nightmare dangers suggested by the archetypal figure. True, Miller finds appropriate images in the sociological condition of the world he sees—images for his projection of the Feminine. However, it is as a traditional symbol of the unconscious, of the dissolving and destructive, chthonic, infernal, that the archetypal Terrible Mother emerges from his representations of whores, hags, burlesque queens, and dancehall girls. Miller's underworld does not submit to rational panaceas for its improvement or correction: it is the timeless setting for the hero's eternal struggle, a "woods" from which he never finally emerges, through which his "progress" forever moves him. And the inimical elementary character of this world is revealed in the emblems of the archetypal Terrible Mother.

As a cacodemonic representation of the negative, elementary Terrible Feminine, Cleo appears appropriately (as do other cacodemons in Miller's iconography) in the midst of the filthy world [49] to which the hero is irresistibly drawn and by which he is clearly repelled. Here the "filthy world" is represented by the monster-frequented, excrement-smeared "temple-theatre" of the big city burlesque show:

> The fetid odor of the burlesque house! That smell of the latrine, of urine saturated with camphor balls! The mingled stench of sweat, sour feet, foul breaths, chewing gum, disinfectants! The sickening deodorant from the squirt guns levelled straight at you, as if you were a mass of bottle flies! Nauseating? No word for it. Onan himself could scarcely smell worse.

The décor too was something. Smacked of Renoir in the last stages of gangrene. Blended perfectly with the Mardi Gras lighting effects—a flushed string of red lights illuminating a rotten womb. Something disgracefully satisfying about sitting there with the Mongolian idiots in the twilight of Gomorrah, knowing all too well that after the show you would have to trudge it back home on foot. . . . All around you overgrown idiots shelling peanuts or nibbling at chocolate bars, or draining bottles of pop through straws. The Lumpen Proletariat. Cosmic riff-raff.

It was so foul, the atmosphere, that it was just like one big congealed fart. On the asbestos curtain remedies against venereal diseases, cloak and suit ads, fur trappers, tooth-paste delicacies, watches to tell time—as if time were important in our lives! . . .

The ushers. . . . Ratty, jail-bird types, if male, and floozy, empty shits, if the other sex. . . . One could smell their filthy underwear, winter or summer. . . .[50]

Like many of the other women in the confessions, moreover, Cleo reveals her negative elementary character in the Gorgon head ("The head is wrapped in excelsior . . . it moves like a sea urchin struggling with eels. . . .") even without Miller's specific identification (". . . a medusa with a straw wig . . ."). The images are insistently familiar. In fact, they repeat the iconographic message, the appearance over and over again of the same signs of the Archetypal Feminine, that makes the symbolic action of the confessions clearer. The *I* must meet and meet again these "women"—not particular women in a never-ending satyric holiday, but the various manifestations of the archetype. Cleo's navel is a hungry mouth; even though the night is cold, "the queen is naked save for a jock-strap." Again in these details the negative and inimical is revealed, for the "mouths" devour, and the jock-strap reveals the phallic character of the Gorgon:

Thus the terrible aspect of the Feminine always includes the uroboric snake woman, the woman with the phallus, the unity of child-bearing and begetting, of life and death. The Gorgon is endowed with every male attribute: the snake, the tooth, the boar's tusks, the outthrust tongue, and sometimes even with a beard.[51]

Although androgyny in the Gorgon figure (and the analysis of Miller's female "figures" most frequently suggests the Gorgon) is often negative and indicative of the chthonic and inimical powers of the unconscious as symbolized by the Terrible Mother, in other figures created by Miller androgyny demands a different analysis. As Jung pointed out, ancient androgynous figures are not a product of "primitive non-differentiation." The idea of the hermaphrodite appears significantly in the *coniunctio* of Hermetic philosophy and according to Jung survives in contemporary thinking in such areas as Catholic mysticism. Essentially, as civilization "progresses," the androgynous figure assumes a new significance:

> . . . the bisexual primordial being turns into a symbol of the unity of personality, a symbol of the self, where the war of opposites finds peace. In this way the primordial being becomes the distant goal of man's self-development, having been from the very beginning a projection of his unconscious wholeness. Wholeness consists in the union of the conscious and the unconscious personality. Just as every individual derives from masculine and feminine genes, and the sex is determined by the predominance of the corresponding genes, so in the psyche it is only the conscious mind, in a man, that has the masculine sign, while the unconscious is by nature feminine.[52]

In the figure of the female shoemaker Olga, which I discussed earlier, the maternal, providing, positive character of the Great Mother is momentarily, if grotesquely, glimpsed, although such emblematic indications of the Gorgon appear as the excelsior hair. Olga has lost her female organs, "she drips with perspiration, has halitosis, and still wears her Circassian wig that looks like excelsior. She has two big warts on her chin from which there sprouts a clump of little hairs; she is growing a mustache." [53] But Olga is the provider of food, the "maternal" figure for those who depend on her. Hence her androgynous character is not "negative."

The positive elementary character of the Great Mother archetype is apparent occasionally in other female figures who are not androgynous. Such figures are not characters in a mimetic world. They do not seem to belong to the narrative structure. Their appearance is casual and apparently irrelevant. However, they have a considerable role in the symbolic structure of Miller's fictional world, for they are significant in any final analysis of the Archetypal Feminine in Miller. Rebecca— the wife of one of Miller's friends—is one such figure, as is the Aunt Caroline of Miller's boyhood, the "sour rye world":

> Strangely enough, the thick slice of rye bread which his mother handed me each day seems to possess more potency than any other image of that period. I wonder about it . . . wonder deeply. Perhaps it is that whenever she handed me the slice of bread it was with a tenderness and a sympathy that I had never known before. She was a very homely woman, my Aunt Caroline. Her face was marked by the pox, but it was a kind, winsome face which no disfigurement could mar. She was enormously stout and she had a very soft, a very caressing voice. When she addressed me she seemed to give me even more attention, more consideration, than her own son. I would like to have stayed with her always: I would have chosen her for my own mother had I been permitted. . . . If I close my eyes now and I think about it, about the slice of bread, I think almost at once that in this house I never knew what it was to be scolded. I think if I had told my Aunt Caroline that I had killed a boy in the lot, told her just how it happened, she would have put her arms around me and forgiven me—instantly. . . . The day of the murder it [the bread] was even tastier than ever. It had a slight taste of terror in it which has been lacking ever since. And it was received with Aunt Caroline's tacit but complete absolution.[54]

Aunt Caroline is not a maternal figure from the "real" world. Her form is reduced to outline, her "character" to a few clichés—except for the symbolic role she plays in the *I*'s vision of the child's world. This world is neither innocent nor sinful: it is "a primitive world ruled by magic, a world in which fear played the most important role." [55] In such a context the numinous absolution of the maternal figure assumes an ambiguous value: the absolution symbolically granted with the bread is absolution for a meaningless and brutal murder. Aunt Caroline, positive, nourishing, protecting, is beyond the categories of social good and evil.

Another emblematic figure which appears late in Miller's work is the mother of the *I*'s friend Karen Lundquist. A superwoman whose abilities, achievements and charm are so absurdly exaggerated as to make any belief in her "reality" impossible, she symbolizes clearly the highest and perhaps most "positive" form of the Archetypal Feminine, the Sophia figure. Certainly only such significance can justify Miller's description of her:

> Karen's mother! A majestic creature in whose person were combined the diverse qualities of matriarch, hetaera and goddess. She was everything that Karen was not. No matter what she was doing she radiated warmth; her ringing laugh dissolved all problems, assured one of her confidence, trust, benevolence. She was positive through and through, yet never arrogant or aggressive. Divining instantly what you were endeavoring to say, she gave her approval before the words were out of your mouth. She was pure, radiant spirit in a most enchantingly carnal form.
>
> . . . .
>
> The year before she had been to Africa, not big game hunting either, but as an ethnologist. She had penetrated to regions where no white woman had ever set foot. She was fearless but not reckless. She could adapt herself to any circumstances, enduring hardships which made even the stronger sex flinch. She had a faith and a trust which were invincible. No one could come into her presence without being enriched. At times she reminded me of those Polynesian women of royal lineage who preserved, in the far Pacific, the last vestiges of an earthly Paradise. Here was the mother I should like to have chosen before entering the womb. Here was the mother who personified the primal elements of our being, in whom earth, sea and sky were harmonized. She was a natural descendant of the great Sybilline figures, embodying the texture of myth, fable and legend. Terrestrial to the core, she nevertheless lived in a realm of superdimensions. Her consciousness seemed to expand or

contract at will. For the greatest tasks she made no more effort than for the humblest. She was equipped with wings,
fins, tail, feet, claws and gills. She was aeronautic and am-
phibious. She understood all languages yet spoke as a child.
Nothing could dampen her ardor or mutilate her irrepressi-
ble joy. Just to look at her was to take courage. Problems became nonexistent. She was anchored in reality, but a reality
which was divine.

For the first time in my life, I had the privilege of gazing
upon a Mother. Images of the Madonna had never meant
anything to me: they were too bright, too translucent, too
remote, too ethereal. I had formed an image of my own—
darker, more substantial, more mysterious, more potent.[56]

The transformative powers of such a being are acknowledged:
"The superior being is not, as I once supposed, more remote,
more detached, more abstract. Quite the contrary. Only the superior being can arouse in us the hunger which is justifiable,
the hunger to surpass ourselves by becoming what we truly
are. In the presence of the superior being we recognize our
own majestic powers . . . ."[57]

Miller's summary of the attributes of the Sophia archetype
corresponds perhaps somewhat crudely to the historical and
traditional forms assumed by such manifestations of the positive
and transformative nature of the Great Mother.[58] Such a
figure is creative, rather than destructive; she is that aspect of
the Feminine which symbolizes a generating and nourishing,
protective and transformative feminine power. The figure with
which she appears in *Plexus* (again in conceptual rather than
visual terms) is her perfect consort—a Socrates of learning,
connoisseur of wines, intimate of the famous, an expert in
chess, law, ballistics, and a figure in world affairs—such a man is
reduced to an absurd superlative. However, as an allegorical
figure he is the appropriate consort for a "Sophia" as Neumann
has described her:

Thus the spiritual power of Sophia is living and saving; her
overflowing heart is wisdom and food at once. The nourishing life that she communicates is a life of the spirit and of
transformation, not one of earthbound materiality. As spirit

mother, she is not, like the Great Mother of the lower phase, interested primarily in the infant, the child, and the immature man, who cling to her in these stages. She is rather a goddess of the Whole, who governs the transformation from the elementary to the spiritual level; who desires whole men knowing life in all its breadth, from the elementary phase to the phase of spiritual transformation.[59]

As characters in a mimetic fictional world describing actual human beings, such figures are absurd. *The Rosy Crucifixion* (in which the Sophia figure appears) gives a clearer account of Miller's fictional world, one more easily accessible to conscious evaluation of his characters than the twilight states of semiconsciousness frequently reproduced in the confessions of the *Tropics*. But the "characters" are no more "real." Often only as emblems do they have any significance. The Sophia figures which appear abruptly and disappear abruptly round out the outlines of the Archetypal Feminine, which is elsewhere essentially negative, chthonic, elementary. This appearance of the positive Feminine is not isolated. In the same section in which Karen's mother appears, the *I* is reminded of another figure, enigmatic, desirable, unattainable: "an exact replica of one of the medieval French madonnas. All light and grace, chaste, seductive, with golden tresses and sea green eyes. Always silent, always seraphic." Characteristically the figure is challenged by the negative Feminine. When the *I* attempts to write down his memories of the madonna figure, he looks for paper and pencil:

> Finally I found a little stationery store run by an old Jewish woman. She was wearing one of those hideous wigs the color of a cockroach's wings. For some reason she had difficulty in understanding me. I began making signs in the air. She thought I was deaf. She began to yell at me. I yelled back at her, drowning her with oaths. She grew frightened and ran to the back of the store to call for help. Baffled, I stood there a moment, then dashed into the street.[60]

Una, too, the girl he wanted to marry and who frequently appears in his daydreams, is an emblem of the positive, transforming Feminine for Miller.

Like the opposing cities of Dijon and Paris, or New York and Paris, the minor female figures in Miller's fiction resolve into emblems of the Archetypal Feminine—sometimes the positive aspects of this archetype, frequently the negative and destructive. Between these opposites, representing as they do the potentials of the unconscious, moves the hero. When Miller insists that he is writing about his self, and not about a fictional hero in the labyrinths of the twentieth-century city world, his insistence should be taken seriously. Moreover, to approach his characters from the critical premises of mimetic fiction leads the reader to overlook their allegorical possibilities. Whether they succeed as allegorical figures is another question.

Most of the images into which the Archetypal Feminine is fragmented fulfill the requirements of the allegorical image as these are outlined by Angus Fletcher:

> First, it must imply a systematic part-whole relationship; second, it should be capable of including both metonymy and synecdoche; third, it should be capable of including "personifications"; fourth, it should suggest the daemonic nature of the image; fifth, it should allow an emphasis on the visual modality, specifically on visual or symbolic "isolation," not to say surrealism; finally, it should be such that large-scale double meanings would emerge if it were combined with other such images.[61]

The allegorical figure is one means by which Miller can focus on the destructive and transformative nature of the unconscious; it is also suitable for the kind of intellectual dissection of mental attitudes which are the concern of that prose form Frye calls *anatomy*. Formally, Miller can ignore the demands for unity and narrative continuity imposed on him by some traditions of the novel. He can attempt to organize his material in a musical scheme, as he does in *Capricorn*, in which "characters" appear as motifs, or he can focus on the alternating states of conscious control over the frightening destructive forces of the unconscious and demonic possession by these forces, as he does in the broad outline of *Cancer*.

Frye has pointed out that the main difference between the

romance and the novel lies in the concept of characterization. In romance the hero, heroine, and villain are in effect the psychological archetypes of libido, anima, and shadow. For this reason romance often suggests the allegorical. The novelist, however, deals with something we call "personality," or characters in their social masks.[62]

Distinctions between the mimetic characterizations of the novel and those figures which appear in confession and anatomy are equally significant. The "characters" of anatomy are not people, but "mental attitudes." [63] In confession, because the selections of pertinent details depends on the particular theoretical or intellectual interest of the author, the "characters" are those which enable the reader to grasp the central significance of the author's life. Frye argues that the success of an author in integrating his mind on some theoretical and intellectual interest "makes the author of a confession feel that his life is worth writing about." [64] In *Capricorn* the theoretical discussions emerge more importantly than in *Cancer;* but it is in *Cancer* that the "integration of the author's mind" on the subject of the problem of the self is most interesting, for the process of the self's "becoming" is itself the basis of the allegorical pattern.

In twentieth-century confession, it is not surprising that those projections which erupt from the darkness of one's unconscious being—projections which determine one's view of the world outside him and reveal his inner landscape—are the most absorbing subject of concern. Freed from the demands of mimesis, these projections as "characters" can be freely organized in patterns other than those of narrative or chronicle in order to establish the kind of integration necessary for confession. In Rousseau, according to Northrop Frye, the confession form is merged with the novel form, producing eventually the fictional autobiography and the *Künstler-roman.*[65] In Miller, the fictional autobiography moves clearly into the archetypal world of projections. Granted a freedom from mimesis, the illusions of past and present can be ignored; characters can appear or disappear as they are symbolically appropriate, and the reader's interest in their eventual "history" is not stimulated. Their appearance or disappearance establishes a sequence of experiences that have allegorical significance. Hence the autobiographical produces the confession. Indeed, the symbols of the Archetypal Feminine in Miller's fiction can scarcely be considered the representations of a mundane world. As emblems of human heaven and hell they outline the transmundane.

Chapter Three

The Transformative Character

In Miller's major work, the female figure to whom he gives the names of Mona and Mara [1] most closely resembles fictional character. She is a pivotal female figure in the structure of several of the individual works. She appears briefly but significantly in *Tropic of Cancer;* in *Tropic of Capricorn* she dominates the relationship between the self and the Archetypal Feminine. She is a focus for the tensions which are explored in the confessions, appearing sometimes as succubus and sometimes as psychopomp—deadly and destructive one moment, transforming and redeeming the next.

But not until the first volume of *The Rosy Crucifixion,* in which she emerges as a traditional figure from romantic literature, does she fill enough of the requirements of character to be evaluated in conventional terms of literary analysis. (She acquires a history, a human form, and a role in an action sufficiently developed to approximate sustained narrative.) However, she never assumes fully the dimensions of a realistic figure, even in *The Rosy Crucifixion.* In *Sexus,* Mona/Mara appears as the anima figure of romance. And in considering the relationship between this manifestation of the Archetypal Feminine and the forms of fiction, Northrop Frye's distinctions should be recalled.

> The essential difference between the novel and romance lies in the conception of characterization. The romancer does not attempt to create "real people" so much as stylized figures which expand into psychological archetypes. It is in the romance that we find Jung's libido, anima, and shadow reflected in the hero, heroine, and villain respectively.[2]

Even in *Capricorn* and *Cancer*, however, Mona/Mara should be considered a symbol of the anima. To do so explains the roles she assumes and the forms in which she appears. Her role in each of the major works, moreover, becomes clearer. It actually determines the nature of the action. But the temptation to approach Miller from a "realistic" or "naturalistic" point of view persists.

Kingsley Widmer, for example, finds Mona/Mara contradictory, "undeveloped," and unsatisfactory as a realistic figure despite Miller's obvious attempts to make her central and significant. His judgment of Miller's characterization of women is representative:

> A novelist with any feminine identification might have done much with the Dark Lady, but Miller is no novelist, or even an apt storyteller, and he also totally lacks the skill to project into the feminine sensibility. Thus we never get his heroine's thoughts, feelings, motives, or sense of existence.[3]

Although he recognizes that Miller is attempting to give the character "cosmic" significance and a "mythic" role, he insists on irrelevant standards: "The chopped up, willful, egotistically indifferent presentation of Mona does not even achieve minimal character analysis or dramatic coherence." [4] Perhaps other judgments made by Widmer are relevant, but his insistence on "development," "coherent images of reality," and "internal understanding of other persons" in characterization reveals the limitations of his analysis. If the reader approaches Miller's fiction with different expectations, Mona/Mara appears as a consistent figure with a consistent function.

It is difficult, of course, to evaluate the creation of an anima figure. Miller's success or failure may be impossible to estimate without a recognized critical standard. If Simon O. Lesser is correct in his judgment of Miller—that his work arouses aversion because it is too direct a statement of the case for repressed tendencies and lacks sufficient disguise and control [5]—then it is difficult for the critic to attempt an adequate analysis of the elements which organize such material.

Widmer recognizes that Mona/Mara belongs to a literary tradition—the Dark Lady of romantic passion—or, perhaps, to several traditions. He sees in her figure elements of the *"femme fatale* of the romantic, an inverted traditional muse of the artist, the Eve-Lilith of primordial knowledge, a witch-goddess of sexuality and power. . . ." [6] In other comments he points out that Miller makes her a Circe figure, a witch of shifting identities, the machined American love goddess, and a Strindbergian metaphor.[7] Miller himself identifies Mona/Mara with the heroine of H. Rider Haggard's *She*. Widmer considers Miller's eulogy of Haggard and his identification of the two heroines as "pretentiously literary." It is possible, however, that Miller (who borrows freely from many sources) recognized in Haggard's *She* the essential characteristics of the anima archetype, for Jung considered Haggard's novels important literary accounts of the symbolic contexts in which this archetype appears.[8] From the psychoanalytic point of view, then, the parallels between Haggard's *She* and Miller's Mona/Mara would suggest that Miller's figure is also an anima projection.

If we accept Frye's assertion that the suggestion of allegory is constantly appearing around the edges of the projections of libido, anima, and shadow in romance, then Miller's claims for the Mona/Mara figure seem less irrelevant and pretentious than Widmer finds them. Miller insists on her allegorical role:

> For a long time *reality* for me was Woman. Which is equivalent to saying—Nature, Myth, Country, Mother, Chaos. I expatiate—to the reader's amazement, no doubt—on a romance called *She*, forgetting that I dedicated the cornerstone of my autobiography to "Her." How very much there was of "She" in "Her"! In place of the Great Caves of Kôr I de-

scribed the bottomless black pit. Like "She," "Her" also strove desperately to give me life, beauty, power and dominion over others, even if only through the magic of words. "Her's" too was an endless immolation, a waiting (in how awful a sense!) for the Beloved to return. And if "Her" dealt me death in the Place of Life, was it not also in blind passion, out of fear and jealousy? What was the secret of Her terrible beauty, Her fearful power over others, Her contempt for Her slavish minions, if not the desire to expiate Her *crime? The crime?* That she had robbed me of my identity at the very moment when I was about to recover it. In Her I lived as truly as the image of the slain Kallikrates lived in the mind, heart, and soul of Ayesha. In some strange, twisted way, having dedicated myself to the task of immortalizing Her, I convinced myself that I was giving Her Life in return for Death. I thought I could resurrect the past, thought I could make it live again—*in truth.* Vanity, vanity! All I accomplished was to reopen the wound that had been inflicted upon me. The wound still lives, and with the pain of it comes the remembrance of what I was. I see very clearly that I was not this, not that. The "notness" is clearer than the "isness." I see the meaning of the long Odyssey I made; I recognize *all* the Circes who held me in their thrall. I found my father, both the one in the flesh and the unnameable one. And I discovered that father and son are one. More, immeasurably more: I found at last that all is one.

At Mycenae, standing before the grave of Clytemnestra, I relived the ancient Greek tragedies, which nourished me more than did the great Shakespeare. Climbing down the slippery stairs to the pit, which I described in the book on Greece, I experienced the same sensation of horror which I did as a boy when descending into the bowels of Kôr. It seems to me that I have stood before many a bottomless pit, have looked into many a charnel house. But what is more vivid still, more awe-inspiring, is the remembrance that, whenever in my life I have gazed too long upon Beauty, particularly the beauty of the female, I have always experienced the sensation of fear. Fear, and a touch of horror too. What is the origin of this horror? The dim remembrance of being other than I now am, of being fit (once) to receive the blessings of beauty, the gift of love, the truth of God. Why, do we not sometimes ask ourselves, why the fatidical beauty in the

great heroines of love throughout the ages? Why do they
seem so logically and naturally surrounded by death, bol-
stered by crime, nourished by evil? There is a sentence in
She which is strikingly penetrative. It comes at the moment
when Ayesha, having found her Beloved, realizes that physical union must be postponed yet a while. "As yet I may not
mate with thee, for thou and I are different, and the very
brightness of my being would burn thee up, and perchance
destroy thee." (I would give anything to know what I made
of these words when I read them as a boy!) [9]

The extravagance of these comments is typical of the remarks Miller makes about his writing, and frequently obscures
their significance. What is interesting, however, is his insistence
on the allegorical nature of the figure he has reproduced. It is
not Mona/Mara's separateness or uniqueness as autobiographical fact that fascinates him, nor even her similarity to the
Haggard heroine he admires. He immediately offers an allegorical extension and interpretation of her role. She is representative not only of the "fatal woman," but of *reality*. She is destructive, as an archetype, of the uniqueness of the self, what
Miller calls here *identity*. But she is also transformative, striving
"desperately to give me life, beauty, power and dominion over
others, even if only through the magic of words." The two
functions of the figure may appear muddily contradictory, for
the reader is puzzled to find the Gorgonesque figure of *Cancer*
suddenly a psychopomp and muse.

Mona/Mara does suggest the literary cliché of the fatal
woman, *La Belle Dame sans Merci*, whose development into
cliché was traced by Mario Praz. Although Praz recognizes
the long history of the archetype, he prefers to ascribe its appearance more to aspects of "real life" than to the projections
of autonomous archetypes:

> There have always existed Fatal Women both in mythology
> and in literature, since mythology and literature are imagi-
> native reflections of the various aspects of real life, and real
> life has always provided more or less complete examples of
> arrogant and cruel female characters. There is no need,
> therefore, to go back to the myth of Lilith, to the fables of

Harpies, Sirens, and Gorgons, of Scylla and the Sphinx, or to the Homeric poems.[10]

Praz believes that the figures of the Fatal Woman are more numerous "during times in which the springs of inspiration were troubled"[11] and suggests that the shifting role of woman —both in function and ideal—in the nineteenth century is partly responsible for the popularity of the type. But he also recognizes the imaginative projection of neurotic sexual desires in the production of this figure and the images which provide appropriate contexts for it. In the algolagnia of such writers as Swinburne, he finds the psychological source for the "phantoms of the mind" which Swinburne's women represent.[12] In his analysis of Swinburne's fatal women, Praz considers paramount one passage from *Notes on Designs of the Old Masters in Florence*. The passage reproduces the image of the Gorgon archetype: the serpent tresses, "electric hair, which looks as though it would hiss and glitter with sparks if once touched, . . . wound up to a tuft with serpentine plaits and involutions."[13] Unfortunately, he does not comment on the traditional iconography of this figure. For Praz, Swinburne is the sexual outsider whose productions provide more insight into abnormal human passions than into the structure of the human self and its recurrent patterns of significant symbolic action. A Freudian approach to Miller would lead to similar conclusions, perhaps.

A more inclusive hypothesis can explain the obsessive persistence of the particular images in which the negative Feminine appears throughout history. The hypothesis should explain both the significance of the archetype and the context in which it appears. When, for example, Praz ends his chapter on the Fatal Woman, he calls "unintentional humour" lines from a poem by R. Le Gallienne entitled *Beauty Accursed*, "in which the Fatal Woman attracts irresistibly towards herself not only men, but even 'strange creatures,' even cows, toads, and snails!"[14] Kayser's study of the grotesque, however, recognizes the appearance of toads and snails as motifs appropriate and familiar to the invocation of the demonic world in which the Fatal Woman of romantic tradition really belongs.

Kayser has described in different terms the important similarity between the romantic period and our own:

> Such attempts [to invoke and subdue the demonic aspects of the world] have been made throughout the ages. But our survey revealed a marked difference in their density and intensity. In concluding, we may state once again that there are three historical periods in particular in which the power of the "It" was strongly felt: the sixteenth century, the age which extends from the *Sturm und Drang* to Romanticism, and the twentieth century. In these periods the belief of the preceding ages in a perfect and protective natural order ceased to exist. Without being forced to construct a unified world view for the Middle Ages, one must admit that the sixteenth century had experiences unexplained by the *Weltanschauung* of the preceding centuries. *Sturm und Drang* and Romanticism were consciously opposed to the rationalistic world view developed during the Enlightenment; they even questioned the legitimacy of the rationale for such a world view. The modern age questions the validity of the anthropological and the relevance of the scientific concepts of the nineteenth century. The various forms of the grotesque are the most obvious and pronounced contradictions of any kind of rationalism and any systematic use of thought. It was absurd in itself when the Surrealists sought to make absurdity the basis of their system.[15]

Kayser's conclusions focus on the anti-rationalism of periods which produced the literary grotesque rather than on a narrower concern of man with the problems of genital sex.[16] Deliberate and conscious courting of the irrational and the absurd produces the motifs Kayser traces in his history of art and literature. In Praz's study, however, one finds excessive emphasis on the abnormal sexual tendencies of the individual writers who created the fascinating Medusas and deadly lamias of romantic literature. As a result, such images appear to belong only to the sick and decadent; the possibility is evaded that they are produced in the exploration of a psychic reality common to us all.

If invocations of this irrational world will always produce images of Medusas and succubi (however modified by tradition) and the other familiar distortions of the interior world's grotesque landscape, then (as Kayser argues in his comments on the surrealists) they prove the falseness of the contention that such productions relate only intimate personal experiences.[17] These same fearful images of the irrational "confession" appear as well in extra-literary traditions—in the symbolic systems of alchemy, for example. Jung points out in his introduction to *Mysterium Coniunctionis* that the "alchemists, with but few exceptions, did not know that they were bringing psychic structures to light but thought that they were explaining the transformations of matter, . . ." As a result, "there were no psychological considerations to prevent them, for reasons of sensitiveness, from laying bare the background of the psyche, which a more conscious person would be nervous of doing. It is because of this that alchemy is of such absorbing interest to the psychologist." [18]

In *Alchemy and Psychology*, Jung explores the relationship between his concept of the psychology of the unconscious and the symbolic productions of the alchemists. The succubi, sirens, and lamias of romantic literary tradition appear among the representations of the unconscious which occur both in contemporary dreams and in the literature of alchemy. In an analysis of a sequence of dreams Jung draws the parallels:

> The experience of the unconscious is a personal secret communicable only to very few, and that with difficulty; hence the isolating effect we noted above.[19] But isolation brings about a compensatory animation of the psychic atmosphere which strikes us as uncanny. The figures that appear in the dream are feminine, thus pointing to the feminine nature of the unconscious. They are fairies or fascinating sirens and lamias, who infatuate the lonely wanderer and lead him astray. Likewise seductive maidens appear at the beginning of the *nekyia* of Poliphile . . . and the Melusina of Paracelsus is another such figure.[20]

The relationship between the many vaguely defined figures and a single, isolated "unknown woman" is discussed in the analysis of a subsequent dream. All are symbols of the unconscious, but the appearance of the isolated female figure has special significance in Jungian psychology, as it does in the sequence of Henry Miller's confessions. Jung calls this figure the anima:

> The theme of the unknown woman—whose technical name is "anima"—appears here for the first time. Like the throng of vague female forms in dream 4, she is a personification of the animated psychic atmosphere. From now on the figure of the unknown woman reappears in a great many of the dreams. Personification always indicates an autonomous activity of the unconscious. If some personal figure appears we may be sure that the unconscious is beginning to grow active. The activity of such figures very often has an anticipatory character: something that the dreamer himself will do later is now being done in advance.[21]

Without tracing Jung's detailed analysis of this pattern in alchemy, I should mention the emergence of this figure (in a later dream described by Jung and also in alchemical literature) as psychopomp: "The anima, having already anticipated the *solificatio* of alchemy, now appears as the psychopomp, the one who shows the way." [22]

This symbolic pattern, culminating as it does in the appearance of a transformative "anima" figure from the seductive and dangerous visions of the unconscious—the succubi and lamias of man's history—describes one of the patterns of symbolic action in Miller. In the *Tropics*, the figure is not sufficiently differentiated from the other images of the Archetypal Feminine to appear as a human character of romance, but is, as I will attempt to illustrate later in this chapter, in the process of emerging. Later, in *The Rosy Crucifixion*, the figure is clearly human, more clearly in the tradition of romance, and specifically in the tradition of the Fatal Woman, who is also a psychopomp and muse.

When Kingsley Widmer lists the roles assumed by Henry Miller's Mona/Mara—*femme fatale*, Eve-Lilith, witch, Circe, inverted muse—he is in fact naming the roles assumed by the anima figure described by Jung. Perhaps the nature of this figure can be explained by the sadistic-masochistic drives of the writer as Praz has done.[23] But such analysis tells us more about the writer than about the form of his art.

Norman O. Brown observes, moreover, that Bachofen's discovery of the religion of the Great Mother has not been sufficiently exploited by the Freudians, but has been left (unfortunately, in his opinion) to the Jungians.[24] Certainly Neumann's description of the relationship between the anima figure and the symbols of the Archetypal Feminine provides the most successful explanation for the symbolic action that is revealed in the imagery and structure of Miller's texts. It explains the apparently contradictory roles of the anima: on the one hand, alluring and destructive; on the other, transforming and creative:

> The anima is the vehicle par excellence of the transformative character. It is the mover, the instigator of change, whose fascination drives, lures, and encourages the male to all the adventures of the soul and spirit, of action and creation in the inner and the outward world.
>
> With the emergence of something soullike—the anima—from the Archetypal Feminine, the unconscious, not only does a change occur in the relations of ego to unconscious and of man to woman, but the action of the unconscious within the psyche also assumes new and creative forms. While the elementary character of the Feminine tends to dissolve the ego and consciousness in the unconscious, the transformative character of the anima fascinates but does not obliterate; it sets the personality in motion, produces change and ultimately transformation. This process is also fraught with danger, often with mortal peril, but when it actually leads to the destruction of the ego, it is because the Great Mother or even the maternal uroboros is preponderant over the anima; i.e., the detachment of the anima from the mother archetype is incomplete.[25]

Erich Neumann considers this "mixed situation" characteristic of a certain type of creative man: "The Romantics, for example, were wholly dominated by this constellation in which the mother archetype of the collective unconscious overpowers the anima and by its fascination leads to the uroboric incest of the death urge or to madness." [26] Even when the anima figure appears as negative, however, the stimulus to the personality can be creative rather than destructive:

> This means that the anima figure, despite the great danger that is bound up with it, is not terrible in the same way as the Great Mother, who is not at all concerned with the independence of the individual and the ego. Even when the anima is seemingly negative and "intends," for example, to poison the male consciousness, to endanger it by intoxication, and so on—even then a positive reversal is possible, for the anima figure is always subject to defeat. When Circe, the enchantress who turns men into beasts, meets the superior figure of Odysseus, she does not kill herself like the Sphinx, whose riddle Oedipus has solved, but invites him to share her bed.[27]

As we have seen in chapter 2, the iconography of the Terrible Mother archetype is dominant in *Capricorn;* Mona/Mara appears in images little different from the Gorgon images which outline this negative archetype. But Neumann points out that just as the Good Mother (in whom an elementary, uroboric element is dominant) can produce a negative development for the ego (the uroboric incest which dissolves and absorbs), the "Terrible Mother may be associated with a tendency toward the transformative character, i.e., toward the anima; her appearance may introduce a positive development in which the ego is driven toward masculinization and the fight with the dragon, i.e., positive development and transformation."[28]

In the process which the Jungians call *fragmentation,* the "primordial archetype breaks down into a sizable group of related archetypes and symbols."[29] The relationship between the complex of images which defines the anima and those which suggest the outline of the Terrible Mother defines the nature of the "action" in Miller's early fiction. This relationship describes in other terms what he has insisted himself was a struggle for his "life" and for an extension of consciousness. Neumann describes this development as assimilation:

> The split-off archetypes and symbols are now easier to grasp and assimilate, so that they no longer overpower ego con-

sciousness. This discursive experience of the archetypes, one after another and from different sides, is the result of a development in the course of which consciousness learns to protect itself against the effect of the primordial archetype.[30]

Essential in this process is growing clarification; the individual symbols of the Great Mother archetype need to be recognized and assimilated by consciousness. They become increasingly more human in form, less monstrous and non-human. The change of Mara's name to Mona suggests such differences. As Mona, she appears only briefly in *Cancer*, rising out of a "sea of faces" (and images which suggest the elementary Archetypal Feminine), sinking into the Gorgon figure in the cheap Paris hotel, her hair alive with lice. Her discontent in Paris and her rejection in this book of the "filthy" world (insisting on the clean sheets of the Hôtel des Etats-Unis) [31] serve in *Cancer* to separate her from the symbols of the Archetypal Feminine represented by the city of Paris. The *I*'s struggle in *Cancer* is with the elementary symbolic projections of the unconscious, with female figures that suggest but rarely maintain the illusion that they are persons—and with even more important elementary symbols, the great cities. Mona is something "other," belonging to a different order. The narrator of *Cancer* is aware that the relationship with this significant figure is fleeting and insubstantial.

In *Capricorn*, however, the transformative possibilities of the Mara figure are clearer, although the negative and destructive elements in the archetype remain dominant. Her name in this second confession is Mara, a traditional name for her negative roles—succubus, whore, witch. Jung's summary of the anima figure's possibilities of meaning coincides with Miller's "characterization":

> Like the "supraordinate personality," the anima is bipolar and can therefore appear positive one moment and negative the next; now young, now old; now mother, now maiden; now a good fairy, now a witch; now a saint, now a whore. Besides this ambivalence, the anima also has "occult" con-

nections with "mysteries," with the world of darkness in general, and for that reason she often has a religious tinge.[32]

The passages in *Capricorn* in which Mara is described are not passages which attempt character analysis or even character creation. They reflect an effort to produce in symbols the essence and form of the elusive manifestation of the unconscious:

> . . . I walked into the hairy Greek's place one night and ran smack into her. She seemed blue-black, white as chalk, ageless. There was not just the flow to and from, but the endless chute, the voluptuousness of intrinsic restlessness. She was mercurial and at the same time of a savory weight. She had the marmoreal stare of a faun imbedded in lava. The time has come, I thought, to wander back from the periphery. I made a move toward the center, only to find the ground shifting from under my feet. The earth slid rapidly beneath my bewildered feet. I moved again out of the earth belt and behold, my hands were full of meteoric flowers. I reached for her with two flaming hands but she was more elusive than sand. I thought of my favorite nightmares, but she was unlike anything which had made me sweat and gibber. In my delirium I began to prance and neigh. I bought frogs and mated them with toads. I thought of the easiest thing to do, which is to die, but I did nothing. I stood still and began to petrify at the extremities.[33]

The literature of the novel which explores the subtleties and ironic implications of personal relations leaves the reader unprepared to respond to the reactions described in this passage. The *I* begins to *petrify at the extremities,* for he is responding to the petrifying gaze of the Gorgon figure, that aspect of the Archetypal Feminine with which the negative form of the Mona/Mara figure is associated. His response is traditional—in literature, myth, and dream.

Mara appears as a scarcely human figure in this passage—ageless, blue-black, and white as chalk.[34] Her junction with the negative Feminine is obvious from her effect on the narrator. The *I* is neither able to "reach" the figure nor escape it. "Death" is inevitable without a struggle, but it is "the easiest thing to do." The non-human symbols of the Feminine suggest the presence of the Archetypal Feminine in its character of the Great Round, toward the center of which the hero tries to move.[35] However, the process of "crystallization of the anima from the mother archetype," according to Jungian analysis, is the means by which the creative spirit is released. Not until the end of *Capricorn* is this process in any way completed, at which time Mara most nearly approaches and sustains human form.[36]

But in this early passage (the *I* has met Mara for the first time), the transformative possibilities of the anima figure are suggested by the symbolic action and the congeries of symbols which isolate the experience of confrontation. The narrator not only begins to petrify—he senses himself (within) as a horse, prancing and neighing. The positive, creative force held in thrall by the negative Feminine can be released—hence in mythology the emergence of Pegasus from the body of the Medusa.[37] The motif is similar and appears elsewhere in Miller's flying imagery. Pegasus is the symbol *par excellence* of the creative impulse, and release of the creative forces of the self is the "theoretical" subject of Miller's confessions. The priapic significance of the horse in this passage can, of course, be identified without difficulty. Jung, however, argues that libido symbols such as the horse have more than sexual significance, for he identifies the libido with psychic energy as a whole.[38]

The complexity of the relationship between the *I* and Mara is suggested by the name Mara as well as by the symbols which describe her. The name is historically associated with the nightmare or succubus [39] (a form she often assumes in the confessions); it is ascribed to witches and other representations of the negative Feminine. The name is frequently associated with the horse, for Mara is the night-mare. And the night-fiend is often associated with water, a symbol of the unconscious and the maternal.

> Now it is very remarkable that night-fiends who assume the shape of horses are, as we shall presently see, almost always connected with ideas of water. Laistner remarks: "Die Rossgestalt des Alps ist hauptsächlich an dem im Wasser

hausenden Lur haften geblieben." ("The horse guise of the night-fiend has been retained from the Lure who dwells in the water.")

In general the ideas of horse and water have always been closely associated, suggesting that something about a horse instinctively brings to the mind the idea of water. Jähns points out that even the names that denote horse spring from common roots for those that denote water: the Latin *aqua* and *equus* (Old High German *ach* and *ech* respectively) are derived from the old Indo-Germanic *akrâ* (= water) and *akva* (= steed), both of which come from the root *ak* (= to hasten). The same may apply to *Ross* itself, . . . ("For *ur* and *or* are primitive words which many languages use to donate the idea of "source." The Latin *orire* (= to arise) belongs to this root, and it is not improbable that the Old German *ors*, which in many names of places indicates water and thus seems to be a common designation for "horse" and "spring," is also connected with it. . . . That words like *Renner* (= race-horse) and *rinnen* (= to stream) are related is plain enough. A clear example in this connection from classical writings is a guise of Poseidon, that of the Trojan Rhesos so famous for his glistening steeds. For this title simply means "the streamer" . . . and hence has given the name to two rivers, one in Troad, another in Bethynia.") Further than this, the place names formed from horse names generally contain a reference to water as well. Jähns, after giving a list of some six hundred and fifty such words, writes: . . . ("Here one need only call attention to the fact of how extraordinarily rich with every one of these place names is the connection between the word for horse and that for running water. Everywhere we come across names for horses in close conjunction with syllables like: ach, back, bore, brunn, bronn, quell, see, etc.").[40]

As we have noted, Jung considers water one of the commonest symbols of the unconscious, and Neumann has traced the extensive symbolic manifestations of the Archetypal Feminine in water symbolism.[41] It is, then, not unusual that the night-fiend or Mara is often associated with water. In a larger context, both are typical manifestations of aspects of the Archetypal Feminine; both are symbolic of the unconscious.

In the passage from *Capricorn* we have been examining, Miller describes a libido force or a self in thrall and symbolizes this force as horse. But the Mara figure (if only by virtue of her name) also suggests the horse symbol. Such overlapping in the theriomorphic symbolism is common, according to Jung:

> We have already seen that the libido directed towards the mother actually symbolizes her as a horse. The mother-imago is a libido-symbol and so is the horse; at some points the meaning of the two symbols overlaps. But the factor common to both is the libido.[42]

That such horse symbolism is often associated with negative rather than positive feminine characteristics has been noted:

> The goddess of the underworld, Hecate, is sometimes represented with a horse's head. Demeter and Philyra, wishing to escape the attentions of Kronos or Poseidon, change themselves into mares. Witches can easily change into horses, hence the nail-marks of the horseshoe may be seen on their hands. The devil rides on the witch's horse, and priests' housekeepers are changed after death into horses.[43]

But as a libido symbol, the horse is important in the theriomorphic symbolism of the archetype of the self.[44]

This passage in *Capricorn* (chosen because it represents the first important appearance of Mara) reveals, in the images and symbols into which the mimetic action dissolves, a complex system of relationships between the *I* and the anima projection. The traditional, transpersonal values and meanings attached to the symbols are developed in an apparently intimate personal account of a shabby relationship in a twentieth-century city in which the heroic exploits of mythical challengers can have only an inverted existence. Miller moves from an obvious insistence on mythical significance for his figures (Mara is a Circe and a Lilith) toward what Frye calls *displacement*, or "indirect mythologizing,"[45] in which an author's techniques try to focus the reader's attention on the apparent reality of his figures. Thus Miller's confessions appear to be the boasts of an oversexed New York Thoreau or accounts of the ingenuous copulations of an aging Huckleberry Finn—a "real American" in the nightmare world of the twentieth century. Yet closer analysis of his symbols and characters always reveals a symbolic struggle between the Archetypal Feminine and the developing self.

When Mara "appears" in *Capricorn,* she is gradually differentiated from the negative and elemental symbols of the archetype; she assumes a "human" form and the *I* attempts to establish a relationship with this projection. As a human figure, however, she is unstable, and the congeries of symbols which erupt in Miller's prose when he attempts to describe her elusive nature reveal the elemental forms of the Great Mother archetype.

At the beginning of her appearance, the "surreal" episodes are overwhelmingly dominant, and Mara is seldom isolated and controlled by the conscious awareness of the *I*. At these moments the sense of demonic possession and the helplessness of the *I* reveal him unmistakably as an allegorical agent, or the "demonic agent" as Angus Fletcher has described him.[46] The reader has no choice except to respond to the symbolic possibilities of the relationships:

> Prod her a bit and she would become a rose, a deep black rose with the most velvety petals and of a fragrance that was overpowering. It was amazing how marvelously I learned to take my cue; no matter how swift the metamorphosis I was always there in her lap, bird lap, beast lap, snake lap, rose lap, what matter: the lap of laps, the lip of lips, tip to tip, feather to feather, the yolk in the egg, the pearl in the oyster, a cancer clutch, a tincture of sperms and cantharides. Life was Scorpio conjunction Mars, conjunction Venus, Saturn, Uranus, et cetera; love was conjunctivitis of the mandibles, clutch this, clutch that, clutch, clutch, the mandibular clutch-clutch of the mandala wheel of lust. Come food time I could already hear her peeling the eggs, and inside the egg *cheep-cheep,* blessed omen of the next meal to come. I ate like a monomaniac: the prolonged dreamlit voracity of the man who is thrice breaking his fast. And as I ate she purred, the rhythmic predatory wheeze of the succubus devouring her young. What a blissful night of love! Saliva, sperm, succubation, sphincteritis all in one; the conjugal orgy in the Black Hole of Calcutta.[47]

Mara appears in images and symbols which suggest the Archetypal Feminine; there is no mimetic human figure produced, nor is coitus described with mimetic intent. Instead, the orgiastic, destructive character of the Archetypal Feminine is described and Mara reveals her connection with the elemental, traditional, mythological roles of the uroboric Great Mother: at the same time nourishing and destructive, she "feeds" her male victim and she devours him.[48]

But Miller ascribes these roles to a particular character whose numinous significance he insists on throughout his fiction; she becomes the focus of the meanings of the unconscious, enabling consciousness to assimilate these meanings. In this passage, for example, Mara is also a Lady of the Beasts; her lap is "bird lap, snake lap, beast lap . . . ." According to Neumann, the psychic projections which created the Lady of the Beasts in mythology mark a distinctive phase in the development of man's awareness of his nature and potential as a conscious being. If we take seriously Miller's insistence that his confessions record the birth struggles of the self, then the stages in which the Archetypal Feminine manifests itself need to be remarked. Neumann's observations on the appearance of the Lady of the Beasts are relevant:

> The history of the natural sciences shows that man's view of nature develops parallel to his experience of his own nature. When in a later phase of development man seems to be centered in consciousness, ego, and will, a patriarchal god of heaven "governs" nature. But in the matriarchal unconscious phase, a feminine self creates an inner hierarchy of powers. Her image in the human psyche manifests the unconscious and unwilled, but purposive, order of nature. Cruelty, death, and caprice stand side by side with supreme planning, perfect purposiveness, and immortal life. Precisely where man is a creature of instinct living in the image of the beast or half-beast, i.e., where he is wholly or in large part dominated by the drives of the unconscious, the guiding purpose, the unconscious spiritual order of the whole, appears as a goddess in human form, as a Lady of the Beasts.
>
> Man's experience of this goddess in human form is the first indication that he now knows the multiplicity of his own

instinctual drives, which he had experienced in projection
upon animals, to be inferior to the human principle that is
specific to him. He experiences the authority that condi-
tions and orders the instinctual drive. The Great Goddess is
an embodiment of all those psychic structures that are superior to instinct. In this phase the male ego, with its independent will, its consciousness, and its patriarchal values, is
not yet dominant; but it has become clear that the nature of
man contains spiritual forces superior to instinct, even
though they are not yet freely available to the ego but must
be experienced by the ego as a numinous godhead outside
it.[49]

However, the elemental, uroboric character of the Archetypal Feminine is still obvious in the passage we are examining,
and its presence explains one of the relationships between the
developing personality and the unconscious:

> Wherever the harmful character of the Great Mother pre-
> dominates or is equal to her positive and creative side, and
> wherever her destructive side—the phallic element—appears
> together with her fruitful womb, the uroboros is still opera-
> tive in the background. In all these cases, the adolescent
> stage of the ego has not been overcome, nor has the ego yet
> made itself independent of the unconscious.[50]

In *Capricorn*, even at the end, the figure of the anima
(Mara) is only partially separated from the more elemental
forms of the Feminine. The developing *I* gains only a measure
of independence from the numinous fascination the unconscious exerts. Any casual reading of the confessions reveals a
sense of dependence, a reluctance to act on the part of the
hero. But this passivity assumes a different significance if the
figures of the Feminine which pursue the *I* or hold him fascinated are recognized as symbols of the unconscious rather than
realistic figures in a world of bizarre personal relations. The
danger faced by the *I* is the danger of assimilation; the reward
is transformation and development if the struggle of consciousness to become independent is successful. Stability can be
achieved only by a union of opposites, not a rejection of unconscious negative elements. Moreover, the passivity of the

hero suggests not that he is weak, but that he is controlled by autonomous archetypal processes.

The motif of assimilation appears in the metabolic symbolism of *Capricorn.* Such symbolism expresses both the dangers and the transformative possibilities in the relationship between the *I* and the unconscious.[51] The *I* eats "like a monomaniac: the prolonged dreamlit voracity of the man who is thrice breaking his fast." Mara peels the eggs at mealtime; the *cheep-cheep* inside suggests the meals to come. But she is also a "succubus devouring her young," and her "rhythmic predatory wheeze" threatens rather than comforts. Throughout this section of *Capricorn* the *I* is threatened with an assimilation that would destroy it. But the *I* also assimilates the products of the unconscious. Using Jung's insights, Erich Neumann analyzes the motif of eating in mythology and religious ritual in terms of its relationship to the maternal uroboros:

> Thus, on the primitive level, conscious realization is called eating. When we talk of the conscious mind "assimilating" an unconscious content, we are not saying much more than is implied in the symbol of eating and digesting.
>
> The examples from Indian and Egyptian mythology could be multiplied at will, for this sort of elementary food symbolism is archetypal. Wherever liquor, fruit, herbs, etc., appear as the vehicles of life and immortality, including the "water" and "bread" of life, the sacrament of the Host, and every form of food cult down to the present day, we have this ancient mode of human expression before us. The materialization of psychic contents, by which contents that we would call "psychic"—like life, immortality, and death—take on material form in myth and ritual and appear as water, bread, fruit, etc., is a characteristic of the primitive mind. Inside is projected outside, as we say. In reality there is a "psychization" of the object: everything outside us is experienced symbolically, as though saturated with a content which we co-ordinate with the psyche as something psychic or spiritual. This material object outside is then "assimilated," i.e., eaten. Conscious realization is "acted out" in the elementary scheme of nutritive assimilation, and the ritual act of concrete eating is the first form of assimilation known to man. Over this whole sphere of symbolism looms

the maternal uroboros in its mother-child aspect, where
need is hunger and satisfaction means satiety.[52]

The development of the individual parallels the development in mythology:

> In the language of symbols, in ritual, myth, dreams, and
> childhood reality, these contents are "eaten," "incorpo-
> rated," and so "digested." By such acts of introjection and
> the assimilation of previously projected contents the psyche
> builds itself up, the subject and the ego-centered conscious
> personality acquiring more and more "weight" as more and
> more contents are taken in. But, as we have already noted
> when discussing the fragmentation of archetypes, it is only
> through image formation—the giving of form to the form-
> less—that conscious assimilation is made possible.[53]

The result of assimilation is the strengthening of the *I* and
the ultimate decrease in power of the effects of the transpersonal archetypes on the individual. The *I*'s orgy in *Capricorn*'s
"Black Hole of Calcutta" is the journey into the belly of the
whale, the confrontation of the archetype which frees the hero
if he is successful.

The Mara of *Capricorn*, insofar as she is an identity separated from the elementary Feminine, is the dramatic representation of the anima figure developing in the fragmentation of
archetypes. As the purring succubus, however, her negative
characteristics reveal her connection with the more elemental
forms of the Archetypal Feminine. The anima figure, moreover, can appear in "higher" and "lower" forms. Mara un-
questionably resembles the negative anima, and for this reason
she is associated with the city of New York. The orgiastic relationship with her is described by Miller as the "mandala wheel
of lust," one of the numerous negative wheel symbols found in
his work. The name *Mara*, moreover, is associated with the
negative samsara wheel: Mara is the name of the prison of
death.[54]

The struggle of the *I* in *Capricorn* to separate itself from
the deadly fascination of the unconscious and achieve independence is dramatized in relationships between symbols rather
than in a narrative structure. These symbolic actions and the

larger pattern of conversion into opposites, which Jung called *enantiodromia*,[55] are compulsive "actions," which will be discussed in the final section of this study. Perhaps it should be noted here, however, that a stage in this process is completed at the end of *Capricorn,* and the confession does not end without recording the significant effect of transformation in a section I refer to here and elsewhere as "the Easter Sunday episode":

> It is Sunday, the first Sunday of my new life, and I am wearing the dog collar you fastened around my neck. A new life stretches before me. It begins with the day of rest. I lie back on a broad green leaf and I watch the sun bursting in your womb. What a clabber and clatter it makes! All this expressly for me, what? If only you had a million suns in you! If only I could lie here forever enjoying the celestial fireworks!

> I lie suspended over the surface of the moon. The world is in a womblike trance: the inner and the outer ego are in equilibrium. You promised me so much that if I never come out of this it will make no difference. It seems to me that it is exactly 25,960 years since I have been asleep in the black womb of sex. It seems to me that I slept perhaps 365 years too many. But at any rate I am now in the right house, among the sixes, and what lies behind me is well and what lies ahead is well. You come to me disguised as Venus, but you are Lilith, and I know it. My whole life is in the balance; I will enjoy the luxury of this for one day. Tomorrow I shall tip the scales. Tomorrow the equilibrium will be finished; if I ever find it again it will be in the blood and not in the stars. It is well that you promise me so much. I need to be promised nearly everything, for I have lived in the shadow of the sun too long. I want light and chastity—and a solar fire in the guts. I want to be deceived and disillusioned so that I may complete the upper triangle and not be continually flying off the planet into space. I believe everything you tell me, but I know also that it will all turn out differently. I take you as a star and a trap, as a stone to tip the scales, as a judge that is blindfolded, as a hole to fall into, as a path to walk, as a cross and an arrow. Up to the present I traveled the opposite way of the sun; henceforth I travel two ways, as sun and as moon. Henceforth I take on two sexes, two hemispheres, two skies, two sets of everything. Hence-

forth I shall be double-jointed and double-sexed. Everything that happens will happen twice. I shall be as a visitor to this earth, partaking of its blessings and carrying off its gifts. I shall neither serve nor be served. I shall seek the end in myself.

I look out again at the sun—my first full gaze. It is blood-red and men are walking about on the rooftops. Everything above the horizon is clear to me. It is like Easter Sunday. Death is behind me and birth too. . . . I am going to live the spiritual life of the pygmy, the secret life of the little man in the wilderness of the bush. Inner and outer have changed places. Equilibrium is no longer the goal—the scales must be destroyed. Let me hear you promise again all those sunny things you carry inside you. Let me try to believe for one day, while I rest in the open, that the sun brings good tidings. Let me rot in splendor while the sun bursts in your womb. I believe all your lies implicitly. I take you as the personification of evil, as the destroyer of the soul, as the maharanee of the night. Tack your womb up on my wall, so that I may remember you. We must get going. Tomorrow, tomorrow. . . .[56]

These last three paragraphs of *Capricorn* summarize a new state of being for the *I:* they are a stage in the *I*'s progress toward integration and totality. Conscious awareness and acceptance of the treacherous and deceitful nature of the anima appear among the achievements of the *I* in this passage.

But the positive aspect of the anima is not unrecognized: she may be Lilith, but she has a sun in her womb. (The pun is undoubtedly intentional.) In each paragraph the sun is an important image: the sun bursting in the womb, the sun the *I* becomes, the Easter morning blood-red sun of resurrection and transformation. The blessing of the sun is not unmixed: the *I* "must try to believe for one day . . . that the sun brings good tidings." The sun is a symbol of something that has been achieved, for the sun receives the *I*'s "first full gaze." According to Jung (and this interpretation is supported by the other images in the passage), the archetypal symbol of the sun "usually denotes consciousness, illumination, understanding." [57] The sun in this section, moreover, is a rising sun, a bursting sun, the sun of the *I*'s new beginning. After a dark struggle with the Archetypal Feminine in the "womb," the meaning of the *I*'s experience is clear.

A transformation has been achieved and a measure of stability as Neumann describes it: "Differentiation of the ego, separation of the World Parents, and dismemberment of the primordial dragon set man free as a son and expose him to the light, and only then is he born as a personality with a stable ego." Neumann continues:

> The world begins only with the coming of light which constellates the opposition between heaven and earth as the basic symbol of all other opposites. Before that, there reigns the "illimitable darkness," . . . With the rising of the sun or . . . the creation of the firmament, which divides the upper from the lower, mankind's day begins, and the universe becomes visible with all its contents.
>
> In relation to man and his ego, the creation of light and the birth of the sun are bound up with the separation of the World Parents and the positive and negative consequences which ensue for the hero who separates them.[58]

Consciousness is still subject to the treachery of the unconscious and subject even to the disillusionment and pain which consciousness will bring. ("Let me try to believe for one day . . . that the sun brings good tidings.")

Consciousness, moreover, is only part of the total personality, and the other symbols in the passage must be read as an allegorical account of the temporary achievement of a union of opposites, of totality of personality. This experience is more than the emergence of consciousness (as sun); it includes union of sun with the chthonic world (the moon of the night sky). The antinomial nature of the *I* is clearly recognized at the end of *Capricorn* in the experience of totality:

> Up to the present I traveled the opposite way of the sun; henceforth I travel two ways, as sun and as moon. Henceforth I take on two sexes, two hemispheres, two skies, two sets of everything.

The androgynous vision of the self appears, as do other symbols of the archetype of the self. The hermaphrodite and homunculus are archetypal symbols of the self and the process of individuation Jung has described as a *"mysterium coniunctionis"* in which the self is experienced "as a nuptial union of opposite halves." [59]

The geometrical symbol in this passage can be identified as a symbol of the self, especially in the context of these final paragraphs of *Capricorn*. In discussing geometrical and arithmetical symbols of the self, Jung observed:

> Three can be regarded as a relative totality, since it usually represents either a spiritual totality that is a product of thought, like the Trinity, or else an instinctual, chthonic one, like the triadic nature of the gods of the underworld—the "lower triad." Psychologically, however, three—if the context indicates that it refers to the self—should be understood as a defective quaternity or as a stepping-stone towards it. Empirically, a triad has a trinity opposed to it as its complement. The complement of the quaternity is unity.[60]

Miller speaks of his need for the unconscious, his need to be "deceived and disillusioned" so that he may "complete the upper triangle" and achieve, thereby, the quaternity Jung considers among the most important of the symbols of the self.

The relationship with Mara, which represents allegorically the struggle between consciousness and the unconscious, produces at least temporarily in *Capricorn* the experience of totality. The experience, however, is recognized as one that is never final, for one can never do away with the threat of the unconscious, nor, indeed, would this be desirable, for the unconscious is the source of the energy needed for transformation.

Miller's dramatization of this process is only partly in terms of human "characters" in *Capricorn*, yet by the time he writes *The Rosy Crucifixion* the figure of Mara is more and more realized in human form. Although she continues to manifest her highly symbolic significance and her negative aspects, especially in *Sexus*, she also becomes an identity in the outside world. She must be "won" in a travesty of romantic involvements; she is even mysteriously isolated and "guarded." Her form, for the reader, is clearer, more human. In fact, she is capable of generating a plot of sorts. At the same time she retains her numinous fascination for the *I*. In *Plexus* and *Nexus*, however, she appears even more ordinary—human and eccentric rather than mysteriously and magically significant. She "belongs" much more to the external world and her numinous significance is largely lost. Widmer remarks that she changes from the demonic Dark Lady into "an ordinary woman to be exploited—the somewhat erratic female who indulged, supported, and encouraged Miller. . . ." [61]

She is, in fact, more "ordinary" in the later volumes, although Miller makes her more ordinary by controlling her through conscious assertion of the power of analysis. He even "divides" her into parts—for Anastasia is a shadow figure for Mona, helping the *I* to isolate and assimilate the negative "masculine" aspect of the anima.[62] She is assimilated, and separated from the Archetypal Feminine by the increasing integration of the *I*. At the end of *Nexus* (and even earlier) she is no longer a threat. One is tempted to extend Frye's suggestions about the anima figure in romance and argue that romance as a literary form arises from a certain stage in the realization of the anima. Certainly the fragmentation of the Archetypal Feminine which produces this all-powerful figure, the anima, produces the allegorical structure of Miller's confessions.

PART TWO

symbols of the self

Chapter Four

Ne te quaesiveris extra

Symbols in the Easter Sunday section at the end of *Capricorn* identify the emerging self of the confessions as an androgynous union of opposites, of negative and positive —a totality in which conscious and unconscious elements are in provisional equilibrium.[1] Art and the life of the artist become ways by which Miller explores this self, as his endless theoretical discussions of the creative process confirm. But the formal traditions of art and even Miller's apparently anti-traditional literary productions are acknowledged sublimations. They will be eventually abandoned in favor of life and the achievement of a human perfection which fully reconciles the repressed or negative elements of human nature with the acceptable or positive. Such achievement means the full emergence and stability of the self.

It is not surprising that Miller explores this self in bizarre or grotesque symbols and symbolically distorted scenes of human coitus to which the reader has no comfortable and familiar responses. Nor is it necessary to dismiss Miller's visions of the self as muddy surrealism or clumsy naturalism. He belongs securely in a romantic tradition with which he has been identified.[2]

Moreover, the problem is complicated by the significance of the term *self*, which can be used in a more general and vague sense to describe the "total personality" in Miller's fiction and in a more specific, Jungian, sense to describe what seems close to being Jung's archetype of the self. The strangeness of Miller's symbols (if they are strange), the seeming incongruity or the deliberate incongruity of their combinations, and his deliberate seeking after the symbols of other cultures may be inevitable in a twentieth-century exploration of an alien self estranged from community.

Hans Jonas has noted some broad historical parallels between such contemporary circumstances and those in which the symbolic productions of Gnosticism appeared. The estrangement from community, the "awakening of the inner self from the slumber or intoxication of the world," the ethical disturbances of antinomianism—these were significant elements of Gnosticism. Such experiences are central in Miller's confessions for Miller also insists on the Gnostic demand that "alienation from the world is to be deepened and brought to a head, for the extrication of the inner self which only thus can gain itself." [3]

The confrontation, fragmentation, and assimilation of the Archetypal Feminine as a symbol of the unconscious [4] and a deepening alienation from the world are interdependent patterns of symbolic action in *Capricorn*. The *I*'s utter rejection of various roles (husband, wage earner, father) which determine what he is or should be and his antinomianism are necessary to the long inward journey into the self, the search for transformation, which he proposes at the beginning of *Capricorn*.

In the inward search and outward alienation, Miller on occasion produces satire or polemic. His narrator's exploitation of people, for example, functions to reveal their weaknesses and not the moral inadequacies of the narrator himself. In effect, they exploit themselves; he does not exploit them, because their weaknesses (revealed by Miller's consistent vision of the self) make them suitably vulnerable. Whenever this occurs, Miller's form could be described more accurately as *anatomy*, and in later volumes of *The Rosy Crucifixion* and in the *Big Sur and the Oranges of Hieronymous Bosch*, he moves closer to unmixed anatomy; action in *Big Sur*, for example, is engulfed by the intellectual dissection of the world.

In the confessions, however, the *I*'s impulse to move inward toward the "aboriginal self" is analogous to the pattern of symbolic action in *Walden*. Miller's interest in Thoreau and Emerson might best be explained by R. W. B. Lewis' suggestions for a Jungian analysis of the New England transcendentalists. Lewis, however, points out that a special psychological vocabulary is not necessary to understand what Thoreau was seeking to explain.[5] The symbolic language in which Miller's self is explored, however, is not as readily accessible. He has moved much closer to the language of dream and has explored more fully the negative and destructive productions of the unconscious, pushing life even further into its corner. He is closer to the tradition of the romantic grotesque. Moreover, the Necropolis of the twentieth century is Miller's Concord and his alienation is more intense, exacerbated by an utterly depersonalized culture.

Hence the parallel with Gnosticism is not altogether arbitrary. The comparison, moreover, reveals some suggestive formal similarities. The Gnostic attempt to define and explore the alienated self, for example, was expressed frequently in sexual symbolism that is openly obscene by twentieth-century literary standards. The figure of Christ (a central symbol in both Gnosticism and in Miller for the archetypal self or the "inner man reached by the path of self-knowledge" [6]) appears in the context of sexual symbolism. According to Jung's analysis, the experience of the archetype of the self in Gnosticism and elsewhere is "circular," moving around a center.[7] Miller's dramatization of the self in his fiction takes precisely such forms. Traditional and numinous symbolic manifestations of the Archetypal Feminine, moreover, are frequently obscene, and coitus serves Miller as a means of expressing relationships between the unconscious and conscious aspects of the *I*. Images of castration, sexual enslavement, and demonic possession by sexual energy are among his most effective means of describing the inward journey and of providing an iconography of the inner world.

The problem of the exploration of the self is for the writer, as Miller recognized in his rejection of traditional novel forms, an inescapable formal problem. If it is possible to gain access to inner layers of being, to explore a guessed-at aboriginal self, the geography of that world must be described. Jung's study of the symbols of the archetype of the self in such systems as Gnosticism and alchemy provides a few maps which corroborate the discoveries of Miller.

To attempt a description of the Miller self from a literary point of view is not without its perils. Like the female figures of his confessions, the *I* represents various aspects of the archetype, sometimes pure "consciousness," sometimes "trickster," "clown," "Christ," "Anti-Christ," or "child." The *I* can appear as fire, fish, light, or eye, or in one of the most significant non-human images—the rock. Occasionally a critical, analytical "consciousness," at other times little more than the symbolic suggestion of pure energy, the *I* cannot be considered a fictional or even autobiographical "character" with a consistent or developing personality readily accessible to the reader. Jung's description of the archetype of the self best approaches a summary of these characteristics. He insists that the self is not the equivalent of the "ego," but it includes the ego and what are called conscious and unconscious elements:

> The ego is, by definition, subordinate to the self and is related to it like a part to the whole. Inside the field of consciousness it has, as we say, free will. By this I do not mean anything philosophical, only the well-known psychological fact of "free choice," or rather the subjective feeling of freedom. But, just as our free will clashes with necessity in the outside world, so also it finds its limits outside the field of consciousness in the subjective inner world, where it comes into conflict with the facts of the self . . . the self acts upon the ego like an *objective occurrence* which free will can do very little to alter. It is, indeed, well known that the ego not

only can do nothing against the self, but is sometimes actually assimilated by unconscious components of the personality that are in the process of development and is greatly altered by them.[8]

For Jung, the self is an archetype of the collective or transpersonal unconscious. As an archetype, its form is autonomous and only its contents can be assimilated or integrated into the "ego-personality." The search for the self, the increase in self-knowledge, is an attempt on the part of consciousness to establish a "critical approach" to the unconscious. This turning inward toward the numinous and autonomous archetypes is a process experienced in images and an experience *of* images, especially images in the visual sense.[9] The process, moreover, has an essentially rhythmical nature:

> Its development usually shows an enantiodromian structure like the text of the *I Ching*, and so presents a rhythm of negative and positive, loss and gain, dark and light. Its beginning is almost invariably characterized by one's getting stuck in a blind alley or in some impossible situation; and its goal is, broadly speaking, illumination or higher consciousness, by means of which the initial situation is overcome on a higher level. . . . The chief danger is that of succumbing to the fascinating influence of the archetypes, and this is most likely to happen when the archetypal images are not made conscious.[10]

Miller's fiction is a dramatization of this process. Jung has described the process of a human lifetime, and Miller, although he insists that his fiction can never be completed until his life is completed, has in his several volumes and especially in *Cancer* and *Capricorn* succeeded in dramatizing stages in the process, or if not stages, significant events in the process which can be singled out, rounded off, and unified: in *Cancer*, for example, the confrontation of the unconscious symbolized as the Archetypal Feminine in its elementary form; in *Capricorn*, the emergence of Mara as the anima figure.

The confrontation or recognition of such archetypes is one stage in the movement toward integration of the *I* or personality. It is preceded by recognition and assimilation of the

shadow (or negative aspects of the individual): suggestions of
this shadow archetype appear in many of the *I*'s male companions in the confessions, figures which he is both identified
with and separated from. Each is an *alter ego* who acts out
symbolically negative roles in the *I*'s development. The charge
often repeated that Miller has no ability to create character is
justified but irrelevant. These figures are projections of aspects
of the *I*. And the confrontation of the anima is possible only
after the *I* recognizes the shadow elements in himself: [11]

> I should like to emphasize that the integration of the
> shadow, or the realization of the personal unconscious,
> marks the first stage in the analytic process, and that without
> it a recognition of the anima and animus is impossible. The
> shadow can be realized only through a relation to a partner,
> and anima and animus only through a relation to the oppo-
> site sex, because only in such a relation do their projections
> become operative. The recognition of anima or animus
> gives rise, in a man to a triad, one third of which is tran-
> scendent: the masculine subject, the opposing feminine sub-
> ject, and the transcendent anima. . . . The missing fourth
> element that would make the triad a quaternity is, in a man,
> the archetype of the Wise Old Man. . . . These four consti-
> tute a half immanent and half transcendent quaternity, an
> archetype which I have called the *marriage
> quaternio.* . . . The self, on the other hand, is a God-image,
> or at least cannot be distinguished from one. Of this the
> early Christian spirit was not ignorant, otherwise Clement
> of Alexandria could never have said that he who knows him-
> self knows God.[12]

This scheme is not repeated here for the purpose of suggesting an exact parallel with Miller's fictional dramatization of
the search for the experience of "totality"; however, it serves
to suggest a relationship between the self and the other archetypes I have described and does indeed seem to describe some
of the action in the confessions and anatomies.

In reading Miller the distinction between ego and self must
be kept in mind, for the pronoun *I* serves to identify both consciousness and the elemental symbols of self which the writer
produces. Such an inside view does away with "people," with

the novelist's "character," and even with character as narrator, but the *I* can stand for those aspects of the self (in Jung's wider sense) which are being either confronted or assimilated by consciousness. The *I* can sometimes stand for the totality, that is, can be fully identified with one of the symbols (as in the Christ figure) or it can be described through rapid juxtaposition of a whole gamut of symbols ranging from the inorganic to organic and "appear" as "energy" rather than "character."

The *I* as analytical consciousness also belongs to a wider world of ideas and is responsible for the theoretical passages in which Miller attempts to establish an intellectual context (usually through the partial assimilation of ideas from his eclectic reading) which is also necessary for the equilibrium the *I* seeks. For psychic health, consciousness can neither be assimilated by the self, nor the self by consciousness, according to Jung. The peculiar moving back and forth between these two often accounts for the incongruous juxtaposition of formal elements—fantasy and essay, dream and satire—in Miller.

In *Capricorn*, for example, the *I* describes the most pleasurable dream he knows, one in which dissolution and assimilation occur:

> Just as I go toward this house the lot on which I am standing begins to grow vague at the edges, to dissolve, to vanish. Space rolls in on me like a carpet and swallows me up, and with it of course the house which I never succeed in entering.

> There is absolutely no transition from this, the most pleasurable dream I know, to the heart of a book called *Creative Evolution*.[13]

But the analysis of *Creative Evolution* that follows leads to the intellectual recognition that the experience of the book was an initiation rite, and experience of "disorientation and reorientation," of revelation, a "moving day for the soul." The fantasy experience of dissolution brought the *I* close to the house (possibly a symbol of the self because it is located in the middle of a great open space [14] in the *Capricorn* passage), although he never enters. In the "essay" on Bergson, an experience of disorientation (followed by reorientation) is assimilated by the conscious intellectual examination of the meaning of *Creative Evolution* for the *I*.

It is not always necessary, however, to rely on such a schematization of psychic processes to note numerous relationships between Miller's ideas and his dramatic passages, although Jung's insights provide considerable illumination. Most of Miller's theoretical discussions are concerned with the problems of art: the artist in society, the artist and the creative process, art and tradition, art and life. His underlying assumption is that a social structure which alienates the artist and destroys the creative impulses in man commands no allegiance from the individual.

Miller's antinomianism is not new or unfamiliar, and those who point out that his ideas are borrowed and often trite are undeniably correct. But he is a utopian whose real concern is not the future of art but the future of human life. Art is a sublimation which will be eventually unnecessary. His exploration of inner psychic processes is an attempt to discover what the greater self is; his acceptance of opposites is the familiar attempt to reconcile the negative and positive aspects of man's nature (including the drive toward death); his speculations on society, an attempt to postulate a utopia in which this reconciled self finds full expression. Following one utopian tradition, Miller rejects work as a necessary sublimation of aggressive or negative elements in man. Art, too, is to be rejected, although it is a sublimation of a different order. The full manifestation of the total personality is more important, and all of Miller's speculations on the nature of art and the artist should be considered in these terms. His position is asserted emphatically in *Cancer:* "Everything that was literature has fallen from me. There are no more books to be written, thank God." [15]

Miller's utopian vision sees a world in which an unknowable and unknown self can flourish—a self whose nature can be described only in symbols and which is only partly accessible to consciousness.[16] The utopia in which it will flourish will not be found among the utopian worlds of the eighteenth or nineteenth centuries, moreover. In *Black Spring* he describes the plight of the eighteenth and nineteenth centuries: "What fascinated men of the eighteenth century was the vision of the end. They had enough. They wanted to retrace their steps, climb back into the womb again." [17] Robinson Crusoe is the "first genuine neurotic, a man who had himself shipwrecked in order to live outside his time in a world of his own which he could share with another human being. . . ." And after Crusoe, "everyone is running away from himself to find an imaginary desert isle, to live out this dream of Robinson Crusoe." They all find, instead, the plague of modern progress:

> Follow the classic flights, of Melville, Rimbaud, Gauguin, Jack London, Henry James, D. H. Lawrence . . . thousands of them. None of them found happiness. Rimbaud found cancer. Gauguin found syphilis. Lawrence found the white plague. The plague—that's it! Be it cancer, syphilis, tuberculosis, or what not. *The plague!* The plague of modern progress: colonization, trade, free Bibles, war, disease, artificial limbs, factories, slaves, insanity, neuroses, psychoses, cancer, syphilis, tuberculosis, anemia, strikes, lockouts, starvation, nullity, vacuity, restlessness, striving, despair, ennui, suicide, bankruptcy, arterio-sclerosis, megalomania, schizophrenia, hernia, cocaine, prussic acid, stink bombs, tear gas, mad dogs, auto-suggestion, auto-intoxication, psychotherapy, hydrotherapy, electric massages, vacuum cleaners, pemmican, grape nuts, hemorrhoids, gangrene. No desert isles. No Paradise. Not even *relative* happiness. Men running away from themselves so frantically that they look for salvation under the ice floes or in tropical swamps, or else they climb the Himalayas or asphyxiate themselves in the stratosphere. . . .[18]

The alienated self in Miller, however, must return to itself. His utopia belongs among those utopian fantasies of the twentieth century which Frank Manuel considers a "characteristic resurgence of the Adamite utopia in a mechanized society." [19] In such visions, the negative and positive, the opposites of man's nature are no longer sublimated by his culture nor controlled and directed by his social institutions, but are fully reconciled and functioning as part of the total individual. Although Manuel does not consider such marginal literary figures as Miller in his analysis of utopias, his discussion of the views of human nature, or the psychologies which give various utopias their peculiar form, indicates the relationship between Miller's utopian vision and the nature of the self Miller dramatizes. Manuel points out that among the new utopians peculiar to our age are those who recognize the challenge presented by Freud's insights into what is considered the irreconcilable opposition of Eros and Thanatos. Miller insists on the acceptance of death in order to live; the fear of death, for him, is what produces the fear of life.[20] His vision, when it is clear, insists on a world where the reconciled opposites are eternally at play, a world in which the symbol of the whole self, the androgynous figure, is manifest and fully alive. The machine will disappear:

> The new civilization, which may take centuries or a few thousand years to usher in, will not be *another* civilization —it will be the open stretch of realization which all the past civilizations have pointed to. The city, which was the birth-place of civilization, such as we know it to be, will exist no more. There will be nuclei of course, but they will be mobile and fluid. The peoples of the earth will no longer be shut off from one another within states but will flow freely over the surface of the earth and intermingle. There will be no fixed constellations of human aggregates. Governments will give way to management, using the word in a broad sense. The politician will become as superannuated as the dodo bird. The machine will never be dominated, as some imagine; it will be scrapped, eventually, but not before men have understood the nature of the mystery which binds them to their creation. The worship, investigation and subjugation of the machine will give way to the lure of all that is truly occult. This problem is bound up with the larger one of power—and of possession. Man will be forced to realize that power must be kept open, fluid and free. His aim will be not to possess power but to radiate it.[21]

And in the distant future the androgynous figure appears:

> The years immediately ahead of us will be a false dawn, that is my belief. We cannot demolish our educational, legal and

economic pediments overnight, nor even our phony religious superstructures. Until these are completely overthrown there is not much hope of a new order. . . .

I do not believe that this repetitious cycle of insanity which is called history will continue forever. I believe there will be a great break through—within the next few centuries. I think that what we are heralding as the Age of Technic will be nothing more than a transition period, as was the Renaissance. We will need, to be sure, all our technical knowledge and skill to settle once and for all the problem of securing to every man, woman and child the fundamental necessities. We will make a drastic revision, it also goes without saying, of our notion of necessities, which is an altogether crude and primitive one. With the concomitant emancipation of woman, entailed by this great change, the awakening of the love instinct will transform every domain of life. The era of neuters is drawing to a close. With the establishment of a new and vital polarity we shall witness the birth of male-and-female in every individual. What then portends in the realm of art is truly unthinkable. Our art has been masculine through and through, that is to say, lop-sided. It has been vitiated by the unacknowledged feminine principle. This is as true of ancient as of modern art. The tyrannical, subterranean power of the female must come to an end. Men have paid a heavy tribute for their seeming subjugation of the female.[22]

If we remember Frye's definition of the confession, we can understand the formal as well as the thematic relationship between the dramatization of psychic events in Miller and the passages on such theoretical subjects as the nature of society and the role of the artist:

Most autobiographies are inspired by a creative, and therefore fictional, impulse to select only those events and experiences in the writer's life that go to build up an integrated pattern. This pattern may be something larger than himself with which he has come to identify himself, or simply the coherence of his character and attitudes. We may call this very important form of prose fiction the confession form, following St. Augustine, who appears to have invented it, and Rousseau, who established a modern type of it.[23]

The theoretical and intellectual interest which according to Frye plays a leading role in the confession, is, in Miller's work, the nature of the self, not the personal self of a Henry Miller, but a transpersonal self whose nature is explored and experienced by a fictional Henry Miller.

Chapter Five

The Gorilla of Despair

So we dance, to an ice-cold frenzied rhythm, to short waves and long waves, a dance on the inside of the cup of nothingness, each centimeter of lust running to dollars and cents. We taxi from one perfect female to another seeking the vulnerable defect, but they are flawless and impermeable in their impeccable lunar consistency. This is the icy white maidenhead of love's logic, the web of the ebbed tide, the fringe of absolute vacuity. And on this fringe of the virginal logic of perfection I am dancing the soul dance of white desperation, the last white man pulling the trigger on the last emotion, the gorilla of despair beating his breast with immaculate gloved paws. I am the gorilla who feels his wings growing, a giddy gorilla in the center of a satin-like emptiness; . . .[1]

The symbols of the transpersonal unconscious which represent its feminine nature for consciousness appear in Miller as the manifestations of the Archetypal Feminine, but the archetype of the self is also a form of the unconscious and appears, as we have noted, in a different complex of images. Its contents are no less difficult to experience, assimilate, or confront. Jung, moreover, describes a hierarchy of value judgments in the relationships between the archetypes and ego-consciousness:

If, therefore, in dealing with psychic contents one makes allowance not only for intellectual judgments but for value judgments as well, not only is the result a more complete picture of the content in question, but one also gets a better idea of the particular position it holds in the hierarchy of psychic contents in general. The feeling-value is a very important criterion which psychology cannot do without, because it determines in large measure the role which the content will play in the psychic economy. That is to say, the affective value gives the measure of the intensity of an idea, and the intensity in its turn expresses that idea's energic tension, its effective potential. The shadow, for instance, usually has a decidedly negative feeling value, while the anima, like the animus, has more of a positive one. Whereas the shadow is accompanied by more or less definite and describable feeling tones, the anima and animus exhibit feeling qualities that are harder to define. Mostly they are felt to be fascinating or numinous. Often they are surrounded by an atmosphere of sensitivity, touchy reserve, secretiveness, painful intimacy, and even absoluteness. The relative autonomy of the anima- and animus-figures expresses itself in these qualities. In order of affective rank they stand to the shadow very much as the shadow stands in relation to ego-consciousness. The main affective emphasis seems to lie on the latter; at any rate, it is able, by means of a considerable expenditure of energy, to repress the shadow, at least temporarily. But if for any reason the unconscious gains the upper hand, then the valency of the shadow and of the other figures increases proportionately, so that the scale of values is reversed. What lay furthest away from waking consciousness and seemed unconscious assumes, as it were, a threatening shape, and the affective value increases the higher up the scale you go: ego-consciousness, shadow, anima, self.[2]

The hierarchy of psychic contents of which Jung speaks is in fact what lends "cosmic order" to the symbolic arrangement of Miller's work. The formlessness of his confessions begins to disappear when this order is explored; instead, an obsessive and rigid, if not altogether accessible, order or cosmos appears to underlie his fictional confessions. Angus Fletcher has suggested that imagery and symbolism which reflect a hierarchy produce the essential type of allegorical image, and he proposes to revive the term *kosmos* as the proper term for such "ornamental diction":

> Just how kosmos is the essential type of an allegorical image will appear as soon as the term is defined. It signifies (1) a universe, and (2) a symbol that implies a rank in a hierarchy. As the latter it will be attached to, or associated with, or even substituted for, any object which the writer wants to place in a hierarchical position.[3]

The archetype of the self, manifested in traditional symbols which rescue Miller's allegorical dramatization of psychic processes from solipsism, is sometimes described in his fiction as the "gorilla of despair" locked within, sometimes as the numinous hermaphrodite which "consciousness" must "seek" in order to achieve totality and maturity. Neumann's description of this movement toward "wholeness" suggests both the significance of androgyny and its hierarchical values:

> Structural wholeness, with the self as center of the psyche, is symbolized by the mandala, by the circle with a center, and by the hermaphroditic uroboros. But this uroboric circle now [as the individual moves toward maturity] has the luminous core of the self for a center. Whereas in the beginning the uroboros existed at the animal level only, so that the ego germ contained in its midst was almost hidden, in the unfolding flower of the mandala the animal tension of opposites is overcome, transcended by a self which blossoms forth into a corolla of opposites. At the beginning of the development, consciousness was all but extinguished by the crushing superiority of the unconscious; at the end, it is broadened and strengthened by its connection with the self. This combination of the self with the stability of the ego serves to subdue and bind in a magic circle all contents, whether of the world or the unconscious, outside or inside.

> The self-differentiating structure of the psyche is reflected in a world cleft asunder by the principle of opposites into outside and inside, conscious and unconscious, life and spirit, male and female, individual and collective. But to the maturing psyche, slowly integrating itself under the sign of the hermaphrodite, the world, too, assumes the appearance of the hermaphroditic ring of existence, within which a

human center takes shape, be it the individual who comes to self-realization between the inner and outer worlds, or humanity itself. For humanity as a whole and the single individual have the same task, namely, to realize themselves as a unity. Both are cast forth into a reality, one half of which confronts them as nature and the external world, while the other half approaches them as psyche and the unconscious, spirit and daemonic power. . . .

. . . .

But only when the conscious development of mankind as a whole, and not merely of single individuals, has reached this stage of synthesis, will the supra-individual uroboros situation truly be overcome, and with it, the collective power of the dragon. The collective unconscious of mankind must be experienced and apprehended by the consciousness of mankind as the ground common to all men. Not until the differentiation into races, nations, tribes, and groups has, by a process of integration, been resolved in a new synthesis, will the danger of recurrent invasions from the unconscious be averted. A future humanity will then realize the center, which the individual personality experiences today as his own self-center, to be one with humanity's very self, whose coming to birth will finally vanquish and cast out that old serpent, the primordial uroboric dragon.[4]

Within this visionary projection of Erich Neumann's hope for the evolving consciousness of man, the process which Miller's confessions dramatize is postulated as the process all humanity will undergo before the realization of the utopian dream. Neumann's intellectual scheme, moreover, is strikingly analogous to the hierarchical cosmos created in Miller's fiction and commented on in his essays. Actually only within such a scheme does Miller's celebration of the wholeness of self become fully clear, as do his symbols for the self and his search for the center. Miller's insistence, for example, that he is the rock or stone, "the happy rock," is an assertion of wholeness in archetypal terms: ". . . diamond, stone, or rock, as symbols of the self, represent the indestructibility and permanence of something that can no longer be split apart by the opposites." [5]

In tracing the significance of the stone as an autonomous

symbol of the self appearing in the projections of the alchemists, Jung has described its relationship to water, especially to the dark depths of the sea, the place of darkness that is the source of life. This darkness suggests the *nigredo* of the alchemical process from which the stone issues. The dramatization of the psychic awareness of the archetypal self in *Capricorn* is symbolically analogous. The following is one example among many:

> It is only after the third meal that the morning gifts, bequeathed by the phony alliance of the ancestors, begin to drop away and the true rock of the self, the happy rock sheers up out of the muck of the soul. With nightfall the pinhead universe begins to expand. It expands organically, from an infinitesimal nuclear speck, in the way that minerals or star clusters form. It eats into the surrounding chaos like a rat boring through store cheese. All chaos could be gathered together on a pinhead, but the self, microscopical at the start, works up to a universe from any point in space. This is not the self about which books are written, but the ageless self which has been farmed out through millenary ages to men with names and dates, the self which begins and ends as a worm, which *is* the worm in the cheese called the world. Just as the slightest breeze can set a vast forest in motion so, by some unfathomable impulse from within, the rocklike self can begin to grow, and in this growth nothing can prevail against it. It's like Jack Frost at work, and the whole world a windowpane. No hint of labor, no sound, no struggle, no rest; relentless, remorseless, unremitting, the growth of the self goes on. Only two items on the bill of fare: the self and the not-self. And an eternity in which to work it out. In this eternity, which has nothing to do with time or space, there are interludes in which something like a thaw sets in. The form of the self breaks down, but the self, like climate, remains. In the night the amorphous matter of the self assumes the most fugitive forms; error seeps in through the portholes and the wanderer is unlatched from his door. This door which the body wears, if opened out on to the world, leads to annihilation. It is the door in every fable out of which the magician steps; nobody has ever read of him returning home through the selfsame door. If opened inward there are infinite doors, all resembling trapdoors: no horizons are visible, no airlines, no rivers, no maps, no tickets.

Each *couche* is a halt for the night only, be it five minutes or ten thousand years. The doors have no handles and they never wear out. Most important to note—there is no end in sight. All these halts for the night, so to speak, are like abortive explorations of a myth. One can feel his way about, take bearings, observe passing phenomena; one can even feel at home. But there is no taking root. Just at the moment when one begins to feel "established" the whole terrain founders, the soil underfoot is afloat, the constellations are shaken loose from their moorings, the whole known universe, including the imperishable self, starts moving silently, ominously, shudderingly serene and unconcerned, toward an unknown, unseen destination. All the doors seem to be opening at once: the pressure is so great that an implosion occurs and in the swift plunge the skeleton bursts asunder. It was some such gigantic collapse which Dante must have experienced when he situated himself in Hell; it was not a bottom which he touched, but a core, a dead center from which time itself is reckoned. Here the comedy begins, for here it is seen to be divine.[6]

In this passage Miller describes the self as the product of the night experience, sheering up from the muck of the soul only at nightfall when the world of light—consciousness, day, tradition (the morning gifts)—is in eclipse. The rebirth of the self requires a traditional descent into the dead core or into "Hell." Self is more than ego, and it is archetypal, accessible to all men, ageless—not the "self about which books are written." The symbols which describe the psychic process here are elemental in the sense that they are not "human." The night, Hell, the long corridors into the inner world, rooms—all suggest the womb in its archetypal sense: the Feminine as a symbol of the unconscious. The self as archetype is also "in" the unconscious and is accessible to consciousness only symbolically: the rock sheering up out of the muck, the universe which expands, for example.

The dark route inward leads either to transformation or annihilation; hence Miller's insistence on danger in his fiction. It is significant in the allegorical structure of *Capricorn* that this description of the continuing process undergone by the individual in quest of the archetypal self occurs just before the narrator mentions (anticipating) that he meets the transformative character (Mara) in a dance hall, after which he is "shunted back to some timeless vector where the process of growth is kept in abeyance." [7] To read Miller's fiction as the wish to return to the womb, in any simple sense, is to miss the significance of these passages, and indeed the allegorical pattern of the whole. The night journeys, the descents into Hell, the returns to the womb, to the sea, to the night, to the primal stuff, are all symbols of the movement into the inner world, the unconscious from which the *I* must emerge transformed, if it survives the numinous fascination of the unconscious and is not devoured, dissolved, or spiritually castrated. The self and salvation cannot be sought by stepping outside "the door which the body wears" into the world.[8] The way to the self is inward. And since this self as archetype can only be "glimpsed" symbolically, in a single passage it may appear in many apparently unrelated images: a "happy rock," a "universe," or a "worm." [9]

At the end of the section of *Capricorn* called "Interlude" in which these passages occur, the narrator "realizes" symbolically the nature of his life as he approaches the totality of the *I*. At these moments, such elements of the unconscious as are symbolized by the Archetypal Feminine and the archetype of the self (that is, the images in which they appear) become temporarily assimilated by consciousness. This assimilation provides the *I* with enormous psychic energy:

> You live like a happy rock in the midst of the ocean: you are fixed while everything about you is in turbulent motion. You are fixed in a reality which permits the thought that nothing is fixed, that even the happiest and mightiest rock will one day be utterly dissolved and fluid as the ocean from which it was born.

> This is the musical life which I was approaching by first skating like a maniac through all the vestibules and corridors which lead from the outer to the inner. My struggles never brought me near it, nor did my furious activity, nor my rubbing elbows with humanity. All that was simply a move-

ment from vector to vector in a circle which, however the perimeter expanded, remained withal parallel to the realm I speak of. The wheel of destiny can be transcended at any moment because at every point of its surface it touches the real world and only a spark of illumination is necessary to bring about the miraculous, to transform the skater to a swimmer and the swimmer to a rock. The rock is merely an image of the act which stops the futile rotation of the wheel and plunges the being into full consciousness. And full consciousness is indeed like an inexhaustible ocean which gives itself to sun and moon and also *includes* the sun and moon. Everything which is born out of the limitless ocean of light—even the night.

Sometimes, in the ceaseless revolutions of the wheel, I caught a glimpse of the nature of the jump which it was necessary to make. To jump clear of the clockwork—that was the liberating thought. To be something more, something *different,* than the most brilliant maniac of the earth! The story of man on earth bored me. Conquest, even the conquest of evil, bored me. To radiate goodness is marvelous, because it is tonic, invigorating, vitalizing. But just *to be* is still more marvelous, because it is endless and requires no demonstration. To be is music, which is a profanation of silence in the interest of silence, and therefore beyond good and evil. Music is the manifestation of action without activity. It is the pure act of creation swimming on its own bosom. Music neither goads nor defends, neither seeks nor explains. Music is the noiseless sound made by the swimmer in the ocean of consciousness. It is a reward which can only be given by oneself. It is the gift of the god which one is because he has ceased thinking about God. It is an augur of the god which every one will become in due time, when all that *is* will *be* beyond imagination.[10]

In this passage Miller sums up the significance of the integration of the *I* toward which his fiction moves. The rock is acknowledged as the center, the archetypal self which permits the individual to escape from the meaninglessness of the wheel of experience, that is, the wheel of life in its negative sense—a traditional symbol of fate and death which is associated with the Terrible Mother.[11]

The wheel symbolism is negative here, but the wheel can

become a magic and positive circle, associated in Jung's system with mandala symbolism and the search for the center, the self:

> As I have said, mandala means "circle." There are innumerable variants of the motif, . . . but they are all based on the squaring of a circle. Their basic motif is the premonition of a centre of personality, a kind of central point within the psyche, to which everything is related, by which everything is arranged, and which is itself a source of energy. The energy of the central point is manifested in the almost irresistible compulsion and urge to *become what one is,* just as every organism is driven to assume the form that is characteristic of its nature, no matter what the circumstances. This centre is not felt or thought of as the ego but, if one may so express it, as the *self.* Although the centre is represented by an innermost point, it is surrounded by a periphery containing everything that belongs to the self—the paired opposites that make up the total personality. This totality comprises consciousness first of all, then the personal unconscious, and finally an indefinitely large segment of the collective unconscious whose archetypes are common to all mankind. A certain number of these, however, are permanently or temporarily included within the scope of the personality and, through this contact, acquire an individual stamp as the shadow, anima, and animus, to mention only the best-known figures. The self, though on the one hand simple, is on the other hand an extremely composite thing, a "conglomerate soul," to use the Indian expression.[12]

The center or self is the source of creative change, hence the transformation:

> But if the life-mass is to be transformed a *circumambulatio* is necessary, i.e., exclusive concentration on the centre, the place of creative change. During this process one is "bitten" by animals; in other words, we have to expose ourselves to the animal impulses of the unconscious without identifying ourselves with them and without "running away"; for flight from the unconscious would defeat the purpose of the whole proceeding. We must hold our ground, which means here that the process initiated by the dreamer's self-observation must be experienced in all its ramifications and then articulated with consciousness to the best of his understanding. This often entails an almost unbearable tension because of

> the utter incommensurability between conscious life and the
> unconscious process, which can only be experienced in the
> innermost soul and cannot touch the visible surface of life at
> any point. The principle of conscious life is: "Nihil est in
> intellectu, quod non prius fuerit in sensu." But the principle
> of the unconscious is the autonomy of the psyche itself, re-
> flecting, in the play of its images, not the world but its own
> self, even though it utilizes the illustrative possibilities of-
> fered by the sensible world in order to make its images
> clear.[13]

Transformation and illumination are the ends sought by the
I, for these bring about the integration of the individual. The
possibility that the conscious mind can lose touch with the center, however, continues to exist; hence the process can never
fully end. The self toward which the narrator moves is the
highest point in Miller's hierarchy of values. The negative
forces of the unconscious, those which threaten spiritual castration and enthrallment, are the nadir. In *Capricorn*, these negative aspects of the Feminine are represented by the cold, mechanical frozen city of New York in which the *I* finds himself.

But *Capricorn* is an allegory of the beginning awareness of
the self and the growth of a more integrated consciousness. As
the activity of consciousness begins, the "male experiences himself as a living, active, and savage animal," [14] the gorilla of despair beating his breast with immaculate paws, recognizing
himself as still subordinate to the negative forces. The necropolis of New York is a projection of Miller's inner world, yet
so successfully is it a symbol of man's negative impulses, those
which deny the self, that it becomes more than a private symbol: the twentieth-century city lends itself as content to the
form of the Terrible Mother archetype.

The experiences of symbolic manifestations of the self
archetype occur throughout *Capricorn* in structurally significant passages which help to define the larger musical pattern of
the confession, a pattern I will comment on later. One particularly important passage in which dissolution is desired should
be considered here. Miller has been describing his narrator's life
as married man and employment manager for Western Union.

This passage sums up the meaninglessness of this experience and his desire for dissolution:

> It went on and on that way, day in and day out for almost five solid years. The continent itself perpetually wracked by cyclones, tornadoes, tidal waves, floods, droughts, blizzards, heat waves, pests, strikes, hold-ups, assassinations, suicides . . . a continuous fever and torment, an eruption, a whirlpool. I was like a man sitting in a lighthouse: below me the wild waves, the rocks, the reefs, the debris of ship-wrecked fleets. I could give the danger signal but I was powerless to avert catastrophe. I *breathed* danger and catastrophe. At times the sensation of it was so strong that it belched like fire from my nostrils. I longed to be free of it all and yet I was irresistibly attracted. I was violent and phlegmatic at the same time. I was like the lighthouse itself —secure in the midst of the most turbulent sea. Beneath me was solid rock, the same shelf of rock on which the towering skyscrapers were reared. My foundations went deep into the earth and the armature of my body was made of steel riveted with hot bolts. Above all I was an eye, a huge searchlight which scoured far and wide, which revolved ceaselessly, pitilessly. This eye so wide-awake seemed to have made all my other faculties dormant; all my powers were used up in the effort to see, to take in the drama of the world.

> If I longed for destruction it was merely that this eye might be extinguished. I longed for an earthquake, for some cataclysm of nature which would plunge the lighthouse into the sea. I wanted a metamorphosis, a change to fish, to leviathan, to destroyer. I wanted the earth to open up, to swallow everything in one engulfing yawn. I wanted to see the city buried fathoms deep in the bosom of the sea. I wanted to sit in a cave and read by candlelight. I wanted that eye extinguished so that I might have a chance to know my own body, my own desires. I wanted to be alone for a thousand years in order to reflect on what I had seen and heard—*and in order to forget*. I wanted something of the earth which was not of man's doing, something absolutely divorced from the human of which I was surfeited. I wanted something purely terrestrial and absolutely divested of idea. I wanted to feel the blood running back into my veins, even at the cost of annihilation. I wanted to shake the stone and the

light out of my system. I wanted the dark fecundity of nature, the deep well of the womb, silence, or else the lapping
of the black waters of death. I wanted to be that night
which the remorseless eye illuminated, a night diapered
with stars and trailing comets. To be of night so frighten-
ingly silent, so utterly incomprehensible and eloquent at the
same time. Never more to speak or to listen or to think. To
be englobed and encompassed and to encompass and to en-
globe at the same time. No more pity, no more tenderness.
To be human only terrestrially, like a plant or a worm or a
brook. To be decomposed, divested of light and stone, varia-
ble as the molecule, durable as the atom, heartless as the
earth itself.[15]

Early in *Capricorn*, before the narrator has given up his
marriage and his employment, he is involved in, even enam-
oured of, the world accessible to the eye. The savage rejection of the contemporary horror revealed to the narrator by
the eye of consciousness [16] is more than the recognition of the
inadequacy of our technological paradise. It is the antithesis, of
course, of the paradise of the archetypal longing which Miller
has projected onto his utopian world (a utopia, it should be remembered, that can be achieved *in time* and is a significant part
of Miller's hierarchy of values). The external human order,
whatever its horrors, is savagely rejected primarily because it is
irresistibly attractive to the narrator. The personality is not integrated, but dominated by this narrow consciousness.

A longing for this "light" to be extinguished is more than
the anti-intellectualism with which Miller is usually (and easily) charged, although he is more properly an anti-rationalist.
At this point in *Capricorn* the unknown and dark areas of the
unconscious also exert a fatal and numinous attraction for the
narrator. The attraction to the night suggests (as do other images) a deadly, compelling desire to return to the Great
Mother, a desire for the uroboric incest which destroys consciousness. Images of the archetypal Great Mother in her elemental nature reveal the narrator's object: he wishes to plunge
into the sea, to "become" the leviathan, to "become" the night.
Womb, death, water, whale—all are traditional symbols of the

unconscious appearing as the Great Mother. This is a return to the womb, but to the womb as symbol of the unconscious, which, if it overcomes the ego, offers dissolution and destruction. He is fatally attracted at this moment to the power of the unconscious and his longing becomes a chant.

The movement inward is dramatized in the sections following. As the movement develops, consciousness confronts various aspects of the Archetypal Feminine. Although the characters who appear seem to have their existence in the world of ordinary experience, they are the projections of the *I*'s inner world that we have examined in part 1:

> It was just about a week before Valeska committed suicide that I ran into Mara. The week or two preceding that event was a veritable nightmare. A series of sudden deaths and strange encounters with women.[17]

In spite of the narrator's longing for dissolution outlined at the end of the first section of *Capricorn*, the unconscious is a threat to be resisted, and his real end is transformation and rebirth. But the unconscious contents must be projected onto the real world so that they can become accessible to consciousness and experienced. The consciousness which is then reborn (as it is in the Easter Sunday section at the end of *Capricorn*) is moving toward the integration of the personality in which the self is the core. This core, like the Archetypal Feminine, has a new relationship with a stronger consciousness at the end of the book: "I look out again at the sun—my first full gaze. . . . Inner and outer have changed places."

Erich Neumann has described the process of projection and assimilation in his speculations on the progressive development in both the individual and the race. The description traces the pattern of Miller's confessions:

> This progressive assimilation of unconscious contents gradually builds up the personality, thus creating an enlarged psychic system which forms the basis of man's inner spiritual history as this makes itself increasingly independent of the collective history going on all round him. This process, initiated in the first instance by philosophy, has today

reached what is chronologically its latest stage in psychology, still of course only in its infancy. Hand in hand with this there goes a "psychization" of the world. Gods, demons, heaven and hell are, as psychic forces, withdrawn from the objective world and incorporated in the human sphere, which thereupon undergoes a very considerable expansion. When we give the name of "sexuality" to what was once experienced as a chthonic divinity, or speak of "hallucination" instead of revelation, and when the gods of heaven and the underworld are recognized as dominants of man's unconscious, it means that an immense tract of external world has dropped into the human psyche. Introjection and psychization are the other side of the process by which a world of psychical objects becomes visible, and this world can no longer be modified by projections to the degree that it could before.

What now happens, however—and this is the most important result of secondary personalization so far as the individual is concerned—is that transpersonal contents are projected upon persons. Just as in the historical process god-images were projected upon human beings and were experienced in them, so now archetypal figures are projected into the personal environment, and this leads to a necessary but exceedingly dangerous confusion of the person with the archetype.[18]

Mara's name is first mentioned in *Capricorn* immediately after the thematic passage at the end of the first section, but only mentioned. She is only introduced—a "musical" theme; the development of her significance is yet to come. The "strange encounters" with women that the *I* mentions have been described earlier in the discussion of the Archetypal Feminine. They are, in effect, the proliferation of female figures which Jung saw as appearing before the manifestation of the single, significant anima figure in the psychic process of transformation. The long section in *Capricorn* describing the sexual encounters with numerous aggressive and negative figures serves to dramatize this stage in the narrator's psychic development. He does not succumb to the incestuous longing for dissolution recorded at the end of the first section. The energy of white desperation, the animal energy of the gorilla of despair whose wings are growing identify him as the "hero." The "eye" has new experiences. It meets the figures of the Archetypal Feminine and finds the inner world suddenly accessible:

> I no longer look into the eyes [19] of the woman I hold in my arms, but I swim through, head and arms and legs, and I see that behind the sockets of the eyes there is a region unexplored, the world of futurity, and here there is no logic whatever, just the still germination of events unbroken by night and day, by yesterday and tomorrow. The eye, accustomed to concentration on points in space, now concentrates on points in time; the eye sees forward and backward at will. The eye which was the I of the self no longer exists; this selfless eye neither reveals nor illuminates. It travels along the line of the horizon, a ceaseless, uninformed voyager.[20]

The experience dramatized in this passage is positive, moreover, as opposed to the earlier desire for incestuous "death"; it is filled with suggestions of potential and expresses a different stage of the process of moving inward than did the longing for dissolution in the earlier passage. Here, however, the difficulty of achieving integration is acknowledged, for the contemporary world provides the narrator with no assistance: "I must have the ability and the patience to formulate what is not contained in the language of our time, for what is not intelligible is meaningless." The scaffold of the city's "mad logic" is no help. "Therefore I close my ears, my eyes, my mouth." [21]

In the next passage Miller speaks of his becoming a garden or a park, "a sort of natural park in which people come to rest, to while away the time." The *I* wishes to be a "bit of breathing space, a stretch of green, a little fresh air, a pool of water." But all of this looks forward; he will be these things "before I shall have become quite a man again." [22]

Miller's park, his natural park, will exist in the center of the "nightmare of perfection" which he identifies with the symbol of the negative Feminine—New York. It is the "still, unshakeable dream in the midst of frenzied activity," a kind of *hortus conclusus* or *temenos* which Jung has described as one of the analogues of the self. He points out that in a movement "into the depths of the sea, into the unconscious, . . . the dreamer reaches the shelter of the *temenos* as a protection against the splintering of personality caused by his regression to childhood." [23] Continuing his analysis of the same symbolic action (similar to that we find in Miller), Jung discusses the symbols of a later dream which he is comparing to the symbolic manifestations of alchemy. In this dream, a gibbon is to be "reconstructed" in the center [24]—Miller's gorilla with its immaculate paws, a gorilla of despair which must be "reconstructed" before integration occurs.

The *I*'s projection of himself as garden and his summary of the action to come serve as a thematic statement which is followed by a dramatization of the "inner process." In the next few pages the narrator returns to the "savage world" of his childhood and develops the thematic material of the meaning of childhood. This return to childhood is the beginning of the way toward realization and integration. It is not an end in itself, not a retreat, but part of the process which the confessions explore. The childhood world, moreover, is not one of innocent security. There the power of magic is recognized and fear is the most important force.[25] The air is full of tension and both outer and inner worlds are charged with meaning.

Childhood belongs to what Jung calls the personal unconscious, and before the *I* can "enter" the world of the collective unconscious, he must deal with the children's land.[26] For Jung, the assimilation of this world means that the man takes the place of the intellect. Miller's narrator recognizes this change when he remarks that before he becomes a man he will exist as a park. When he rejected the "eye" of limited consciousness for the "eye" that will see forward and backward at will, he also moved away from a limited definition of self as intellect or consciousness. In the childhood land the *I* seeks an inviolate sense of this larger self, a "well-defined identity." [27] The return to the sour rye world is part of the centering process.

The *I* recognizes, however, that the return is one step on the way back to a still brighter world which he cannot describe, but which has been discovered by another—Hamilton.

Hamilton, like many of Miller's minor characters, is casually introduced and almost immediately dropped; his name is unimportant. But he represents, symbolically, a significant step toward the realization of the total personality, for Hamilton has discovered the self and appeals to the germ of the *I*'s self, "the being who would eventually outgrow the naked personality, the synthetic individual, and leave me truly alone and solitary in order to work out my own proper destiny." [28] The "return to the womb," so numinous and consequential an experience, is a return so that the self may be transformed and undergo a new integration, developing a "higher consciousness."

For this reason all of the *I*'s crucifixions are rosy crucifixions:

> . . . I had been born free of the need to suffer—and yet I knew no other way to struggle forward than to repeat the drama. . . . Suffering has never taught me a thing; for others it may still be necessary, but for me it is nothing more than an algebraic demonstration of spiritual inadaptability. The whole drama which the man of today is acting out through suffering does not exist for me: it never did, actually. All my Calvaries were rosy crucifixions, pseudo-tragedies to keep the fires of hell burning brightly for the real sinners who are in danger of being forgotten.[29]

The importance of the phrase *rosy crucifixion* for Miller and the symbolic context in which it appears in his total work suggest that the rosy crucifixion has the same significance in his symbolism as the "per crucem ad rosam" of alchemical symbolism which became the Rosy Cross of the Rosicrucians. The way to the rose through the cross symbolized spiritual transformation,[30] and the connection of rose and Christ was common in alchemical symbolic structures: rosy blood corresponded to the blood of Christ, "who is 'compared and united' with the stone. He is the 'heavenly foundation-stone and corner-stone.' The rose-garden is a 'garden enclosed,' and like the rose, a soubriquet of Mary, the parallel of the 'locked' prima materia." [31]

In Miller's fiction the crucifixion most frequently appears in scenes in which the narrator is closest to the symbolic manifestations of the Archetypal Feminine, as in this section from *Black Spring* which we examined from another point of view in chapter 2:

> Over the foot of the bed is the shadow of the cross.[32] There are chains binding me to the bed. The chains are clanking loudly, the anchor is being lowered. Suddenly I feel a hand on my shoulder. Some one is shaking me vigorously. I look up and it is an old hag in a dirty wrapper. She goes to the dresser and opening a drawer she puts a revolver away.
>
> There are three rooms, one after the other, like a railroad flat. I am lying in the middle room in which there is a walnut bookcase and a dressing table. The old hag removes her wrapper and stands before the mirror in her chemise. She has a little powder puff in her hand and with this little puff she swabs her armpits, her bosom, her thighs. All the while she weeps like an idiot. Finally she comes over to me with an atomizer and she squirts a fine spray over me. I notice that her hair is full of rats.
>
> . . . .
>
> Winding a pair of cobras about my arms I go for the old hag with murder in my eyes. From her mouth, her eyes, her hair, from her vagina even, the cobras are streaming forth, always with that frightful steaming hiss as if they had been ejected fresh from a boiling crater. In the middle of the room where we are locked an immense forest opens up. We stand in a nest of cobras and our bodies come undone.
>
> I am in a strange, narrow little room, lying on a high bed. There is an enormous hole in my side, a clean hole without a drop of blood showing. I can't tell any more who I am or where I came from or how I got here. The room is very small and my bed is close to the door. I have a feeling that some one is standing on the doorsill watching me. I am petrified with fright.[33]

Christ, stone, gorilla—these important and traditional symbols of the archetypal self appear in the confessions with myriad other symbolic manifestations of the archetype, for as an archetype, the self is accessible only through symbols and through the same fragmentation in which the Archetypal Feminine appeared. The apparent incongruity in the nature of these symbols is characteristic, as is the range of symbols—inanimate objects, human forms, animal figures, geometrical configurations.

Jung's exhaustive analysis of the manifestations of this archetype provides a reading for Miller that is thoroughly substantiated by formal analysis of passage after passage. And without this insight into traditional symbolism of the self, the total organization of Miller's confessions remains obscure. If we wish to understand the transcendent and non-human archetypal aspect of this symbolism, we must see significant relationships between Miller's expository digressions and his fantasy episodes. The non-human images by which he identifies himself, what he was, and what he will become—"happy rock," "garden," "gorilla of despair"—become significant (as Angus Fletcher argues in his study of allegory) in terms of the large scale meanings that appear when they are combined with similar images. They can also be "traditional" and "cosmic." Jung's analysis of alchemical, Christian, and Gnostic images makes their traditional nature clear to us:

> Alchemical symbolism has produced, aside from the personal figures, a whole series of non-human forms, geometrical configurations like the sphere, circle, square, and octagon, or chemical symbols like the Philosophers' Stone, the ruby, diamond, quicksilver, gold, water, fire, and spirit (in the sense of a volatile substance). This choice of symbols tallies more or less with the modern products of the unconscious. I might mention in this connection that there are numerous theriomorphic spirit symbols, the most important Christian ones being the lamb, the dove, and the snake (Satan). The snake symbolizing the Gnostic Nous and the Agathodaimon has a pneumatic significance (the devil, too, is a spirit). These symbols express the non-human character of the totality or self, as was reported long ago when, at Pentecost, the spirit descended on the disciples in tongues of fire.[34]

Chapter Six

Pervious and Maculate

The progress of Miller's narrator toward integration also requires the recognition, experience, and assimilation of the negative elements of the archetype of the self. This process is frequently expressed in traditional Christian symbols, yet traditional responses to these symbols may obscure the action. Miller's fierce religiosity is that of the prophet who rejects tradition in favor of revelation. His Second Coming is the arrival of the self, and his "traditional" symbols are best recognized as projections of the archetypes. The *I* at the same time may rail against the Christian opposition of good and evil and identify himself with Christ without violating consistency. Miller's Christ generates an Anti-Christ; and, insisting on the psychological validity of the experience of totality, the *I* will also appear as Devil:

> I felt almost as if I had been shot forward into a round of existence which for the rest of mankind had not yet attained its full rhythm. I was obliged to mark time if I were to remain with them and not be shunted off to another sphere of existence. On the other hand, I was in many ways lower than the human beings about me. It was as though I had

come out of the fires of hell not entirely purged. I had still a tail and a pair of horns, and when my passions were aroused I breathed a sulphurous poison which was annihilating. I was always called a "lucky devil." The good that happened to me was called "luck," and the evil was always regarded as a result of my shortcomings. Rather, as the fruit of my blindness. Rarely did anyone ever spot the evil in me! I was as adroit, in this respect, as the devil himself. But that I was frequently blind, everybody could see that. And at such times I was left alone, shunned, like the devil himself. Then I left the world, returned to the fires of hell—voluntarily. These comings and goings are as real to me, more real, in fact, than anything that happened in between.[1]

Jung argues that because "Christianity has insisted on God's goodness as a loving Father and has done its best to rob evil of substance," the figures of Christ and Devil are hopelessly irreconcilable for Christians, and that Christianity has made psychological "wholeness," a totality which includes the opposites, impossible for its believers. Christ, Jung insists, must have his shadow. It is not surprising that the God-Christ image and its implications become as important as they do in Miller's fiction. If Jung's description of symbolic processes is plausible, and if, as he argues, *the destruction of the God-image is followed by the annulment of the human personality*," [2] then any attempt to explore the process of moving toward wholeness will rediscover the God-image as one of the most important manifestations of the archetype of the self.

The reconciliation of opposites is the object of the *I*'s quest. Miller dramatizes this psychic process of integration or centroversion [3] in which a wider consciousness is achieved. But only through a transformation in which the symbolic "contents" of the archetypes are assimilated or in which consciousness establishes an attitude toward them can the integration be achieved. Such a dramatization, moreover, produces the alternating identification of the *I* with Christ and Devil. Understood as psychic projections, the significance of these symbols is clearer and more acceptable. The relationships among these symbols, the movement from one complex to another, and the description of the attitude of the *I* toward various symbols or symbolic experiences are not arbitrary. Such states as demonic "possession," despair, assurance, dissolution, and reorientation arise out of the nature of the experience. The repetitions of these actions and states vary in intensity and effect. Moments when the *I* reaches the numinous center around which psychic contents are organized, for example, are obviously more significant than other moments of illumination.

The transition from outer to inner experience in Miller can appear especially obscure, however, unless his apparently mimetic reality is also recognized as a projection of psychic contents. The reader encounters in Miller's exploration of the self the dilemma described by Burke in his discussion of the psychology of mysticism: "We find ourselves trying to chart a fluctuant situation in which merger and division keep changing places." We are, in fact, in the world of Burke's super-person, "envisaged *beyond* language but *through* language" or the "transcendent Self." [4]

The language, for example, moves toward formula and the magical repetition of formulas: all Miller's crucifixions are rosy; his receptivity to the unconscious finds him "pervious and maculate"; all systematic, rationalistic approaches to the problem of self are "doomed to failure"; to be sane everyone must become crazy. Even when these formulas are familiar clichés—perhaps especially when they are clichés—they represent ways of dealing with a threatening reality: the reality of the archetypes with which consciousness is threatened, but to which it must turn for vitality.[5] Miller's catalogues consist of such formulas and indicate the relationship between the forms of his fiction and other allegorical structures. Fletcher has called these devices aspects of "defensive" ritual:

> The response to ambivalence is of course what counts, since mixed attitudes in themselves are natural in all human thought. We cannot escape ambivalence, but we can respond differently to situations which arouse this state of feeling. Here also there is an aesthetic rationale for the allegorical mode.

Ritual is its characteristic allegorical way of showing the human response to ambivalence. Under "ritual" I subsume all those devices of symmetry and balance which allegory carries to such extremes. It has to be clearly understood that there are other ways of responding to the intense simultaneous mixture of love and hate. One can respond by a hysterical outburst of rage or affection, which are likely to bring on tears and violent outcries. One can respond by a gradual cooling off, under the control of the intellect, but at the same time without the distinct coldness and detachment that marks compulsive behavior. One can lapse into daydream and free fantasy, and then we have something which might be called a "mythical" symbolic response. The allegorist responds otherwise, as I have argued. He creates a ritual which by virtue of its very repetition and symmetry "carries off" the threat of ambivalent feelings, and shows this same process of displacement occurring in the fiction. The central characteristic of the compulsive response to ambivalence is the ordered ritual which gives to this particular behavior its form. Its effect is to allow a degree of certainty in a world of flux. By making lists (naturalism), by creating complicated "double plots" (pastoral), by building "summation schemes" and antithetical polarities in "debate" (*psychomachia*), the allegorist slows and regulates the pace of the existence his fiction represents. He furthermore keeps the threatening ambivalence from taking up any focal point other than those defined by the strictest polar frame of reference. The tendency toward polarization may not always operate in practice, but underneath surface complications and subtleties one can always discern a subtending structure which opposes the powers of darkness to the powers of light.[6]

The vulnerable *I*—accessible to the contents and forms of the unconscious—must confront powers of darkness that have not only numinous fascination for consciousness, but are the source of both death (dissolution of consciousness) and life (extension of consciousness and creative power). Early in *Capricorn* Miller describes this *I* as charged with potential but still not ready for birth:

> Of those with fever few hatched, among them myself still unhatched, but pervious and maculate, knowing with quiet ferocity the ennui of ceaseless drift and movement.[7]

It is an *I* both changing and changeable, but aware of the seed of the archetypal self within, which provides it with order in the midst of chaos:

> I was really afraid of myself, of my appetite, my curiosity, my flexibility, my permeability, my malleability, my geniality, my powers of adaptation. No situation in itself could frighten me: I somehow always saw myself sitting pretty, sitting inside a buttercup, as it were, and sipping the honey.[8]

The movement inward toward the self is not a movement toward the unique and individual. Miller insists that the *I* seeks an "ageless self which has been farmed out through millenary ages to men with names and dates," [9] a self for which Jung's term archetype is appropriate, for it is collective and transpersonal. Miller calls the process an initiation and again his description seems to echo Jung: the "disorientation and reorientation which comes with the initiation into any mystery is the most wonderful experience which it is possible to have." [10]

This self includes evil, for the total personality cannot be "cleansed" of evil. The negative *I* and the negative God can neither be denied nor exorcised: they must be recognized and assimilated. The acceptance of evil on which Miller insists is not a simple acceptance of the social horror he sees about him. It demands recognition and assimilation of the negative aspects of the self. Miller's male figures serve this end, for the male companions in the narrator's erotic adventures are projections of negative aspects of the *I*. Like Miller's female figures, they are not characters from mimetic fiction, although in the later *Rosy Crucifixion* they are less obviously projections and could be described accurately as the characters of anatomy: the "pedants, bigots, cranks, parvenus, virtuosi, enthusiasts, rapacious and incompetent professional men of all kinds" [11] who appear in Menippean satire as Frye has described it. These stylized figures belong both to Miller's confessions and to the later fiction which is closer to anatomy. The section from *Big Sur and the Oranges of Hieronymous Bosch* published separately as *Devil in Paradise* is almost pure anatomy in its portrayal of the maddened intellect of Conrad Moricand. One is scarcely aware of the experiences of the narrator, except for his relentless underlining of Moricand's grotesque limitations.

I would argue that all Miller's fictional characters are projections, an explanation that makes irrelevant Kingsley Widmer's observation that Miller seldom writes well of people "except from disgust or malice" and his argument that Miller is incapable of producing fictional characters.[12]

Certainly in the *Tropics* many of the male figures clearly symbolize negative aspects of the *I* and serve as allegorical agents in the dramatization of the process of integration. Miller's underground is a mental basement, not a social reality, and the grotesques which decorate his cities are the products of projection and stylization. But many are more than decoration, however necessary such decoration is for any dramatic exploration of the inner underworld. These negative figures suggest the archetype of the shadow, which, according to Jung, is the easiest of the archetypes to experience. The contents of the shadow belong largely to the personal rather than the transpersonal unconscious, and represent the negative aspects of personality that are frequently projected onto individuals in the environment.[13] Moreover, before the individuation process can proceed to a confrontation of the anima, the individual must become conscious of the shadow, and its contents must be assimilated.[14] The projections must be recognized. Because they are projected onto individuals of the same sex, the process demands that the individual have a companion. The archetypal shadow "hides" the self and stands somewhere between the personal conscious and the collective unconscious.[15]

Neumann points out that in myths the shadow appears as the dark brother, a companion and friend, as well as a hostile brother. This motif is unmistakable in various passages in *The Rosy Crucifixion*. George Marshall, for example, identified as the narrator's "twin," his companion-brother. This identification is preserved until George deceives the narrator on one important occasion.[16] Until then he appears in numerous episodes during which certain of his characteristics are examined, to be admired or deplored. By insisting on identifying himself with George, the narrator uses him as a means of isolating his own characteristics, frequently negative characteristics. George's "end" as a member of the social structure is by implication what the narrator has escaped:

> "As I was saying before, Hen, George is a different guy. He's at loose ends. Hates his work, loathes his wife, and the kids bore him to death. All he thinks of now is tail. And boy, does he chase it! Picks 'em younger and younger all the time. The last time I saw him he was in a hell of a mess with some fifteen year old—from his own school. (I still can't picture George as a principal, can you?) It began right in his office, it seems. Then he takes to meeting her at the dance hall. Finally he has the nerve to take her to a hotel—and register as man and wife." [17]

Few of the narrator's male companions and acquaintances are presented for admiration; he is incisive about their shortcomings, their ugly and vicious habits, their crude sexuality. They are without exception stylized figures. A few traits or characteristics serve to identify them and no development of the character exists. Longer treatments of them are likely to be repetitious; frequently these result in extensive elaboration and grotesque decoration of their figures. But they do function as the shadow of the *I*. Commenting on the suicide of a man whom he knew slightly and admired, but was unable to claim as a friend, the narrator reveals the significance of the dramatic range of the male figures:

> All these aspects of the man, plus the fact that he was debonair, adroit, thoroughly sophisticated, utterly tolerant and forgiving, had endeared him to me. Not one of my friends possessed these qualities. They had better and worse traits, traits all too familiar to me. They were too much like myself *au fond*, my friends. All my life I had wanted, and still crave, as a matter of fact, friends whom I could look upon as being utterly different from myself. Whenever I succeeded in finding one I also discovered that the attraction necessary to maintain a vital relationship was lacking. None of these individuals ever became more than "potential" friends.[18]

Through the anatomy or analysis of the shadow figures Miller isolates and fixes the negative characteristics of the self, although even the shadow figures are not unmixed evil. And, although the *I* is aware of the identity of these companions in the *Tropics*, in the later volumes of *The Rosy Crucifixion*, the psychic process of the development of the individual is much more accessible to conscious speculation and analysis. Hence, the greater clarity of Miller's later volumes, for there is less presentation of the process of transformation and more explanation.[19] The meaning of various figures is explained more often than it is experienced, as, for example, in *Sexus* when the "separation" between George Marshall and the *I* is described:

> Thinking of George Marshall, I began to make more faces; I did it so well that I began to get a little frightened of myself. For, suddenly I remembered the day when for the first time in my life I looked into the mirror and realized that I was gazing at a stranger. It was after I had been to the theatre with George Marshall and MacGregor. George Marshall had said something that night which disturbed me profoundly. I was angry with him for his stupidity, but I couldn't deny that he had put his finger on a sore spot. He had said something which made me realize that our twinship was over, that in fact we would become enemies henceforth. And he was right, though the reasons he had given were false. From that day forth I began to ridicule my bosom friend George Marshall. I wanted to be the opposite of him in every way. It was like the splitting of a chromosome.
>
> George Marshall remained in the world, with it, of it; he took root and grew like a tree, and there was no doubt but that he had found his place and with it a relatively full measure of happiness. But as I looked in the mirror that night, disowning my own image, I knew what George Marshall had predicted about my future was only superficially correct. George Marshall had never really understood me; the moment he suspected I was *different* he had renounced me.[20]

This experience is followed by a "profound disturbance" and the melancholy recognition that he is in a state of inertia which he loathes. The question that he poses, "Which is the true self?" seems unanswerable. His identification of himself with George Marshall has been naive; the self-knowledge he acquires when he rejects the image of George is a withdrawal of projection. It is a step toward facing the psychic reality of the individual (which he is reluctant to do) in the quest for self-knowledge. Shortly after recalling the break with George as *alter ego,* Miller sums up the meaning of the experience for the *I:* "What I disliked most in George Marshall, in Kronski, in Tawde and the incalculable hosts which they represented, was their surface seriousness. . . . The man who is forever disturbed about the condition of humanity either has no problems of his own or has refused to face them." [21]

The inertia, the melancholy, and the "opposition" which follow the confrontation of the shadow (here, George) should be expected in any account of the process Miller is dramatizing. George is of interest only as a means of reaching an understanding of the self and experiencing the totality toward which the narrator forever moves. In *The Rosy Crucifixion,* Miller is looking back at the experience of transformation, seeing it from the perspective of one who now understands the significance of events in *Cancer* and *Capricorn.* Because the process is consciously analyzed more often than it is dramatically presented, the density of images, the incongruous juxtapositions which lend the confessions their character, have cleared considerably. The dark experiences of *Capricorn* are subjected to analysis and are organized more clearly in *The Rosy Crucifixion.* The confrontation of the shadow is remembered, and the characters, subjected constantly to intellectual analysis, become the characters of anatomy. The problem is the same, however. What is the true self?

Again Miller's analysis of the process of transformation appears to echo Jung:

> There is a time when ideas tyrannize over one, when one is just a hapless victim of an other's thoughts. This "possession" by another seems to occur in periods of depersonalization, when the warring selves come unglued, as it were. Normally

one is impervious to ideas; they come and go, are accepted or rejected, put on like shirts, taken off like dirty socks. But in those periods which we call crises, when the mind sunders and splinters like a diamond under the blows of a sledge-hammer, these innocent ideas of a dreamer take hold, lodge in the crevices of the brain, and by some subtle process of infiltration bring about a definite, irrevocable alteration of the personality. Outwardly no great change takes place; the individual affected does not suddenly behave differently; on the contrary, he may behave in more "normal" fashion than before. This seeming normality assumes more and more the quality of a protective device. From surface deception he passes to inner deception. With each new crisis, however, he becomes more strongly aware of a change which is no change, but rather an intensification of something hidden deep within. Now when he closes his eyes he can really look at himself. He no longer sees a mask. He sees without seeing, to be exact. Vision without sight, a fluid grasp of intangibles: the merging of sight and sound: the heart of the web. Here stream the distant personalities which evade the crude contact of the senses; here the overtones of recognition discreetly lap against one another in bright, vibrant harmonies. There is no language employed, no outlines delineated.[22]

The "distant personalities" at the "heart of the web," personalities whose outlines overlap and are "seen" without vision, are strikingly analogous to the experience of the archetypes described by Jung.[23] The *Bildung* of the *I* is the rediscovery of the archetypal and the assimilation of the transcendental world. Such an "education" requires the recording and analysis of inner experiences. And in the next paragraph, Miller insists that it is "memory" which saves the individual from dissolution by reintroducing him to the transpersonal world of the mind. Even the external world is a projection of this inner reality: "Everything external is but a reflection projected by the mind machine." [24]

Miller is interested in art and the life of the artist precisely because art has access to both worlds—the inner, and the external world which is formed by projections from within: "Creation is the eternal play which takes place at the border-line." [25]

Art, moreover, gives the artist power and control over these worlds.[26]

In *The Rosy Crucifixion*, the analysis of the inner process by which the *I* is integrated becomes part of the anatomy of the external world. The stylized figures which decorate the external world, the social underworld of New York, are criticized and denigrated in terms of their failure to recognize themselves and become ideally integrated and autonomous human beings. Hence, George Marshall remains "in the world," defined forever and destroyed forever by his social roles of husband, father, school principal. Miller's MacGregor, the *alter ego* of *Capricorn* who also appears in *The Rosy Crucifixion*, is equally self-destructive. He has little substance as a character of mimetic fiction, but interests Miller precisely because he *has* no character: his is a singularly stylized and limited approach to life. (The approach to life is the central problem in each of the figures Miller analyzes.) MacGregor drives himself toward a goal he cannot even imagine:

> On my way home, an hour or so later, I got to thinking of all the wild projects he had hatched, beginning from the time I first knew him—when he was still going to prep school. How he had always complicated his life trying to make things easier for himself. I thought of the hours he had spent doing drudge work, so that "later" he might be free to do as he pleased, though he never did know precisely what it was he would do when he would be able to do only what he pleased. To do nothing at all, which he always pretended was the *summum bonum*, was thoroughly out of the question. If I went to the beach for a holiday he was sure to bring his notebook along, and a law book or two, or even a few pages from the unabridged dictionary which he had been reading, a page at a time, for years. If we flung ourselves into the water he would have to race someone to the raft or propose that we swim around the point or suggest we play water polo. Anything but float quietly on our backs. If we stretched out in the sand he would suggest we shoot craps or play cards. If we started a pleasant conversation he would turn it into an argument. He was never able to do anything in peace or contentment.[27]

MacGregor is possessed by irrational drives within him and tantalized by the prizes the world offers:

> "Tess has all sorts of connections, you know. She'd like to see me on the bench. The thing is, I can't run for judge and start divorce proceedings—*see what I mean?* Besides, I'm not so sure I want to be a judge. Even on the bench you can't keep your skirts clean, you know that. Still, I'm not much good as a lawyer, to be frank with you. Can't work up any enthusiasm. . . ." [28]

He is still the victim of his social roles. In fact, identification with the *persona* is another of the dangers faced in the development of the *I* and leads to the characteristic human limitations of the figures of anatomy. The *persona* is a false self, an "acquired personality arising from perverted beliefs" or "the general idea of our nature which we have built up from experiencing our effect upon the world around and its effect upon us." [29] The projections which serve Miller as shadow figures in the confessions become the satirical figures of the anatomies, although the same figure can be both at the same time.

Jung's remarks on the problem of identification with the *persona* as a danger in the development of personality provide a relevant comment on the *I*'s rejection of social roles and responsibility, for it is this identification which destroys the possibility of establishing relationships with the source of energy and life, the distant personalities of the transcendental world. Identification with the *persona* results in possession—the mastery of an individual by "some content, an idea or part of the personality." [30]

Such possession (and the examples are numerous in Miller's gallery of grotesques) leaves an individual "in the world" but little more than a psychic cripple, even when he is successful in his adaptation to a social role:

> A common instance of this is identity with the persona, which is the individual's system of adaptation to, or the manner he assumes in dealing with, the world. Every calling or profession, for example, has its own characteristic per-

sona. It is easy to study these things nowadays, when the photographs of public personalities so frequently appear in the press. A certain kind of behavior is forced on them by the world, and professional people endeavor to come up to these expectations. Only, the danger is that they become identical with their personas—the professor with his textbook, the tenor with his voice. . . . One could say, with a little exaggeration, that the persona is that which in reality one is not, but which oneself as well as others think one is. . . .[31]

Miller's male figures are essentially symbols in an allegory, even when they correspond more closely to mimetic reality than obviously iconographic figures. Each gesture, opinion, action is necessary to a delineation of their symbolic role, whether this role functions in *anatomy* in which the characters are subjected to analysis and castigation as failures in the process of living, or in the *confession* as projections of the *I*'s inferior nature, his shadow. The forms overlap, although the earlier *Tropics* and *Black Spring* are more properly confessions in which consciousness is struggling to understand and interpret the process of integration. In the later *The Rosy Crucifixion*, events, figures, and places appear somewhat more real and are more accessible to conscious analysis and castigation. The *I* of the confessions is involved in the process of integration; in *The Rosy Crucifixion*, the *I* is more often onlooker (except in *Sexus*) than participant. The *I* of the *Tropics* is "pervious and maculate," ready for the experience of transformation. In *The Rosy Crucifixion*, the *I* recalls the experiences which surround the transformation in *Capricorn*, and the sense of analysis and recall is pervasive.

The shadow figures of the *Tropics* play clearly symbolic roles in assisting the *I* in the process of transformation and integration. In the *Tropic of Cancer*, for example, the satyriasis of Van Norden illuminates a particular symbolic relationship between the unconscious (as symbolized by the Archetypal Feminine) and consciousness: that of possession. The unity of the male figures in Paris is underlined by the name they call one another: "I call him Joe because he calls me Joe. When Carl is with us he is Joe too. Everybody is Joe because it's easier that way. It's also a pleasant reminder not to take yourself too seriously."[32] Van Norden's possession leaves him helpless and unsatisfied. He is spiritually castrated, possessed by the Archetypal Feminine and reduced to a phallic instrument. The fusion of fantasy and the external world underscores the meaning of Van Norden for the *I* in numerous scenes such as the one in which the narrator helps Van Norden move into a filthy hotel:

> Ever since we have mounted the stairs Van Norden has kept silence. But his looks are eloquent. When he opens the door of 57 I have for a fleeting moment the sensation of going mad. A huge mirror covered with green gauze and tipped at an angle of 45 degrees hangs directly opposite the entrance over a baby carriage which is filled with books. Van Norden doesn't even crack a smile; instead he walks nonchalantly over to the baby carriage and picking up a book begins to skim it through, much as a man would enter the public library and go unthinkingly to the rack nearest to hand. And perhaps this would not seem so ludicrous to me if I had not espied at the same time a pair of handle bars resting in the corner. They look so absolutely peaceful and contented, as if they had been dozing there for years, that suddenly it seems to me as if we had been standing in this room, in exactly this position, for an incalculably long time, that it was a pose we had struck in a dream from which we never emerged, a dream which the least gesture, the wink of an eye even, will shatter. But more remarkable still is the remembrance that suddenly floats up of an actual dream which occurred only the other night, a dream in which I saw Van Norden in just such a corner as is occupied now by the handle bars, only instead of the handle bars there was a woman crouching with her legs drawn up. I see him standing over the woman with that alert, eager look in his eye which comes when he wants something badly. The street in which this is going on is blurred—only the angle made by the two walls is clear, and the cowering figure of the woman. I can see him going at her in that quick, animal way of his, reckless of what's going on about him, determined only to have his way. And a look in his eye as though to say—"you can kill me afterwards, but just let me get it in . . . I've got to get it in!" And there he is, bent over her, their heads knocking against the wall, he has such a tremendous erection that

it's simply impossible to get it in her. Suddenly, with that disgusted air which he knows so well how to summon, he picks himself up and adjusts his clothes. He is about to walk away when suddenly he notices that his penis is lying on the sidewalk. It is about the size of a sawed-off broomstick. He picks it up nonchalantly and slings it under his arm. As he walks off I notice two huge bulbs, like tulip bulbs, dangling from the end of the broomstick, and I can hear him muttering to himself "flowerpots . . . flowerpots." [33]

Van Norden seeks the dissolution and deadly comfort of loss of consciousness, a communion with the unconscious which is the dangerous (because utterly destructive) yearning for uroboric incest, for the return to the Mother in her symbolic role:

"I get so goddamned mad at myself that I could kill myself . . . and in a way, that's what I do every time I have an orgasm. For one second like I obliterate myself. There's not even one me then . . . there's nothing . . . not even the cunt. It's like receiving communion. Honest, I mean that. For a few seconds afterward I have a fine spiritual glow. . . ." [34]

Van Norden's relationship with women is the symbolic expression of his demonic possession by the unconscious and his inability to establish independence from the unconscious. As the shadow of Miller's *I*, he isolates and dramatizes what the *I* must "experience in images" before he can integrate the partial personalities in himself. The *I* frees himself in this way from the fatal urge to return to the Archetypal Feminine as an eternal lover, forever fascinated. The Joes of Paris are like the strugglers who may attempt to free themselves from the Great Mother, but who fail to become heroes and turn against themselves in self-destruction, mutilation, and suicide.[35] In *Capricorn*, in which the Archetypal Feminine is further fragmented and the figure of the anima (Mara) appears, MacGregor is the *I*'s companion, the shadow figure who joins the *I* in a relentless pursuit of the "sacred whores" of the middle section of *Capricorn:* the multiple female figures who appear prior to the Mara. It is through MacGregor, or the shadow, that the *I* approaches the Archetypal Feminine. MacGregor brings Paula to meet the narrator—Paula, the nymphomaniac who is the "incarnation of the hallucination of sex." [36] MacGregor is the "glutton for sex," and his weaknesses are also the weaknesses of the man committed to the world: "like all men who practice willpower he was absolutely flabby inside." He represents the limitations of the self imposed by the external world:

> He was brought up on the North Side, not very far from the neighborhood in which I had spent my childhood. He was very much a product of the North Side, too, and that was one of the reasons why I liked him. The way he talked, out of the corner of his mouth, for instance, the tough air he put on when talking to a cop, the way he spat in disgust, the peculiar curse words he used, the sentimentality, the limited horizon, the passion for playing pool or shooting craps, the staying up all night swapping yarns, the contempt for the rich, the hobnobbing with politicians, the curiosity about worthless things, the respect for learning, the fascination of the dance hall, the saloon, the burlesque, talking about seeing the world and never budging out of the city, idolizing no matter whom so long as the person showed "spunk," a thousand and one little traits or peculiarities of this sort endeared him to me because it was precisely such idiosyncrasies which marked the fellows I had known as a child.[37]

His sexual appetite, moreover, symbolizes his inability to separate himself from the hallucination of sex—from possession by the Archetypal Feminine. By confronting the negative dimensions of the *I*, the totality of the personality can be glimpsed, and the process of integration and development dramatized. At the end of *Nexus*, in a conversation with Mac-Gregor, Miller turns on him, rejects the sentimental claims of friendship and frees himself from both the shadow and the temptation to identify with the persona.

> "Listen," I said, "once we were as close as peas in a pod, you, George Marshall and me. We were like brothers. That was a long, long time ago. Things happened. Somewhere the link snapped. George settled down, like a reformed crook. His wife won out. . . ."
>
> "And *me?*"

"You buried yourself in your law work, which you despise. One day you'll be judge, mark my words. But it won't change your way of life. You've given up the ghost. Nothing interests you any more—unless it's a game of poker. And you think *my* way of life is cockeyed. It is, I'll admit that. But not in the way you think."

His reply surprised me somewhat. "You're not so far off the track, Hen. We *have* made a mess of it, George and myself. The others too, for that matter. (He was referring to the members of the Xerxes Society.) None of us has amounted to a damn. But what's all that got to do with friendship? Must we become important figures in the world to remain friends? Sounds like snobbery to me. We never pretended, George or I, that we were going to burn up the world. We're what we are. Isn't that good enough for you?"

"Look," I replied, "it wouldn't matter to me if you were nothing but a bum; you could still be my friend and I yours. You could make fun of everything I believed in, if you believed in something yourself. But you don't. You believe in nothing. To my way of thinking one's got to believe in what he's doing, else all's a farce. I'd be all for you if you wanted to be a bum and become a bum with all your heart and soul. But what are you? You're one of those meaningless souls who filled us with contempt when we were younger . . . when we sat up the whole night long discussing such thinkers as Nietzsche, Shaw, Ibsen. Just names to you now. You weren't going to be like your old man, no sir! They weren't going to lasso *you*, tame *you*. But they did. Or *you* did. You put yourself in the straitjacket. You took the easiest way. You surrendered before you had even begun to fight." [38]

The shadow figure—or the negative figure—stands between the external world of social demands and the figures of the transpersonal unconscious which Miller has described as the distant personalities. Only when the shadow is recognized in some form is access to the other figures of the unconscious possible. Jung states this insight in images that remind one of Miller:

The meeting with oneself is, at first, the meeting with one's own shadow. The shadow is a tight passage, a narrow door, whose painful constriction no one is spared who goes down to the deep well. But one must learn to know oneself in order to know who one is. For what comes after the door is, surprisingly enough, a boundless expanse full of unprecedented uncertainty, with apparently no inside and no outside, no above and no below, no here and no there, no mine and no thine, no good and no bad. It is the world of water, where all life floats in suspension; where the realm of the sympathetic system, the soul of everything living, begins; where I am indivisibly this *and* that; where I experience the other in myself and the other-than-myself experiences me.[39]

Perhaps the experience described here—the mystical experience—can be approached only dramatically. Certainly this is Miller's problem: to visualize and dramatize the limits of the self and the limitlessness of the self. He needs the negative figures of his confessions and anatomies, for they are part of the process of integration. The *I* is maculate and pervious, marked by its shadow and subject to the threatening invasions of the unconscious. The journey into the self is the journey into the "land of the dead" or the belly of the whale—and only the hero can return. He must stop his ears for he must not hear his own desires to succumb to dissolution.

Frye has suggested that the villain, hero, and heroine of romance are projections of Jung's shadow, libido, and anima, and that these projections appear as aspects of personality in the "archetypal masque." [40] I have argued that complex manifestations of these archetypes make their appearance in the confessions of Miller. Miller's subject and the process he is describing correspond to the archetypal experiences of the human psyche whose symbolic representations Jung has attempted to categorize and analyze. The figures of the anatomy—which I suggest is the form of the later autobiographical volumes—are often *personae*, the social masks with which the human self can become identified, and hence destroyed. Such figures are the proper subjects of satire because their failure is a "moral" failure: they have "fallen in line," a position Miller insists is meaningless: "But whatever I do, whatever I take up, it'll be because

I believe in it. I won't float with the tide. I'd rather go down fighting . . . a failure, as you say. I loathe doing like everyone else, falling in line, saying yes when you mean no." [41]

Out of context the position seems naive; but the context must be recognized as part of the declaration. And the context requires the recognition of the negative figures as shadow figures of the self.

Other characters, sometimes crudely archetypal in significance, appear in *The Rosy Crucifixion*. Claude, for example, is Jung's child archetype.[42] Miller's Claude obviously has symbolic significance for the self, and he is certainly not a convincing figure as far as any realistic standards for fiction are concerned. Miller's archetypes manage to succeed as part of his allegory when they are better disguised than Claude, and the mimetic surface of his fiction is not destroyed. Claude is too obvious and insufficiently disguised. He has an exotic origin, an "Oriental" cast to his form, a strange and mysterious past, and mysterious powers of empathy and prophecy. Jung claims that such figures have "clearest and most significant manifestation" in "the maturation process of personality induced by the analysis of the unconscious, which I have termed the process of *individuation*." [43] Such figures appear in dreams and can be made conscious; frequently the child is modeled after the Christ child. It is often Indian or Chinese. Claude has all the signs of this archetype, and Miller underlines his symbolic role by an account of a dream (In the anatomies, Miller frequently fails to fuse the real world and the fantasy as successfully as in *Cancer;* comments on the meaning of scenes or figures is mechanically done by dreams which are carefully recorded—another indication of the conscious analysis of the process of integration.):

> I fell asleep with difficulty. Claude kept reappearing, like a vision, each time in a different aspect. Though he always had the figure of a boy, his voice sounded like the voice of the ancient one. No matter what language he spoke I was able to follow him. I wasn't the least amazed, curiously enough, to hear myself talking Hungarian. Nor was I

amazed to find myself riding a horse, riding bareback with bare feet. Often we carried on our discussions in foreign lands, in remote places such as Judea, the Nubian desert, Turkestan, Sumatra, Patagonia. We made use of no vehicles; we were always there where our thoughts roamed, without effort, without the use of the will. Aside from certain sexual dreams I don't believe I had ever had such a pleasant dream. It was more than pleasant—it was instructive in the highest sense. This Claude was more like an *alter ego*, even though at times he did strikingly resemble the Christ. He brought me great peace. He gave me direction. More than that—he gave me reason for being. I was at last something in my own right and no need to prove it to anyone. I was securely in the world yet not a victim. I was participating in a wholly new way, as only a man can who is free from conflict. Strangely, the world had grown much smaller than I thought it to be. More intimate, more understandable. It was no longer something against which I was pitted; it was like a ripe fruit which I was inside of, which nourished me, and which was inexhaustible. I was one with it, one with everything—that's the only way I can put it.[44]

Such figures are not uncommon in the Miller world, but Claude is perhaps the most obvious. Certainly unless he is seen as part of the total allegorical reality Miller is producing, his appearance is absurd and meaningless. He carries no conviction as a mimetic character.

Moreover, many incidents, encounters, or scenes are meaningful only when they are seen as part of the total allegorical structure. The symbols appear with relentless repetition: the wheels and bridges which symbolize the narrator's psychic states, for example. His movement from one psychic state to another is frequently symbolized by the bridge he crosses. The bridge motif assumes enormous importance in *Capricorn* when a final bridge, the bridge to insanity, appears, and the *I* refuses to cross:

> I pass on. Not the stabbing horror of disaster and calamity, I say, but the automatic throwback, the stark panorama of the soul's atavistic struggle. A bridge in North Carolina, near the Tennessee border. Coming out of lush tobacco fields, low cabins everywhere and the smell of fresh wood burning.

The day passed in a thick lake of waving green. Hardly a soul in sight. Then suddenly a clearing and I'm over a big gulch spanned by a rickety wooden bridge. This is the end of the world! How in God's name I got here and why I'm here I don't know. *How am I going to eat?* And if I ate the biggest meal imaginable I would still be sad, frightfully sad. I don't know where to go from here. This bridge is the end, the end of me, the end of my known world. This bridge is insanity: there is no reason why it should stand there and no reason why people should cross it. I refuse to budge another step, I balk at crossing that crazy bridge. Nearby is a low wall which I lie against trying to think what to do and where to go. I realize quietly what a terribly civilized person I am—the need I have for people, conversation, books, theater, music, cafés, drinks, and so forth. It's terrible to be civilized, because when you come to the end of the world you have nothing to support the terror of loneliness.[45]

The motif of eating appears in this passage with its archetypal significance clearly manifest. Eating is an act of assimilation, symbolically the assimilation of the contents of the unconscious and the real world—the other than *I*. It is a psychic assimilation.[46] In this passage, the *I* faces that which is beyond assimilation, a bridge which it refused to cross. Throughout Miller's fictional world, however, eating is usually a successful means of ritual assimilation, and the ritual crossing of bridges successfully moves the *I* from one state to another.

When the scenes of Miller's confessions and anatomies are read allegorically, they appear far more integrated and orderly than if their symbolic patterns are overlooked or slighted. The narrator at the end of *Nexus*, about to leave for Paris, encounters a horse in a "vision" after the conversation with Mac-Gregor in which the past is rejected:

At the corner I come upon a horse wandering in the middle of the street. The most forlorn, broken down nag ever a man laid eyes on. I try to speak to this lost quadruped—it's not a horse anymore, not even an animal. For a moment I thought it understood. For one long moment it looked me full in the face. Then, terrified, it let out a bloodcurdling neigh and took to its heels.[47]

A little later, in a conversation with Mona in which they are discussing the trip to Europe the narrator will take, the motif of the horse reappears:

> *"Horses.* That's what I'm thinking. I wish we were going to Russia first. You remember Gogol and the troika? You don't suppose he could have written that passage if Russia was motorized, do you? He was talking horses. *Stallions,* that's what they were. A horse travels like the wind. A horse *flies.* A spirited horse, anyway. How would Homer have rushed the gods back and forth without those fiery steeds he made use of? Can you imagine him maneuvering those quarrelsome divinities in a Rolls-Royce? To whip up ecstasy . . . you've got to make use of cosmic ingredients. Beside arms, legs, hooves, claws, fangs, marrow and grit you've got to throw in the equinoctial precessions, the ebb and flow of the tide, the conjunctions of sun, moon and planets, and the ravings of the insane. Beside rainbows, comets and the Northern lights you've got to have eclipses, sun spots, plagues, miracles . . . all sorts of things, including fools, magicians, witches, leprechauns, Jack the Rippers, lecherous priests, jaded monarchs, saintly saints . . . but *not* motorcars, *not* refrigerators, *not* washing machines, *not* tanks, *not* telegraph poles."

> Such a beautiful Spring morning. Did I mention Shelley? Too good for his likes. Or for Keats or Wordsworth. A Jacob Boehme morning, nothing less. No flies yet, no mosquitoes. Not even a cockroach in sight. Splendid. Just splendid.

> . . . .

> Yes, even if MacGregor were to suddenly appear I could not fall from grace. I would sit him down and tell him of Masaccio or of the *Vita Nuova.*[48]

The symbol of the horse as a theriomorphic symbol of the self is the archetypal expression of Miller's quest for integration and totality: the libido as Pegasus, the flying horse that combines the negative and positive and symbolizes the release of creative energy.[49]

In such a state (a "Jacob Boehme morning," "even if MacGregor were to suddenly appear I could not fall from grace"), the shadow figure can still appear, but the *I* has successfully assimilated his significance.

For Miller this integration is the end of all his actions, although it is an end that either eludes the hero or is obviously a temporary achievement. Occasionally the fiction reaches a climax or a stage in the search for such integration. A temporary resolution of the opposites or the tension within occurs, an "Easter Sunday," or a "Jacob Boehme morning." But the movement is progressive, toward still greater integration and extension of consciousness. Miller's fiction dramatizes process, and its forms are properly arranged in a total *progress*.

PART THREE

toward a union of opposites

Chapter Seven

Enantiodromia *and Progress*

Near the end of *Nexus,* the narrator speaks of confronting MacGregor with a new sense of power and the temporary conviction that he can not fall from grace. But the warning is apparent. His Jacob Boehme morning, the aurora of his Pegasus, is a temporary state and part of a never-ending progress: "No flies yet, no mosquitoes. Not even a cockroach in sight." [1] The *yet* suggests what is to come, for *Nexus* ends before the visit to Paris chronicled in *Tropic of Cancer,* before this most important excursion into the filthy world to which the lice and cockroaches belong—the world of the demonic and irrational. In each of the six volumes of the two autobiographical trilogies the same states occur: moments of epiphany followed by descents into chaos for confrontations with the Archetypal Feminine that threaten dissolution or possession.

In the later volumes of *The Rosy Crucifixion,* these encounters are stylized and self-conscious. They are often introduced by a dream formula.[2] Such self-consciousness is characteristic of the later form of Miller's fiction, the anatomy. In the earlier confessions, the distinction between the two worlds—the inner and the outer—is not made as consciously and deliberately.

Fantasy episodes are often experienced as inseparable correlatives of external events.

The goal of the *I*'s progress is androgyny,[3] the androgynous self of the utopian vision as symbol of the reconciliation of opposites: "Beside rainbows, comets and the Northern lights you've got to have eclipses, sun spots, plagues, miracles . . . all sorts of things, including fools, magicians, witches, leprechauns, Jack the Rippers, lecherous priests, jaded monarchs, saintly saints. . . ." The opposites are light and darkness, the negative and positive potentials of the individual, and insofar as these are projected on the external world, the negative elements must be assimilated and integrated. This theme is substantially corroborated by the analysis of the symbols of the Archetypal Feminine and the self.

More remains to be said, however, about the larger patterns into which these symbolic manifestations of the progress are organized. No permanent equilibrium in the psychic system is ever reached, for the possibility of *enantiodromia*, or reversal, always remains.[4] This is the essential significance of Miller's insistence that his book about the self can never be finished. Those who have described Miller's world as a rejection of external reality in favor of a return to the womb miss his insistence on the experience of rebirth. The womb (as symbol) is only one of the sacred centers in Miller's fictional world. Among others are the "dead center," the *hortus conclusus*, the great cities, the child-world, and the center of the wheel. These are sacred centers in Mircea Eliade's sense: zones of absolute reality. Such zones are reached by difficult roads:

> This is verified at every level of reality: difficult convolutions of a temple (as at Borobudur); pilgrimage to sacred places (Mecca, Hardwar, Jerusalem); danger-ridden voyages of the heroic expeditions in search of the Golden Fleece, the Golden Apples, the Herb of Life; wanderings in labyrinths; difficulties of the seeker for the road to the self, to the "center" of his being, and so on. The road is arduous, fraught with perils, because it is, in fact, a rite of the passage from the profane to the sacred, from the ephemeral and illusory to reality and eternity, from death to life, from man to the di-

vinity. Attaining the center is equivalent to a consecration, an initiation; yesterday's profane and illusory existence gives place to a new, to a life that is real, enduring, and effective.[5]

Not all the centers in Miller's fiction are positive, however. Many are also threatening (for example, the womb is both positive and negative), for they can destroy the hero through possession or dissolution. They are hells to which the *I* must journey *and from which he must return*, having attained a greater measure of vitality and reached a higher consciousness. Miller's acceptance of an inevitable catastrophe toward which we move in our time, moreover, is fully in accord with the principle of *enantiodromia* and his utopian vision: in order to achieve utopian ends, regeneration of society is necessary, and this parallels the need for regeneration of the *I*.[6] Miller's vision is analogous to Eliade's description of the myth of eternal return in pre-Christian thought:

> In the "lunar perspective," the death of the individual and the *periodic* death of humanity are necessary, even as the three days of darkness preceding the "rebirth" of the moon are necessary. The death of the individual and the death of humanity are alike necessary for their regeneration. Any form whatever, by the mere fact that it exists as such and endures, necessarily loses vigor and becomes worn; to recover vigor, it must be reabsorbed into the formless if only for an instant; it must be restored to the primordial unity from which it issued; in other words, it must return to "chaos" (on the cosmic plane), to "orgy" (on the social plane), to "darkness" (for seed), to "water" (baptism on the human plane, Atlantis on the plane of history, and so on).[7]

Such a vision is, of course, essentially optimistic and accounts for Miller's "cosmic joy" and his indifference to rational projects for social salvation. Whether we take his cyclic visions seriously or not, his affinity for these convictions should be recognized, and even more important, their relationship to the role of the individual's transformations acknowledged, for many of the apparent contradictions in Miller's fictional world are revealed as only apparent. On the contrary, a rigid consistency in his vision and projects emerges.

The progress of the self is central, however, for the transformation of the external world will occur in a distant future.[8] For Miller, the transformation of the individual can occur in the midst of the historical process, and separately:

> I lived out the social problem by dying: the real problem is not one of getting along with one's neighbor or of contributing to the development of one's country, but of discovering one's destiny, of making a life in accord with the deep-centered rhythm of the cosmos.[9]

Paralleling the individual psychic process with the historical or the cosmic process is intrinsic to the formal structure of Miller's fiction. Fletcher has discussed this aspect of allegorical form as one of the "magical devices" the allegorist uses to enjoin his audience to accept certain "intellectual or moral or spiritual attitudes":

> Ultimately the imitative magic of allegory is based on the correspondence between microcosmos and macrocosmos, since it is necessary to have systems of images and agents that can be placed in a symmetrical relationship to each other.[10]

The paralleling, with its "magic" implications for the hero of Miller's fiction, extends to the shadow figures I have discussed. Fletcher acknowledges this potential of allegory in somewhat different terms from the ones I have used:

> We can say that when a main character of an allegory generates more than one double for himself, when he is fractionated into a number of other partial characters, this portrayal greatly increases the amount of plot symmetry. Each partial aspect that has been generated out of the main character is now available to the author for its development parallel to every other partial aspect.[11]

The male figures (such as Van Norden and MacGregor) are generated by the *I*. Their relationships with either the manifestations of the Archetypal Feminine or the demands of the social world enable Miller to explore in parallel actions his

problem of the self. Because Miller is writing confession, moreover, plot is not essential to his progress. The fundamental
concern is theoretical, and the allegorical process serves these
theoretical ends more obviously than is apparent in romance.
(Both Fletcher and Frye consider romance essentially allegorical.) Moreover, the doubles that are "generated" by the hero
achieve only partial mimetic dimension. As I have indicated in
the earlier chapters of this study, their forms often dissolve into
the non-human symbols characteristic of certain archetypal
manifestations. It is perhaps inevitable that in *Capricorn* especially Miller's form appears to imitate—at least partially—a musical structure, for the articulation between motifs is not one
that requires a narrative line.

But the causal interdependence remains: the *I* responds to
figures and events, to the archetypal manifestations we have
recognized. These responses are "ritually or symmetrically
ordered" [12] in the structure in which they occur, the ritual
serving to bring something under control (in Miller, the ex-
crescences of the unconscious and the threats of social reality).
Such symbolic actions as eating have this function, for by eating the *I* assimilates the contents of the archetypal forms and
converts them. Coitus is *par excellence* the ritual act for Miller,
and, as we have seen, is a means by which the nature of the relationship with the unconscious is explored.

The detail with which coitus is described by Miller functions magically. (Readers who consider such details "realistic"
demonstrate that they have failed to recognize the essentially
symbolic and allegorical nature of Miller's work.) The words
and images serve as a barrier between the demonic figures of
the inner world that Miller evokes or sees projected on the
external world—especially the Gorgon figures of the Archetypal Feminine. They enable him to "control" the archetypes
by naming and describing their parts. Fletcher recognizes this
function in his discussion of metonymy:

> Metonymies are above all *names*, and are emphatically kept
> to serve the needs of labeling and fixing the magical value of
> whatever they are applied to. When one chronicles a set of

names which label aspects of a virtue or vice, one is making a catalogue, and this in turn constitutes a ritual.[13]

Enormous sections of *Capricorn* and *Cancer* consist of these ritual catalogues, suggesting in their total effect the dimensions of a chant.[14] Both the device of paralleling microcosm and macrocosm and that of ritual cataloguing coexist in many passages, as, for example, in this description of America prompted by the narrator's insights into the failures of a clinic for the mentally ill:

> The purpose of [the doctor's] treatment was to render the subject fit for society. But no matter how fast he worked, no matter whether he was successful or not successful, society was turning out more and more misfits. Some of them were so marvelously maladapted that when, in order to get proverbial reaction, he slapped them vigorously on the cheek they responded with an uppercut or a kick in the balls. It's true, most of his subjects were exactly what he described them to be—incipient criminals. The whole continent was on the slide—is still on the slide—and not only the glands need regulating but the ball-bearings, the armature, the skeletal structure, the cerebrum, the cerebellum, the coccyx, the larynx, the pancreas, the liver, the upper intestine and the lower intestine, the heart, the kidneys, the testicles, the womb, the Fallopian tubes, the whole goddamned works. The whole country is lawless, violent, explosive, demoniacal. It's in the air, in the climate, in the ultra-grandiose landscape, in the stone forests that are lying horizontal, in the torrential rivers that bite through the rocky canyons, in the supra-normal distances, the supernal arid wastes, the overlush crops, the monstrous fruits, the mixture of quixotic bloods, the fatras of cults, sects, beliefs, the opposition of laws and languages, the contradictoriness of temperaments, principles, needs, requirements. The continent is full of buried violence, of the bones of antediluvian monsters and of lost races of man, of mysteries which are wrapped in doom. The atmosphere is at times so electrical that the soul is summoned out of its body and runs amok. Like the rain everything comes in bucketsful—or not at all. The whole continent is a huge volcano whose crater is temporarily concealed by a moving panorama which is partly dream, partly fear, partly despair. From Alaska to Yucatan it's the same story.

Nature dominates, Nature wins out. Everywhere the same fundamental urge to slay, to ravage, to plunder. Outwardly they seem like a fine, upstanding people—healthy, optimistic, courageous. Inwardly they are filled with worms. A tiny spark and they blow up.[15]

"Naming" controls not only the threat from social reality: the appearance of symbols of the unconscious inevitably prompts the *I* to name. The threatening elements of the archetype can be "contained" by these names, as in the description of Paula/Laura in a passage I discussed earlier:

She has the loose, jaunty swing and perch of the double-barreled sex, all her movements radiating from the groin, always in equilibrium, always ready to flow, to wind and twist and clutch, the eyes going tic-toc, the toes twitching and twinkling, the flesh rippling like a lake furrowed by a breeze. This is the incarnation of the hallucination of sex, the sea nymph squirming in the maniac's arms. . . . The music is sprinkled with rat poison, with the rattlesnake's venom, with the fetid breath of the gardenia, the spittle of the sacred yak, the bolloxed sweat of the muskrat, the leper's sugar-coated nostalgia. The music is a diarrhea, a lake of gasoline, stagnant with cockroaches and stale horse piss. The drooling notes are the foam and dribble of the epileptic, the night sweat of the fornicating nigger frigged by the Jew. . . . The octopus is dancing like a rubber dick. . . . In the belly of the trombone lies the American soul farting its contented heart out. Nothing goes to waste—not the least spit of a fart. In the golden marshmallow dream of happiness, in the dance of the sodden piss and gasoline, the great soul of the American continent gallops like an octopus, all the sails unfurled, the hatches down, the engine whirring like a dynamo. The great dynamic soul caught in the click of the camera's eye, in the heat of rut, bloodless as a fish, slippery as mucus, the soul of the people miscegenating on the sea floor, popeyed with longing, harrowed with lust. The dance of Saturday night, of cantaloupes rotting in the garbage pail, of fresh green snot and slimy unguents for the tender parts. . . . The dance of the magneto world, the spark that unsparks, the soft purr of the perfect mechanism, the velocity race of a turntable, the dollar at par and the forests dead and mutilated. The Saturday night of the soul's

hollow dance, each jumping jigger a functional unit in the
St. Vitus' dance of the ringworm's dream. Laura the nym-
pho brandishing her cunt, her sweet rose-petal lips toothed
with ballbearing clutches, her ass balled and socketed.[16]

The sentences in such passages are structured paratactically,
producing the rhythm of chant. By such ritual catalogues, the
historical, external, social darkness which threatens the *I* is contained, as well as the threatening inner reality:

> It's only a stretch of a few blocks, from Times Square to Fif-
> tieth Street, and when one says Broadway that's all that's
> really meant and it's really nothing, just a chicken run and a
> lousy one at that, but at seven in the evening when every-
> body's rushing for a table there's a sort of electrical crackle
> in the air and your hair stands on end like antennae and if
> you're receptive you not only get every flash and flicker but
> you get the statistical itch, the *quid pro quo* of the interac-
> tive, interstitial, ectoplasmatic quantum of bodies jostling in
> space like the stars which compose the Milky Way, only
> this is the Gay White Way, the top of the world with no
> roof above and not even a crack or a hole under your feet to
> fall through and say it's a lie. The absolute impersonality of
> it brings you to a pitch of warm human delirium which
> makes you run forward like a blind nag and wag your delir-
> ious ears. Every one is so utterly, confoundedly not himself
> that you become automatically the personification of the
> whole human race, shaking hands with a thousand human
> hands, cackling with a thousand different human tongues,
> cursing, applauding, whistling, crooning, soliloquizing, orat-
> ing, gesticulating, urinating, fecundating, wheedling, cajol-
> ing, whimpering, bartering, pimping, caterwauling, and so
> on and so forth.[17]

Fletcher draws attention to the ambivalent attitudes which
lie behind such allegorical rituals, an ambivalence which we
have observed specifically in the response of the *I* to manifestations of the Archetypal Feminine.[18] The dramatic paralysis
which the *I* frequently suffers is a response to the magical
power of the anima and the other figures of the unconscious.
In fact, the loss of the anima's power to possess, which is recorded in the last two volumes of *Plexus* and *Nexus* and manifests itself in the increasing lack of significance of the character

Mona/Mara, represents a stage in the *I*'s progress; for the anima loses her demonic power and autonomy.[19]

As threatening and autonomous archetypes, however, the anima and other figures of the Archetypal Feminine are often approached through coitus. In fact, the "possession" which the unconscious exerts on the *I* acquires perfect expression in the impersonal and demanding obsession with sexuality in the early volumes.[20] Symbolic coitus, as it occurs in various scenes in the confessions, involves the threat of contagion. The possession or castration of the hero means that the *I* is "diseased," for the Feminine, as a symbol of the unconscious, has "captured" or dissolved or perverted consciousness. The *I* can, of course, and does in various passages, move to "sacred centers" that are free from contagion. (We have identified many of these centers as images of the archetype of the self.) Such movement is ritual in significance, for the *I* thereby reorganizes itself and recovers from the threat of dissolution by the unconscious, or (if the threat comes from without) from social reality. This centering process Jung associates with the process of individuation, the development of the individual personality.[21]

A "retreat" to the symbols of the self as center provides the *I* with sanctuary and power. But as we have pointed out not all the centers toward which the symbolic action moves and from which the *I* returns are positive. The "dead centers" of the wheel, the hells of the inner world, the Ixion figures with which the *I* occasionally identifies, the destroying womb—these are numinous, negative sacred centers. The *I*, moreover, harbors ambivalent attitudes toward the dead centers. In this ambivalence lies the real reconciliation of opposites that Miller speaks of, for it is a recognition of the fecundating and destructive powers of the transpersonal unconscious. Coitus is symbolically the entrance to the transpersonal world:

> It was a personal tour in the impersonal world, a man with a tiny trowel in his hand digging a tunnel through the earth to get to the other side. The idea was to tunnel through and find at last the Culebra Cut, the *ne plus ultra*, of the honeymoon of flesh. And of course there was no end to the dig-

ging. The best I might hope for was to get stuck in the dead center of the earth, where the pressure was strongest and most even all around, and stay stuck there forever. That would give me the feeling of Ixion on the wheel, which is one sort of salvation and not entirely to be sneezed at. On the other hand I was a metaphysician of the instinctivist sort: it was impossible for me to stay stuck anywhere, even in the dead center of the earth. It was most imperative to find and to enjoy the metaphysical fuck, and for that I would be obliged to come out on to a wholly new tableland, a mesa of sweet alfalfa and polished monoliths, where the eagles and the vultures flew at random.[22]

The descent into the inner world is the difficult way to rebirth and renewal. And contact with the unconscious as it is symbolized by the negative Feminine brings with it the fear of contagion. Miller's frequent association of the female with disease and destruction is the symbolic expression of the fear of such contagion:

She could break down the most "personal" hard on in the world. Break it down with laughter. At the same time it wasn't quite as humiliating as one might be inclined to imagine. There was something sympathetic about this vaginal laughter. The whole world seemed to unroll like a pornographic film whose tragic theme is impotence. You could visualize yourself as a dog, or a weasel, or a white rabbit. Love was something on the side, a dish of caviar, say, or a wax heliotrope. You could see the ventriloquist in you talking about caviar or heliotropes, but the real person was always a weasel or a white rabbit. Evelyn was always lying in the cabbage patch with legs spread open offering a bright green leaf to the first comer. But if you made a move to nibble it the whole cabbage patch would explode with laughter, a bright, dewy, vaginal laughter such as Jesus H. Christ and Immanuel Pussyfoot Kant never dreamed of, because if they had the world would not be what it is today and besides there would have been no Kant and no Christ Almighty. The female seldom laughs, but when she does it's volcanic. When the female laughs the male had better scoot to the cyclone cellar. Nothing will stand up under that vaginating chortle, not even ferroconcrete. The female, when her risibility is once aroused, can laugh down the hyena or the

> jackal or the wildcat. Now and then one hears it at a lynch-
> ing bee, for example. It means that the lid is off, that every-
> thing goes. It means that she will forage for herself—and
> watch out that you don't get your balls cut off! It means that
> if the pest is coming SHE is coming first, and with huge
> spiked thongs that will flay the living hide off you. It means
> that she will lay not only with Tom, Dick, and Harry, but
> with Cholera, Meningitis, Leprosy; it means that she will
> lay herself down on the altar like a mare in rut and take all
> comers, including the Holy Ghost.[23]

In such contact error can enter, and the self—pervious and
maculate—is threatened.

Nevertheless, the descent is necessary and inevitable for
transformation, and the development of a higher consciousness
which has assimilated greater areas of the total personality.
This ritual pattern is articulated in passage after passage.

Near the end of *Nexus* the *I* describes his state of psychic
ecstasy and the sense of power it lends him. He chooses the
phrase "Jacob Boehme morning." Such an aurora, however,
only follows a darkness, a *nigredo*,[24] a descent into hell, a return to the womb, a journey into the belly of the whale. And,
as it is symbolized by the Archetypal Feminine, the transpersonal unconscious into which the hero descends is the source of
vitality and energy as well as possible (or ultimate) death. It is
the positive aspect of hell that reminds us of Boehme's
Ungrund: [25] Hell is a core, not a bottom, "a dead center from
which time itself is reckoned. Here the comedy begins, *for
here it is seen to be divine.*" [26]

Not all negative centers permit rebirth, however, and the
motif then becomes escape. (America, Miller asserts in *Capricorn*, is incapable of providing for rebirth.) Nevertheless, it is
in the dark abyss that the cosmic process must begin, and it is
in New York that the anima figure emerges in Miller's psychic
drama. (The term "magical causation" serves effectively here
to describe such dramatic relationships, as Fletcher demon-
strates.) I have used the term *escape* because it describes Miller's dramatization of one aspect of the descent into the dark
centers. From Dijon the *I* escapes to Paris; from New York, to

Paris. In the relationship with Mara at the end of *Capricorn*, however, the contact with the anima seems to generate "magically" the transformation and development of the *I*.

Dijon, New York, and Paris (and other cities) are, as I have pointed out in chapter 2, elementary representations of the Archetypal Feminine. They are symbolic cities, "sacred centers" or zones of absolute reality for the hero. And in New York and Dijon, it is the negative aspect of the archetype that is manifest. Nevertheless, the conflict with the negative (or confrontation) stimulates the transformative process. Before the *I* can escape or develop or reorganize itself, the anima figure must be detached from the Mother archetype, or recognized. This process is the most significant action in *Capricorn*, for Mara begins to emerge as a human figure from the cluster of non-human images and symbols in which she first appears. In *Tropic of Cancer* the relationship with the Archetypal Feminine is in terms of more elemental symbols, which explains the relative absence of Mara, although the *I* continues to dream of her. Paris is the city of both negative and positive aspects of the Great Mother. New York and Dijon are symbols of only the deadly aspect.

Neumann's explanation of the symbolic process is helpful here:

> But even where the transformative character of the Feminine appears as a negative, hostile, and provocative element, it compels tension, change, and an intensification of the personality. In this way an extreme exertion of the ego is provoked and its capacity for creative transformation is directly and indirectly "stimulated." But of course the transformative character is not to be understood as a conscious intention of woman, as it appears in the mythological image; it attains to this awareness only late, and in the highest form of femininity. But even the unconscious workings of the feminine transformative character spur the male on to achievement and transformation. Even where the trial by the Feminine is not, as in many myths and tales, consciously planned, it is immanent in the male relation to the feminine transformative character.

This means that the anima figure, despite the great danger that is bound up with it, is not terrible in the same way as the Great Mother, who is not at all concerned with the independence of the individual and the ego. Even when the anima is seemingly negative and "intends," for example, to poison the male consciousness, to endanger it by intoxication, and so on—even then a positive reversal is possible, for the anima figure is always subject to defeat. When Circe, the enchantress who turns men into beasts, meets the superior figure of Odysseus, she does not kill herself like the Sphinx, whose riddle Oedipus has solved, but invites him to share her bed.[27]

The negative centers and the negative figures "cause," then, certain effects: the *I* dissolves, or reorganizes. In *Capricorn* the *I* speaks of these various transformations which lead him away from old relationships and reorganize the self as dramatizations of processes that occurred over long periods of time:

When I think of the book now, and the way I approached it, I think of a man going through the rites of initiation. The disorientation and reorientation which comes with the initiation into any mystery is the most wonderful experience which it is possible to have. Everything which the brain has labored for a lifetime to assimilate, categorize and synthesize has to be taken apart and reordered. Moving day for the soul! And of course it's not for a day, but for weeks and months that this goes on. You meet a friend on the street by chance, one whom you haven't seen for several weeks, and he has become an absolute stranger to you. You give him a few signals from your new perch and if he doesn't cotton you pass him up—*for good*. It's exactly like mopping up a battlefield; all those who are hopelessly disabled and agonizing you dispatch with one swift blow of your club. You move on, to new fields of battle, to new triumphs or defeats. But you move! And as you move the world moves with you, with terrifying exactitude. You seek out new fields of operation, new specimens of the human race whom you patiently instruct and equip with the new symbols. You choose sometimes those whom you would never have looked at before. You try everybody and everything within range, provided they are ignorant of the revelation.[28]

The "disorientation and reorientation" which occurs is necessary to the progress of the self or the development of a
more fully integrated personality. That a positive development
(for it is obvious that such development is positive for Miller)
occurs as the result of the "descents" into the negative centers
is a dramatization of what Jung has called *enantiodromia:* the
regulatory principle of the opposites that bring each other into
existence.

The positive emerges from the negative (we become angels
only after we have become monsters); the hero who escapes
the contaminated and destructive "sacred centers" of the world
and of his being is reborn. Miller, like Boehme, does not accept
the easy opposition of good and evil: his quest for the center
involves more than one center. The recognition of both positive and negative centers in his fiction is essential to an understanding of the movement toward moments of realization, of
power, of "resurrection." The "Easter Sunday" episode at the
end of *Capricorn* is illustrative.

In the spaceless, timeless chaos Miller seeks, and which he
clearly symbolizes as Feminine, centers such as the dead center
of the wheel or the core that is hell do not always appear, however. When they do, they represent a focusing on the negative
aspects of the Feminine (or the unconscious) and are followed
by a movement away or (as in the passage I quoted above) a
conscious assertion that unlike others the *I* will not remain
fixed at the center. The movement or recognition is part of an
endlessly repeated process.

That the experience of chaos and descent is necessary to the
creation of the integrated self is as difficult for some of Miller's
readers to acknowledge as is his notion that out of destruction
of the world will emerge a utopia, and destruction must precede this rebirth. Not that Miller's notions are in any way
unique; I have tried to point out some of the most striking parallels, especially in the work of men to whom he finds himself
drawn, such as Jacob Boehme.[29] Boehme's *Ungrund*, for example, where the "cosmic process" is begun, is described in details
and symbols which are similar to the archetypal symbols I have

traced in Miller's confessions.[30] Perhaps these are processes accessible to the few: we should remember Freud's belief that the mystic has greater access to the unconscious than others,[31] and Jung's conviction that the archetypal processes (such as transformation) are carried on unconsciously and that only rarely is the individual confronted with the archetypes.

Certainly Miller's account of the effect of the negative centers upon the *I* can find numerous parallels; however, what is more important is that the negative and positive centers be recognized as organizing principles in his work. Fletcher finds that most allegorical rituals depend on the symbols of the center for their moments of "particular exuberance, particular intensity, particular vision." [32] Accordingly, all the great allegories move toward such centers:

> It is toward this kind of moment, as toward moments like the descent to the Underworld, . . . that all the great allegories move, and if we do not seek conventional imagery only, we shall find such moments where we would hardly expect them, in so-called "naturalistic" works.[33]

Tropic of Cancer is organized around a "descent" to Dijon and a return to Paris. But there are, in fact, numerous descents (such as the visit to the woman on the dais in the cellar, a scene which I discussed earlier). Numerous encounters with the numinous manifestations of the Archetypal Feminine occur, for the repetition of this pattern achieves ritual significance in Miller. The most formidable descent, however, the nadir of the book's experience, is the stay in the city of ice and darkness: Dijon. The chapter describing this experience (which is the penultimate chapter of the book) ends with the moment of insight that I quoted in another context:

> Going back in a flash over the women I've known. It's like a chain which I've forged out of my own misery. Each one bound to the other. A fear of living separate, of staying born. The door of the womb always on the latch. Dread and longing. Deep in the blood the pull of paradise. The beyond. Always the beyond. It must have all started with the navel. They cut the umbilical cord, give you a slap on the ass, and

presto! you're out in the world adrift, a ship without a rudder. You look at the stars and then you look at your navel. You grow eyes everywhere—in the armpits, between the lips, in the roots of your hair, on the soles of your feet. What is distant becomes near, what is near becomes distant. Inner-outer, a constant flux, a shedding of skins, a turning inside out. You drift around like that for years and years, until you find yourself in the dead center, and there you slowly rot, slowly crumble to pieces, get dispersed again. Only your name remains.[34]

The return to Paris after the stay in Dijon is a return to a positive center, a triumph of escape, "and then only by the stroke of fortune." Paris is a positive center only in that the elements of negative and positive, reflected in the ambivalence which the *I* feels for the city as symbol, are balanced. Dijon, on the other hand, is at the "dead center." Paris may be indifferent to the *I*, but it offers him possibilities. It is springtime in Paris when the *I* returns, and the sun is shining:

At the Pont de Sèvres I got out and started walking along the river, toward the Auteuil Viaduct. It's about the size of a creek along here and the trees come right down to the river's bank. The water was green and glassy, especially near the other side. Now and then a scow chugged by. Bathers in tights were standing in the grass sunning themselves. Everything was close and palpitant, and vibrant with the strong light.[35]

The cold, frozen world of Dijon, the deadly symbol of the negative Feminine, is lost in the *I*'s sense of vigor, his feeling of well-being, his delight in having tricked a treacherous French girl and rescued his friend Fillmore from marriage with her. Most important is his identification with the flow, the artery of Paris:

After everything had quietly sifted through my head a great peace came over me. Here, where the river gently winds through the girdle of hills, lies a soil so saturated with the past that however far back the mind roams one can never detach it from its human background. Christ, before my eyes there shimmered such a golden peace that only a neurotic could dream of turning his head away. So quietly flows the

Seine that one hardly notices its presence. It is always there, quiet and unobtrusive, like a great artery running through the human body. In the wonderful peace that fell over me it seemed as if I had climbed to the top of a high mountain; for a little while I would be able to look around me, to take in the meaning of the landscape.

Human beings make a strange fauna and flora. From a distance they appear negligible; close up they are apt to appear ugly and malicious. More than anything they need to be surrounded with sufficient space—space even more than time.

The sun is setting. I feel this river flowing through me—its past, its ancient soil, the changing climate. The hills gently girdle it about: its course is fixed.[36]

The *I* has returned from the dead center, the frozen world, and has enjoyed a rebirth, a new vision as if from "the top of a high mountain." This passage emphasizes his isolation from a community, and establishes his identification with another destiny. Such isolation frees the self from a decadent social reality (from which, as I suggested earlier, contagion is possible). The reconciliation of the opposites is an inner state, a temporary alleviation of the anxiety which pervades his exploration of the self. Through his identification with the flowing river, he acknowledges, symbolically, the potency and fecundity of the transpersonal unconscious which is no longer dead and frozen. The significance of this ending is further underlined by the contrast between the two cities New York and Paris. In the musings of the narrator, New York suggests a skeleton in the snow:

Suddenly it occurred to me that if I wanted I could go to America myself. It was the first time the opportunity had ever presented itself. I asked myself—"do you want to go?" There was no answer. My thoughts drifted out, toward the sea, toward the other side where, taking a last look back, I had seen the skyscrapers fading out in a flurry of snowflakes. I saw them looming up again, in that same ghostly way as when I left. Saw the lights creeping through their ribs. I saw the whole city spread out, from Harlem to the Battery, the streets choked with ants, the elevated rushing by, the theaters emptying. I wondered in a vague way what had ever happened to my wife.[37]

In such negative centers as Dijon and New York, Miller concentrates the elementary negative symbolism of the Terrible Mother. Paris, on the other hand, although still capable of negative significance for the *I*, is also a city of birth and life. It is experienced in images by the *I*, and "assimilated" in the process of *Cancer*. This process leads to independence rather than the possession suffered by the shadow characters, Carl and Van Norden. Not everyone can experience the unconscious and escape. In section four of *Cancer*, for example, the *I* tried to persuade Carl to act, for his predicament is acknowledged by the *I* as a possible predicament for everyone: "But that's just it! In Europe one gets used to doing nothing. You sit on your ass and whine all day. You get contaminated. You rot." [38] At the same time, the river that flows through Paris provides the city symbol with meaning and life:

> The river is still swollen, muddy, streaked with lights. I don't know what it is rushes up in me at the sight of this dark, swift-moving current, but a great exultation lifts me up, affirms the deep wish that is in me never to leave this land.[39]

New York by contrast is "A whole city erected over a hollow pit of nothingness." [40]

The symbols of the self suggest the whole of the total personality. The *hortus conclusus*, the circles and centers, the childhood worlds, are positive centers toward which the *I* moves, in which he is contained for a while, and from which he re-emerges. When the negative centers are approached, however, they may fatally attract and hold, becoming experiences of captivity. The images of the Great Mother archetype may be both positive and negative, which explains the similarities between some of the symbols of the negative and positive centers: "The function of *holding fast, fixating*, and *ensnaring* . . . indicates the dangerous and deadly aspect of the Great Mother, just as the opposite . . . shows her aspect of life and growth." [41] To this aspect belongs the flowing imagery of the water:

> The Great Goddess is the flowing unity of subterranean and celestial primordial water, the sea of heaven on which sail the barks of the gods of light, the circular life-generating ocean above and below the earth. To her belong all waters, streams, fountains, ponds, and springs, as well as the rain. She is the ocean of life with its life—and death—bringing seasons, and life is her child, a fish eternally swimming inside her, like the stars in the celestial ocean of the Mexican Mayauel and like men in the fishpool of Mother Church—a late manifestation of the same archetype.[42]

If, as Angus Fletcher believes, ambivalence is the central problem of allegory and "we should not assume the polar opposites are really separated by any distance," [43] then the symbolism of the Great Mother and the account of the *I*'s confrontation with the archetypal figures of the unconscious provide Miller's allegories with powerful and traditional experiences. Even his choice of the tabooed words to describe physical functions serves to increase the ambivalence. The twentieth-century necropolis on which these traditional symbols are projected provides him with a visual vocabulary that effectively obscures and controls his subject. Edmund Wilson, for example, speaks of the hero of *Cancer* as "the genuine American bum come to lead the beautiful life in Paris . . ." and sees the theme of the book as "the lives of a group of Americans who have all more or less come to Paris with the intention of occupying themselves with literature but who have actually subsided easily into an existence almost exclusively preoccupied with drinking and fornication. . . ." [44] Yet the meaning of this experience goes unexamined, and Wilson accepts the disguise as the real subject.

Miller's way is the negative way, the route of descent before ascent. The *I*'s rebirth in Paris (which brings him the power to defeat the aggressive Feminine in Ginette) means independence, power, and access to the flowing fecundity of the maternal Paris. Innocence is born in corruption; insight and illumination emerge from the sordid and unpleasant. And the principle of *enantiodromia* provides an arrangement or formal structure for the events in *Cancer*.

In stages of the progress Miller records, the *I* achieves power over the forces of the unconscious in his moments of independence. The dramatic paralysis from which the narrator suffers frequently, the feelings of helplessness or containment, the spiritual castration, however, mark a temporary failure of consciousness to assimilate the threatening contents of the unconscious archetypes. This experience needs further explanation. Although I speak of the narrator's "escape" from Dijon, the term indicates the dramatic action (Miller also used the word *escape*), not the precise relationship between the *I* and the negative center. The center, Jung believes, is the place of creative change, and insists that before we undergo such change, we must be exposed to the transpersonal unconscious without identifying ourselves with it. The *I* must hold its ground, "experience" the unconscious, and then articulate "with consciousness" the meaning of the experience.[45] Such precisely is the action at the end of section fourteen, when the *I* responds to the experience of Dijon. In fact, articulation of the experience of the unconscious might be one way of describing the subject of Miller's confessions.

This articulation of the meaning of his experience is an assertion of the *I*'s energy and independence. The act of understanding is itself a sign of strength. Transformation, Jung argues, requires such focus on the centers about which I have been speaking, and the experience is almost unbearable. (He refers to this experience as a centering process.) One must be strong enough to resist succumbing to the unconscious. That the hero escapes from a negative center, moreover, is part of an immutable pattern which governs his destiny. Miller's narrator, for example, speaks of knowing that he is not among those who will remain at the dead center. He is assured that he is different from others, that he has the power to withstand the unconscious and escape. Yet he needs help. He is, in effect, the demonically controlled hero of allegory. "Dramatic paralysis" successfully describes his inability to act on occasion, just as sexual enslavement and the involuntary nature of erection are significant symbols of possession.

But it is necessary to distinguish between those moments when the *I* is compelled by his sense of immutable destiny and those moments when he recognizes and articulates the meaning of his experience. When he is possessed entirely, as in the section of *Capricorn* in which he first explores a relationship with Mara, or in *Sexus* when he becomes a dog, the paralysis appears fatal. In a ferocious round of sexual encounters in *Capricorn*, for example, the *I* is paralyzed and helpless. Yet here he remains aware of his ultimate destiny:

> The day wore on like that, with lots to eat and drink, the sun out strong, a car to tote us around, cigars in between, dozing a little on the beach, studying the cunts passing by, talking, laughing, singing a bit too—one of many, many days I spent like that with MacGregor. Days like that really seemed to make the wheel stop. On the surface it was jolly and happy-go-lucky; time passing like a sticky dream. But underneath it was fatalistic, premonitory, leaving me the next day morbid and restless. I knew very well I'd have to make a break some day; I knew very well I was pissing my time away. But I knew also that there was nothing I could do about it—*yet*. Something had to happen, something big, something that would sweep me off my feet. All I needed was a push, but it had to be some force outside my world that could give me the right push, that I was certain of. I couldn't eat my heart out, because it wasn't in my nature. All my life things had worked out all right—*in the end*. It wasn't in the cards for me to exert myself. Something had to be left to Providence—in my case a whole lot. Despite all the outward manifestations of misfortune or mismanagement I knew that I was born with a silver spoon in my mouth. And with a double crown, too. The external situation was bad, admitted—but what bothered me more was the internal situation.[46]

He descends even further in *Capricorn*, to a symbolic drowning in the Gulf of Mexico and to the bridge to insanity which he refuses to cross. But it is his resignation from the shadow world or the external world of the *persona* with its social definitions of the self, and his entrance, entirely, into a world dominated by Mara which is the important event at the end of *Capricorn*. This relationship produces the real progress in his life. Mara, crystallized out of the endless manifestations of the Archetypal Feminine, is the most important transformative character, the anima. The experience of this figure *in her symbolic roles* (especially her *negative* aspect) leads to the "resurrection" at the end of *Capricorn*, the Easter Sunday section examined earlier.

The *I* insists on a sacred destiny, yet he does not exert himself. He suffers and assimilates. By his acquiescence to the principle of *enantiodromia*, his salvation occurs. His progress is rhythmical and spiral, for descents and confrontations appear throughout the *Tropics* [47] and *The Rosy Crucifixion*. In this rhythmical movement, contradictions are simply annulled; it is not necessary to exclude them in a rational and rectilinear process.

Miller's *I* never imagines that he is in control of his destiny. His problem is to communicate with his personal destiny: "I wasn't synchronized with my own destiny, so to speak. I was trying to live out the world destiny." [48] Communication with the forces of this destiny may take the form of symbolic coitus, for the most frequent manifestations of the unconscious are feminine. Communication in the real world is almost impossible. The beginning of *Capricorn*, with its long and memorable account of the diseased "cosmodemonic" telegraph company, is suitable as an ironic symbol of the broken-down communication system of man with man. Communication in the real, external, social world is a nightmare of dissent, undelivered or meaningless messages carried by the flotsam and jetsam of the human sea. The *I* is personnel manager for this sick system. Yet the outer world is not ready for transformation. Hence all efforts at reform, at managing are futile, and the *I* resigns. Only the *I* can be transformed, but the *I* is Everyman, ultimately:

> . . . *I wanted to electrify the cosmos!* I meant by that a very simple thing—The Delaware, Lackawanna and Western had been electrified, but the soul of man was still in the covered

wagon stage. I was born in the midst of civilization and I accepted it very naturally—what else was there to do? But the joke was that nobody else was taking it seriously. I was the only man in the community who was truly civilized. There was no place for me—as yet. And yet the books I read, the music I heard assured me that there were other men in the world like myself. I had to go and drown myself in the Gulf of Mexico in order to have an excuse for continuing this pseudo-civilized existence. I had to delouse myself of my spiritual body, as it were.[49]

Nevertheless the *I* cannot bring about his transformation because the archetypal processes of transformation are, as Jung insists, transpersonal (Miller would say "cosmic") and autonomous. The psychological processes which Miller dramatizes are beyond the control of the individual; for if one defines will as belonging only to the area of consciousness, one is helpless beyond this narrow area of self, and the hero cannot determine his destiny. Miller's *I* is a characteristic hero of allegory, for such heroes are never free, according to Fletcher:

> Even when Dante, who follows Pseudo-Dionysius, wants to show that the blessed spirits of the "Paradiso" are free to come and go as they wish, he also in fact shows them *fixed* to certain stages of the progress toward God. This, I think, is the case with all allegorical agents, and when an author is interested in what seem to be free metamorphoses and changes of taste, he is in fact not showing his characters acting freely. He is showing them changing, presto, from one facet of a destiny to another. They remain bound to the Wheel of Fortune, though it turns, rising and falling to give them the illusion of a changed state. The chief metamorphic poet, Ovid, is naturally turned to exegetical use in the *Ovide Moralisé*, since he himself draws attention so often to the opposite of change, namely fixity. The idea that the hero undergoes a change as a result of a *psychomachia* in which he battles, or of an agony, a progress, a voyage to the moon, or whatever typical story we choose, should not blind us to the real lack of freedom in all these stories. Picaresque romances, for example, submit their heroes to the workings of blind chance. These heroes do not choose, they do not "deliberate" but act on compulsion, continually demonstrating a lack of inner control. This is the most interesting in psycho-

logical allegory, in Spenser or Kafka, for example, where the author shows over and over that men suffer from a primary illusion when they imagine they are in control of their own actions. This prideful imagination may be called a sin, but it is also a psychological fact, as common experience tells us.[50]

Although the events of the *I*'s *enantiodromia* are repeated throughout Miller's autobiographical work, they can be arranged in terms of a progress. Each of the major volumes ends in a transformation, and each is different from the others. In fact, their differences are important. The dominant symbolism of *Cancer* and *Capricorn*, for example, is the elemental symbolism of the Archetypal Feminine. However, the nature of the images suggests that different stages in the *I*'s development have been reached in the two works. Despite the fact that the events of *Capricorn* precede those of *Cancer* in the life of the author, *Capricorn* describes a later stage in the integration of the *I*, or the integration has occurred on a higher level. The Archetypal Feminine emerges in *Capricorn* in the form of the anima figure, the transformative figure in almost human form. *Tropic of Cancer*, however, is dominated by elemental city symbolism—Paris and Dijon. The most powerful symbols of the unconscious in *Cancer* are non-human, or scarcely human: city, ice, water, for example. The human females in *Cancer* frequently dissolve into elemental non-human symbols or into scarcely human Gorgon forms, or they are sacred whores, aggressive and symbolically threatening.

The *I* is born in Paris. But another stage of transformation is reached in *Capricorn*. From the beginning of the book, one is aware of an *I* more in control, more conscious of the significance of events than in *Cancer*. The New York of *Capricorn* is not as imposing as the Paris of *Cancer*, although it remains a significant elemental symbol of the negative aspects of the unconscious. The myriad human female figures and the emphasis on the negative Feminine, suggest as we have seen, the crystallization of the anima, who gradually emerges in the figure of Mara.

The volumes of *The Rosy Crucifixion* review the events of

Capricorn at a much later date. Except in *Sexus,* which records the struggle with an anima figure who has assumed more human characteristics and acquired a history, Mona/Mara becomes less important. Events appear more ordinary and there is greater focus on various male figures who are shadow characters, but who are as much the subject of analysis and satire as partners in a psychic experience. Not that their allegorical significance as shadow figures has diminished, but they are more available to the dissection of consciousness; in effect, they have become the characters of anatomy.

Confession, romance, anatomy: these forms merge and coexist in the volumes of Miller's psychic drama. The allegorical progress has been toward a greater and greater awareness, on the part of the *I,* of the significance of the psychic events recorded. Having created his world in the early volumes, he proceeds to analysis in the later. Moreover in the later volumes there is less threat from the numinous figures of the Archetypal Feminine, although episodes of confrontation continue to appear. The cities—the great elemental symbols of the earlier confessions—have receded in their symbolic significance. The anima figure, certainly central in *Capricorn* and in *Sexus,* becomes more ordinary, more realistic in *Nexus* and *Plexus.* In *Sexus* Mona/Mara acquires a life of her own. She appears more often as a woman (although definitely as anima projection) than as a bewildering complex of images. *Sexus* even has the suggestion of narrative and most closely approximates romance.

Confession depends, in Frye's view, on the theoretical concern which dominates the form. In Miller's confession his concern with the nature of self and the processes of becoming provide the theoretical subject on which he seeks to integrate his mind. The action serves to illustrate or to lead to the moments of insight and comment. His confessions are accounts of his struggle to arrive at the meaning of self. His anatomies [51] appear when he no longer has to integrate his vision, but can turn to an analysis of its meaning and an intellectual dissection of its elements.

Miller's vision may be obscured by the difficulty his form

and images present. The repetition of action in his confessions and anatomies, moreover, tends to level the reader's response. But any final evaluation of his achievement as a writer should begin with the recognition that his work dramatizes a psychic process and that his images reveal the nature of an inner world.

notes

Introduction

1. T. S. Eliot, Herbert Read, Aldous Huxley, John Dos Passos, and Ezra Pound offered only "cautious praise." See George Orwell, "Inside the Whale," *Henry Miller and the Critics*, ed. George Wickes (Carbondale, Ill., 1963), p. 31.

2. Herbert Read, *The Tenth Muse* (London, 1957), pp. 250–51.

3. Pierre Brodin, *Écrivains américains du vingtième siècle* (Paris, 1947), p. 151.

4. Leslie A. Fiedler, *Waiting for the End* (New York, 1964), p. 42.

5. Annette Kar Baxter studied Miller's expatriate role and his attitudes toward American civilization. *Henry Miller, Expatriate* (Pittsburgh, 1961). Those who take Miller seriously as a religious writer may overstate their case. See Kenneth Rexroth, *Bird in the Bush: Obvious Essays* (New York, 1955), pp. 161–62, and Richard Colbert Bedford, "The Apocatastasis of Henry Miller" (Ph.D. dissertation, State University of Iowa, 1960). William A. Gordon's sympathetic and important study of Miller appeared too late to be considered carefully here. See *The Mind and Art of Henry Miller* (Baton Rouge, La., 1967). Kingsley Widmer's largely unsympathetic analysis of Miller's work was the first full-length study of the writer. See *Henry Miller* (New York, 1963).

6. Warrington Winters, "Transcendentalist in the Basement," *Saturday Review*, June 19, 1965, p. 39.

7. C. G. Jung, *Modern Man in Search of a Soul,* trans. W. S. Dell and Cary F. Baynes (New York, 1933), pp. 180–81.

8. Ibid., p. 182.

9. Jung's identification of the Archetypal Feminine as symbolic of the unconscious will be documented in the discussion of various motifs in Miller's fiction. The elaboration and extension of Jung's ideas by Erich Neumann's structural analysis of the Archetypal Feminine has been invaluable in suggesting in detail the recurrent patterns of symbolism in which the Archetypal Feminine has appeared. See *The Great Mother,* trans. Ralph Manheim, Bolligen Series XLVII (2d ed.; New York, 1963).

10. C. G. Jung, *The Collected Works,* Vol. IX, Part I: *The Archetypes and the Collective Unconscious,* eds. Sir Herbert Read, Michael Fordham, and Gerhard Adler, trans. R. F. C. Hull, Bolligen Series XX (New York, 1959), p. 38.

Chapter I

1. Widmer, *Henry Miller,* p. 81.

2. Ibid., p. 27.

3. Erich Neumann, *The Origins and History of Consciousness,* trans. R. F. C. Hull, Bolligen Series XLII (New York, 1954), p. 323.

4. Ibid., p. 325.

5. Henry Miller, *The World of Sex* (New York, 1965), p. 16.

6. Simon O. Lesser, *Fiction and the Unconscious* (Boston, 1957), p. 83.

7. Orwell, "Inside the Whale," *Henry Miller and the Critics,* p. 31.

8. See, for example, Widmer's remarks in chapter one and in the notes to that chapter.

9. Northrop Frye, *Anatomy of Criticism* (Princeton, 1957), pp. 307–10.

10. Homer K. Nicholson, Jr., "O Altitudo: A Comparison of the Writings of Walt Whitman, D. H. Lawrence, and Henry Miller" (Ph.D. dissertation, Vanderbilt University, 1957), p. 44.

11. Frank Kermode, *Puzzles and Epiphanies* (London, 1962), p. 143.

12. See Neumann's discussion of these symbols of the Great Mother archetype in *The Great Mother,* p. 283.

13. Henry Miller, *Tropic of Cancer* (New York, 1961), p. 40.

14. Ibid., p. 181.

15. Neumann, *The Great Mother,* p. 162. Jung's discussion of this symbolism appears in *The Collected Works,* Vol. V: *Symbols of Transformation* (New York, 1956), pp. 251–52, and elsewhere in his writings.

16. Miller, *Cancer,* pp. 181–82.

17. Ibid., p. 4.

18. Ibid., p. 46.

19. Ibid., p. 247.
20. Neumann, *The Great Mother*, p. 66.
21. C. G. Jung, *The Collected Works*, Vol. XII: *Psychology and Alchemy* (New York, 1953), pp. 207–08.
22. Ibid., p. 208. The figure of the uroboros appears elsewhere in Miller. Erich Neumann's summary of the meaning of this figure in the differentiation of psychic states suggests its significance in the fictional world Miller creates: ". . . the uroboros, the circular snake biting its tail, is the symbol of the psychic state of the beginning, of the original situation, in which man's consciousness and ego were still small and undeveloped. As symbol of the origin and of the opposites contained in it, the uroboros is the 'Great Round,' in which positive and negative, male and female, elements of consciousness, elements hostile to consciousness, and unconscious elements are intermingled. In this sense the uroboros is also a symbol of a state in which chaos, the unconscious, and the psyche as a whole were undifferentiated—and which is experienced by the ego as a borderline state." *The Great Mother*, p. 18.
23. Miller, *Cancer*, p. 6.
24. Jung, *The Archetypes and the Collective Unconscious*, p. 18. For a summary of the relationship between snake and water symbols as manifestations of the feminine, see Jolande Jacobi, *Complex/Archetype/Symbol*, trans. Ralph Manheim (New York, 1959), pp. 146 ff.
25. Jung, *Psychology and Alchemy*, p. 71. The anima figure will be discussed in Chapter III.
26. Jung, *The Archetypes and the Collective Unconscious*, p. 17.
27. Wolfgang Kayser describes the grotesque as an attempt to invoke the demonic aspects of the world. *The Grotesque in Art and Literature*, trans. Ulrich Weisstein (Bloomington, Ind., 1963), p. 188. Miller's exploration of the irrational world is just such an attempt. Moreover, his characteristic fusing of organic and inorganic in the images of his fictional world is an aspect of the grotesque discussed at length by Kayser.
28. Miller, *Cancer*, p. 5.
29. Ibid., p. 7. Miller's frequent fusion of spatial entities in his prose suggests Ernst Cassirer's "mythical thinking" or "magical anatomy." In this process, "the mere possibility of coordinating certain spatial totalities part for part suffices to make them coalesce. From this point on they are different expressions of one and the same essence, which can assume entirely different dimensions. . . . Thus, just as there is a magical anatomy in which particular parts of the human body are equated with particular parts of the world, there is also a mythical geography and cosmography in which the structure of the earth is described and defined in accordance with the same basic intention." *The Philosophy of Symbolic Forms*, Vol. II: *Mythical Thought*, trans. Ralph Man-

heim (New Haven, 1955), pp. 91–92. Miller's exultation in the inevitability of world catastrophe is related. The world catastrophe is, in essence, a psychic event. Jung identifies such fantasy as a projection of the enantiodromia of life into death in the individual psychic existence. See *The Archetypes and the Collective Unconscious*, p. 438. According to Jung, "the fantasy of world conflagration, of the cataclysmic end of the world in general, is the projected primordial image of the great transformation, the enantiodromia of life into death, which Reubens represents [in his *Last Judgment*] as emasculation by the serpent. The image of the consuming change that dissolves the phenomenal world of individual psychic existence originates in the unconscious and appears before the conscious mind in dreams and shadowy premonitions. And the more unwilling the latter is to heed this intimation, the more frightening become the symbols by which it makes itself known." *Symbols of Transformation*, p. 438.

30. Miller, *Cancer*, pp. 6–7.

31. Ibid., p. 7.

32. Thomas Wright, *The Worship of the Generative Powers during the Middle Ages of Western Europe*, Vol. II of *Sexual Symbolism: A History of Phallic Worship* (New York, 1957), pp. 35–36. Wright's early study of this subject was first published in 1866. See also Neumann's discussion of ritual exhibitionism in *The Origins of Consciousness*, p. 78.

33. "Henry Miller schuf den volkreichsten Kanvas: Myreaden von Brüsten, Nabeln, Vaginas und Penissen; die Bezeichnungen sind deplaciert, Abstraktionen aus medizinischen Lehrbüchern." Ludwig Marcuse, *Obszön* (Munich, 1962), p. 315.

34. Miller, *Cancer*, p. 19.

35. Ibid., p. 20.

36. For Miller in *Cancer*, the "door of the womb" is "always on the latch, always open, ready like the tomb." See, for example, p. 252, and passim.

37. Neumann, *The Origins of Consciousness*, p. 87.

38. Kayser, *The Grotesque in Art and Literature*, p. 182.

39. Miller, *Cancer*, p. 1.

40. Ibid., p. 21.

41. Ibid., p. 62.

42. See Neumann, *The Great Mother*, p. 52, for his discussion of the extent of such imagery.

43. Jung, *The Archetypes and the Collective Unconscious*, p. 343.

44. Ibid., pp. 187–88; my italics.

45. Miller, *Cancer*, pp. 9–10.

46. Neumann, *The Great Mother*, pp. 272–73. Jung has identified the lion as an emblem of the devil in alchemy. It "stands for the danger of being swallowed by the unconscious." *Psychology and Alchemy*, p. 182.

47. Miller, *Cancer*, pp. 126–27.

48. Ibid., p. 40.

49. Ibid., p. 8. "God," as a symbol of the self, will be discussed in Part II.

50. Ibid., p. 36.

51. Isaac Rosenfeld, "Henry Miller," *An Age of Enormity*, ed. Theodore Solotaroff (Cleveland, 1962), p. 115.

52. Neumann, *The Origins of Consciousness*, pp. 236–37.

53. Ibid., p. 48.

54. Ibid., p. 58.

55. Miller, *Cancer*, p. 104.

56. See Jung's discussion of the Cabiri as symbols of the unconscious in Faust II. *Psychology and Alchemy*, pp. 148–51.

57. Jacobi, p. 35.

58. Miller, *Cancer*, p. 2. For a brief discussion of the elementary character of this symbolism, see Neumann, *The Great Mother*, pp. 12–13, 25–28.

59. Jacobi summarizes the relationship between the snake and time, p. 185. A more detailed account can be found in C. G. Jung, *The Collected Works*, Vol. VIII: *The Structure and Dynamics of the Psyche* (New York, 1960), pp. 197–98.

60. Neumann, *The Great Mother*, p. 22.

61. Miller, *Cancer*, p. 15.

62. Ibid., p. 63.

63. A summary of the relationship between the androgyny of primitive deities and the uroboros can be found in Neumann, *The Origins of Consciousness*, p. 75.

64. Neumann, *The Great Mother*, p. 170.

65. Jung, *The Archetypes and the Collective Unconscious*, pp. 140 ff. Jung discusses the assimilation of ancient fish symbolism by the figure of Christ in *The Collected Works*, Vol. IX, Part II: *Aion* (New York, 1959), Chapter VI. The historical significance of the fish as symbol is discussed in detail in Chapter VIII; the role of this ancient symbol in alchemy is covered in Chapter X.

66. Jung, *The Structure and Dynamics of the Psyche*, p. 199. See also Jung's comments on Jacob Boehme's use of the eye as symbol in *The Archetypes and the Collective Unconscious*, p. 381.

67. Miller, *Cancer*, pp. 60–61.

68. Ibid., p. 282.

69. Neumann, *The Great Mother*, p. 177.

70. Miller, *Cancer*, p. 4.

71. Ibid., p. 64.

72. Ibid., p. 287.

73. Jung, *Symbols of Transformation*, p. 123.

74. Miller, *Cancer*, p. 318.

75. Neumann, *The Great Mother*, p. 222.

76. Widmer, p. 26.

77. Miller, *Cancer*, p. 250.

78. Ibid., pp. 257–58. The italics are mine.
79. Neumann, *The Great Mother*, p. 30.
80. Neumann, *The Origins of Consciousness*, p. 17.
81. Ibid., pp. 278–79.

Chapter II

1. Miller, *Cancer*, pp. 16–17.
2. Miller's lavatories are underground or in the depths of buildings. They are appropriate settings for the old women who tend them, for the Great Mother figure is frequently associated with caves. The appearance of a plurality of inimical old and young women in Miller's fictional world suggests Neumann's analysis of the individual who is dominated by his unconscious: "The more unconscious a man is, the more the anima figure remains fused or connected with the mana figure of the mother or of the old woman. In other words, the unconscious psyche of the man is directed by a magical unity of old and young women." *The Great Mother*, p. 295.
3. Henry Miller, *Black Spring* (New York, 1963), pp. 151–53.
4. Neumann, *The Great Mother*, pp. 51–52.
5. Miller, *Tropic of Capricorn* (New York, 1961), pp. 261–62.
6. Ibid., p. 59.
7. Ibid., pp. 254–55.
8. Ibid., pp. 256–57.
9. Ibid., p. 279.
10. Ibid., p. 280.
11. Ibid., pp. 103–04.
12. Angus Fletcher, *Allegory: The Theory of a Symbolic Mode* (Ithaca, N. Y., 1964), p. 64. The ultimate significance of Miller's titles *Tropic of Capricorn* and *Tropic of Cancer* lies in their designation of a mythical world in which man is controlled by demonic agents. Fletcher's comment on astral symbolism is relevant here: "Whenever the poet draws attention to the influence of the stars (a demonic influence in every case), he must at the same time remind us that this is action at a distance, that humans are under the control of distant bodies" (p. 95). Miller's choice of the zodiacal symbols has psychological validity in providing a geographical "reality" for the demonic world in which the hero's self struggles.
13. Jung specifically identifies the figure of the nymph as an anima projection: "Mythologically, nymphs, dryads, etc., are nature- and tree-numina, but psychologically they are anima projections. . . . One can hardly imagine a better description of the feminine archetype that typifies a man's unconscious than the figure of this 'most hazardous beloved' (*incertissima amasia*), who pursues him like a teasing sprite amid the stillness of the 'groves and springs.'" *The Collected Works*, Vol. XIV: *Mysterium Coniunctionis* (New York, 1963), p. 68.

Jung's analysis of a dream in which the dreamer is surrounded by nymphs is significant for an understanding of the entire section of Miller quoted in the text: "The regressive character of the vision is also apparent from the fact that there is a multiplicity of female forms. . . . But this time they are of a classical nature, which . . . points to an historical regression. The splitting of the anima into many figures is equivalent to dissolution into an indefinite state, i.e., into the unconscious, from which we may conjecture that a relative dissolution of the conscious mind is running parallel to the historical regression (a process to be observed in its extreme form in schizophrenia). The dissolution of consciousness or, as Janet calls it, the *abaissement du niveau mental*, comes very close to the primitive state of mind. A parallel to this scene described with the nymphs is to be found in the Paracelsian *regio nymphidica*, mentioned in the treatise *De vita longa* as the initial stage of the individuation process." *Psychology and Alchemy*, p. 85.

14. The motifs of oyster, sea shell, and clam are favorites among Miller's emblematic representations of the Archetypal Feminine. They are inevitably associated with the negative elemental character of the archetype, with the *vagina dentata* and its symbolic danger for consciousness. See Jung's remarks on the oyster image in his discussion of the motif of "devouring." *Symbols of Transformation*, p. 245, n. 72.

15. Here the *vagina dentata* symbolism emerges clearly. Neumann's summary of its archetypal significance extends and reinforces its meaning in this passage and throughout Miller's confessions: "The positive femininity of the womb appears as a mouth; that is why 'lips' are attributed to the female genitals, and on the basis of this positive symbolic equation the mouth, as 'upper womb,' is the birthplace of the breath and the word, the Logos." In the passage quoted from *Capricorn*, Laura's lips are "muted"; her words fall "like pollen through a fog." Neumann continues: "Similarly, the destructive side of the Feminine, the destructive and deathly womb, appears most frequently in the archetypal form of a mouth bristling with teeth. We find this symbolism in an African statuette, where the tooth-studded womb is replaced by a gnashing mask, and in an Aztec likeness of the death goddess, furnished with a variety of knives and sharp teeth. This motif of the *vagina dentata* is most distinct in the mythology of the North American Indians. In the mythology of other Indian tribes a meat-eating fish inhabits the vagina of the Terrible Mother; the hero is the man who overcomes the Terrible Mother; breaks the teeth out of her vagina, and so makes her into a woman." The *vagina dentata* is characteristic of the Gorgon figures: "We know the phallic significance of the lone tooth of the Graeae—those female figures whose names are Fear, Dread, and Terror, and who live at the borders of night and death, in the distant west, on the ocean shore. Their sisters are the Gorgons, the daughters of Phorcys, 'the

Gray,' a child of Pontus, the 'primordial deep.' From all of them terrible mythical monsters are descended. The winged Gorgons with snakes for hair and girdle, with their boar's tusks, beards and outthrust tongues, are uroboric symbols of the primordial power of the Archetypal Feminine, images of the great pre-Hellenic Mother Goddess in her devouring aspect as earth, night, and underworld." In Miller, the motif of exhibitionist females also appears. Neumann identifies the Gorgon with this characteristic: "With her outspread legs, the Gorgon throttling an animal takes the same posture as the exhibitionistic goddesses. Here to be sure the genitals are clothed and invisible, but they are represented by the terrible face with its gnashing teeth." *The Great Mother*, pp. 168–69.

16. Here, again, the motif of the *vagina dentata*. These figures in Roseland appear on "the sea floor," a symbol of the unconscious: "In dreams and fantasies the sea or a large expanse of water signifies the unconscious. The maternal aspect of water coincides with the nature of the unconscious, because the latter (particularly in men) can be regarded as the mother or matrix of consciousness. Hence the unconscious, when interpreted on the subjective level, has the same maternal significance as water." Jung, *Symbols of Transformation*, p. 219.

17. Miller, *Capricorn*, pp. 105–08.

18. Ibid., pp. 108–09.

19. Even though Miller has an actual dance hall in mind, in context the name Roseland has numerous emblematic possibilities, some of which reinforce those demanded by the grotesque figures in the passage. For example, Jung considers the rose a feminine, maternal symbol because, like the lotus, it is vessel shaped. *The Archetypes and the Collective Unconscious*, p. 81. In *Psychology and Alchemy* (pp. 74 ff.) he also analyzes the significance of the rose in the formula *per crucem ad rosam* of the Middle Ages, a formula which became the "Rosie Crosse" of the Rosicrucians. That Miller was consciously aware of the symbolic possibilities of this formula is suggested by his choice of the title *The Rosy Crucifixion* for his trilogy.

20. J. B. Beer reduces all literary demons to "energy." He also recognizes that "the figure of the daemon is rarely far removed from that of the serpent" and that there is a "common connection between daemons and lust." *Coleridge the Visionary* (New York, 1959), p. 135.

21. Henry Miller, *The Rosy Crucifixion*, Vol. I: *Sexus* (New York, 1965), p. 208.

22. Miller, *Capricorn*, pp. 231–32. The significant images into which the figure of Mona dissolves here are analyzed later.

23. Miller, *Cancer*, pp. 246–47.

24. Neumann, *The Origins of Consciousness*, p. 84.

25. Wright, *The Worship of the Generative Powers*, pp. 35–36.

26. Ibid., p. 42.
27. Neumann, *The Origins of Consciousness*, pp. 93–94.
28. Kayser, *The Grotesque in Art and Literature*, pp. 172–73.
29. Fletcher, p. 106.
30. Ibid., p. 107.
31. Miller, *Capricorn*, pp. 251–52.
32. Ibid., p. 261.
33. "The *nigredo* not only brought decay, suffering, death, and the torments of hell visibly before the eyes of the alchemist, it also cast the shadow of its melancholy over his own solitary soul." Jung, *Mysterium Coniunctionis*, p. 350. This is Valeska's role for Miller's narrator.
34. Miller, *Cancer*, p. 77.
35. Edgar Wind, *Pagan Mysteries in the Renaissance* (New Haven, 1958), p. 96.
36. Kayser, p. 188.
37. Miller, *Black Spring*, p. 221.
38. Ibid., pp. 222–23.
39. The navel as a "hungry mouth" reveals the negative aspect of the Feminine when one considers its archetypal significance: "The navel as center of the world is also archetypal. Characteristically, many shrines are looked upon as navels of the world, as, for example, the Temple at Jerusalem, the sanctuary at Delphi, and so forth. For us it is significant that this symbolism unconsciously 'includes' the female symbolism of the earth. The earth in a sense is the womb of a reality seen as feminine, the navel and center from which the universe is nourished. Cf. the shining white Parthian goddess of the luminous moon, who has not only gleaming eyes but also a radiant navel." Neumann, *The Great Mother*, p. 132. The negative elementary character is revealed in the womb as deadly devouring maw.
40. Miller, *Sexus*, pp. 593–94.
41. See Fletcher's discussion of allegorical imagery and surrealism, p. 101.
42. Jung, *The Archetypes and the Collective Unconscious*, pp. 185–86.
43. Neumann, *The Great Mother*, p. 96.
44. Ibid., p. 138. In the umbilical swell with its numinous suggestions of the maternal, the positive aspects of the Archetypal Feminine are revealed. The individual experiences considerable ambivalence toward this archetype, which manifests itself in "positive" and "negative" aspects. The two can appear together. In Cleo, of course, the negative element is dominant. Cleo's belly swells with sewer gas.
45. Miller, *Sexus*, pp. 600–01.
46. Ibid., p. 602.
47. Ibid., p. 603.
48. Kayser, pp. 184, 161.

49. The details of this filthy world, recorded with an insistence that forces them on the reader's attention, have contributed to Miller's reputation for "naturalistic" reporting. Fletcher has argued that naturalism is an allegorical rather than a mimetic mode, a point of view my analysis of Miller's form echoes (pp. 315–16, and elsewhere).

50. Miller, *Sexus*, pp. 589–90.

51. Neumann, *The Great Mother*, p. 170.

52. Jung, *The Archetypes and the Collective Unconscious*, p. 175.

53. Miller, *Cancer*, p. 60.

54. Miller, *Capricorn*, pp. 126–28.

55. Ibid., p. 129.

56. Miller, *The Rosy Crucifixion*, Vol. II: *Plexus* (New York, 1965), pp. 352–54.

57. Ibid., p. 355.

58. The transformative nature of the Great Mother is discussed by Neumann in Chapter XV of *The Great Mother*.

59. Ibid., p. 331.

60. Miller, *Plexus*, pp. 361–62.

61. Fletcher, p. 109.

62. Frye, *Anatomy of Criticism*, pp. 304–05.

63. Ibid., p. 309.

64. Ibid., p. 308.

65. Ibid., p. 307.

Chapter III

1. The narrator's remarks on this name change do not reveal its entire significance. See, however, *Plexus*, p. 41. Mara is identified with Naomi in the Book of Ruth.

2. Frye, *Anatomy of Criticism*, p. 304. The rest of the passage is relevant in any evaluation of Miller's form: "That is why the romance so often radiates a glow of subjective intensity that the novel lacks, and why a suggestion of allegory is constantly creeping in around its fringes. Certain elements of character are released in the romance which make it naturally a more revolutionary form than the novel. The novelist deals with personality, with characters wearing their *personae* or social masks. He needs the framework of a stable society, and many of our best novelists have been conventional to the verge of fussiness. The romancer deals with individuality, with characters *in vacuo* idealized by revery, and, however conservative he may be, something nihilistic and untamable is likely to keep breaking out of his pages" (pp. 304–05).

3. Widmer, *Henry Miller*, p. 73.

4. Ibid., p. 77.

5. Lesser, *Fiction and the Unconscious*, p. 83.

6. Widmer, p. 69.

7. Ibid., pp. 70–73.

8. Jung, *The Archetypes and the Collective Unconscious*, p. 71.

9. Henry Miller, *Books in My Life* (Norfolk, Conn., 1952), pp. 96–97.

10. Mario Praz, *The Romantic Agony*, trans. Angus Davidson (2d ed.; London, 1951), p. 189.

11. Ibid., pp. 189–90.

12. Ibid., p. 217. It is not difficult to identify elements of algolagnia in Miller's description of his relationships with women.

13. Ibid., p. 240.

14. Ibid., p. 271.

15. Kayser, *The Grotesque in Art and Literature*, p. 188.

16. René Wellek and Austin Warren have pointed out that Praz's *The Romantic Agony* is a book about sex and death, that is, the history of man's attitude toward these two experiences. *Theory of Literature* (2d ed.; New York, 1955), pp. 104–05.

17. Kayser, p. 172.

18. Jung, *Mysterium Coniunctionis*, p. xvii.

19. Jung pointed out that the irrational and incomprehensible experience of the unconscious contents erupting into the consciousness of an individual "alienates and isolates him from his surroundings." Kayser considered such alienation central to the grotesque. It is primarily the expression of our failure to orient ourselves in the physical universe. The grotesque is the objectification of the "It." "What intrudes remains incomprehensible, inexplicable, and impersonal" (p. 185).

20. Jung, *Psychology and Alchemy*, p. 52.

21. Ibid., pp. 53–54.

22. Ibid., p. 58.

23. Norman O. Brown points out that Freud is perplexing on the meaning of this pattern, reversing his earlier position on masochism. See Brown's discussion, *Beyond the Pleasure Principle in Life Against Death: The Psychoanalytic Meaning of History* (Middletown, Conn., 1959), p. 88.

24. Ibid., p. 126.

25. Neumann, *The Great Mother*, pp. 33–34.

26. Ibid., p. 34, n. 18.

27. Ibid., p. 35.

28. Ibid., p. 38.

29. Neumann, *The Origins of Consciousness*, p. 321.

30. Ibid., pp. 321–32.

31. Miller, *Cancer*, p. 21.

32. Jung, *The Archetypes and the Collective Unconscious*, p. 199.

33. Miller, *Capricorn*, pp. 199–200.

34. These are traditional characteristics of the Fatal Woman. See Praz, p. 221.

35. The movement toward the center, as an organizing principle in Miller, is discussed in Part III. These symbols of the Great

Round (wheels, mills, circles) are recurrent symbols in Miller. The following analysis from Neumann's *The Origins of Consciousness* is relevant here: "During the phase when consciousness begins to turn into self-consciousness, that is, to recognize and discriminate itself as a separate individual ego, the maternal uroboros overshadows it like a dark and tragic fate. Feelings of transitoriness and mortality, impotence and isolation, now color the ego's picture of the uroboros, in absolute contrast to the original situation of contentment. . . . For the dawning light of consciousness, the maternal uroboros turns to darkness and night. The passage of time and the problem of death become a dominant life-feeling . . ." (p. 45).

Jung's comments on the significance of concentration on the center are also relevant, especially since they occur in his analysis of the emergence of an archetype: "But if the life-mass [the *materia informis* which contains the seed of life] is to be transformed, a *circumambulatio* is necessary, i.e., exclusive concentration on the centre, the place of creative change. During this process . . . we have to expose ourselves to the animal impulses of the unconscious without identifying ourselves with them and without 'running away'; for flight from the unconscious would defeat the purpose of the whole proceeding. We must hold our ground, which means here that the process initiated by the dreamer's self-observation must be experienced in all its ramifications and then articulated with consciousness to the best of his understanding. This often entails an almost unbearable tension because of the utter incommensurability between conscious life and the unconscious process, which can only be experienced in the innermost soul and cannot touch the visible surface of life at any point. The principle of conscious life is: 'Nihil est in intellectu, quod non prius fuerit in sensu.' But the principle of the unconscious is the autonomy of the psyche itself, reflecting, in the play of its images, not the world but its own self, even though it utilizes the illustrative possibilities offered by the sensible world in order to make its images clear." *Psychology and Alchemy*, pp. 138–39.

36. Miller's dramatization of this process reveals its autonomous nature. The significance of such autonomy has been suggested by Neumann: "The unconscious as the elementary character of the Archetypal Feminine is entirely independent and self-contained, as, for example, in the spontaneous processes of the collective unconscious, which are demonstrable also in mental disorder. This means that the processes of the unconscious are here unrelated to the human personality in which they operate. The affected individual does not in reality 'have' the visions; rather, they occur within him as an autonomous natural process. The structure of the transformative character already relates to a personality embracing the spontaneity of consciousness. It relates to a possible future constellation of the total personality and communicates a content or an experience that is of vital importance for the future development of the

personality. That is to say, in the transformative character of the anima, the prospective, anticipatory function of the unconscious has become personified and configured; confronting the ego as the nonego, it attracts it and exerts a spell upon it. The ego, however, does not at first experience this fascination directly in relation to its psyche, but in indirect projection as a demand or stimulus from outside, which for man is usually represented by an anima figure. The soul-guiding animus figure plays a corresponding role for the woman." *The Great Mother*, pp. 35–36.

37. Neumann's analysis of the significance of the symbolic action in the Pegasus myth suggests the pattern of action that Miller explores in the confrontation of the negative Feminine and the isolation of the anima figure: "The profound psychological intuition of the myth is revealed even more strikingly in the fact that Pegasus, on being released from the Medusa, is credited with a creative work upon earth. We are told that, as the winged horse flew up to Zeus amid thunder and lightning, he struck the Fountain of the Muses from the ground. The archetypal affinity between horse and fountain is the same as that between natural impulse and creative fertilization. In Pegasus it takes the form of transformation and sublimation: the winged horse strikes the fountain of poesy from the earth. As we shall see later, this aspect of the Pegasus myth lies at the root of all creativity.

"The destruction of the dragon means not only the liberation of the captive, but the ascent of libido. The process known in psychological theory as the crystallization of the anima from the mother archetype is dynamically portrayed in the myth of Pegasus. The soaring creative forces are set free by the death of the dragon. Pegasus is the libido which, as winged spiritual energy, carries the hero Bellerophon (also called Hipponoüs, 'skilled with the horse') to victory, but he is also inward-flowing libido that wells forth as creative art. In neither case is the release of libido undirected; it rises up in the direction of spirit.

"Thus, to put it abstractly, the hero Perseus espouses the spiritual side, he is the winged one, and the gods of the spirit are his allies in the fight with the unconscious. His foe is the uroboric Gorgon dwelling far to the West, in the land of death, flanked by her hideous sisters the Graeae, denizens of the deep. Perseus defeats the unconscious through the typical act of conscious realization. He would not be strong enough to gaze directly upon the petrifying face of the uroboros, so he raises its image to consciousness and kills it 'by reflection.' The treasure he gains is firstly Andromeda, the freed captive, and secondly Pegasus, the spiritual libido of the Gorgon, now released and transformed. Pegasus is therefore a spiritual and transcendent symbol in one. He combines the spirituality of the bird with the horse character of the Gorgon." *The Origins of Consciousness*, pp. 218–19.

38. See Jung, *Symbols of Transformation*, Chapter II.

39. Ernest Jones, *On the Nightmare* (2d ed.; New York, 1951), pp. 125–26.

40. Ibid., pp. 291–93; see also Jung, *Symbols of Transformation*, pp. 249 ff.

41. Neumann, *The Great Mother*, pp. 47–48 and elsewhere.

42. Jung, *Symbols of Transformation*, p. 275.

43. Ibid., n. 1.

44. Jung, *Aion*, p. 226.

45. Northrop Frye, *Fables of Identity: Studies in Poetic Mythology* (New York, 1963), p. 36.

46. See Fletcher, *Allegory: The Theory of a Symbolic Mode*, Chapter I.

47. Miller, *Capricorn*, pp. 235–36.

48. Neumann, *The Origins of Consciousness*, p. 83.

49. Neumann, *The Great Mother*, pp. 277–78.

50. Neumann, *The Origins of Consciousness*, pp. 87–88.

51. Many readers have noted Miller's interest in food; his descriptions of eating suggest a Herculean capacity and appetite comparable to his sexual appetite. Both activities, however, are more than naive celebrations of the sensual life. The symbolic contexts in which they appear argue for other interpretations. Erich Neumann has discussed the importance of such symbolism in mythology: "Whereas in its later developments centroversion promotes the formation of ego consciousness as its specific organ, in the uroboric phase, when ego consciousness has not yet been differentiated into a separate system, centroversion is still identified with the functioning of the body as a whole and with the unity of its organs. The metabolic symbolism of mutual exchange between body and world is paramount. The object of hunger, the food to be 'taken in,' is the world itself; while the other productive side of the process is symbolized by 'output,' that is, evacuation. The dominant symbol is not the semen; in creation mythology, urine, dung, spit, sweat, and breath (and later, words) are all elementary symbols of the creative principle." *The Origins of Consciousness*, pp. 290–91.

52. Ibid., pp. 30–31.

53. Ibid., p. 336.

54. See Part III for a discussion of negative and positive centers. On the negative wheel symbolism, see Neumann, *The Great Mother*, pp. 234–36.

55. This principle of opposites operates in Miller to explain the relationship between negative and positive "centers," and the role of negative figures in his fiction generally.

56. Miller, *Capricorn*, pp. 347–48.

57. Jung, *The Archetypes and the Collective Unconscious*, p. 379.

58. Neumann, *The Origins of Consciousness*, pp. 106–07.

59. Jung, *Aion*, p. 64.

60. Ibid., p. 224.

61. Widmer, p. 79.

62. I argue later, in Parts II and III, that *The Rosy Crucifixion* belongs in the tradition of romance-anatomy rather than confession-romance. The archetypes become the subject of intellectual and conscious analysis.

Chapter IV

1. Miller's interest in Boehme (recorded in *The Red Notebook* and elsewhere) can be explained by the nature of the self Boehme describes. Norman O. Brown points out that Boehme's mysticism "insists on the androgynous character of human perfection." *Life against Death*, p. 313. Brown's comments on Novalis, Blake, Rilke, Whitehead, Jung, and others in his chapter "The Resurrection of the Body" outline an area of investigation in religion, depth analysis, philosophy, and literature which he sees as a central concern in twentieth-century thought and to which Miller's fictional explorations are related. Brown does not discuss Miller, although he prefaces Part Six of *Life against Death* with a passage from *Sunday after the War* describing Miller's utopian visions of the future.

2. See William Alexander Gordon, "Henry Miller and the Romantic Tradition" (Ph.D. dissertation, Tulane University, 1963). Gordon's *The Mind and Art of Henry Miller* grew out of this study.

3. Hans Jonas, *The Gnostic Religion: The Message of the Alien God and the Beginnings of Christianity* (2d ed. rev.; Boston, 1963), p. 329.

4. Jung's description of the nature of this assimilation seems especially helpful in following the "action" in Miller: "The autonomy of the collective unconscious expresses itself in the figures of the anima and animus. They personify those of its contents which, when withdrawn from projection, can be integrated into consciousness. To this extent, both figures represent *functions* which filter the contents of the collective unconscious through to the conscious mind. They appear or behave as such, however, only so long as the tendencies of the conscious and unconscious do not diverge too greatly. Should any tension arise, these functions, harmless till then, confront the conscious mind in personified form and behave rather like systems split off from the personality, or like part souls. This comparison is inadequate in so far as nothing previously belonging to the ego personality has split off from it; on the contrary, the two figures represent a disturbing accretion. The reason for their behaving in this way is that though the *contents* of anima and animus can be integrated they themselves cannot, since they are archetypes. As such they are the foundation stones of the psychic structure, which in its totality exceeds the limits of consciousness and therefore can never become the object of direct cognition. Though the effects of anima and animus can be made conscious, they themselves are factors transcending consciousness and beyond the reach

of perception and volition. Hence they remain autonomous despite the integration of their contents, and for this reason they should be borne constantly in mind." *Aion*, p. 20.

5. R. W. B. Lewis, *The American Adam: Innocence, Tragedy, and Tradition in the Nineteenth Century* (Chicago, 1955), pp. 26–27.

6. Jung, *Aion*, p. 203.

7. Ibid., p. 219.

8. Ibid., pp. 5–6.

9. Jung cautions against narrow allegorical readings of archetypal symbols: "They are genuine symbols precisely because they are ambiguous, full of half-glimpsed meanings, and in the last resort, inexhaustible." *The Archetypes and the Collective Unconscious*, p. 38.

10. Ibid., pp. 38–39.

11. Jung argues that the archetype of the shadow can be inferred from the contents of the "personal" unconscious: "With a little self-criticism one can see through the shadow—so far as its nature is personal. But when it appears as an archetype, one encounters the same difficulties as with anima and animus. In other words, it is quite within the bounds of possibility for a man to recognize the relative evil of his nature, but it is a rare and shattering experience for him to gaze into the face of absolute evil." *Aion*, p. 10.

12. Ibid., p. 22.

13. Miller, *Capricorn*, p. 219.

14. See Jung's discussion of the house as a symbol of the self. *Aion*, p. 224. It is familiar as a symbol of the Archetypal Feminine, but the movement toward a center earlier in the passage from *Capricorn* identifies it as a symbol of the self.

15. Miller, *Cancer*, p. 1.

16. Miller quotes Miguel de Unamuno on this subject at the beginning of *Black Spring:* "Can I be as I believe myself or as others believe me to be? Here is where these lines become a confession in the presence of my unknown and unknowable me, unknown and unknowable for myself. Here is where I create the legend wherein I must bury myself."

17. Miller, *Black Spring*, p. 46.

18. Ibid., pp. 45–46.

19. Frank E. Manuel, "Toward a Psychological History of Utopias," *Daedalus*, XCIV (Spring, 1965), 315.

20. Miller rejected Freud and Freudian analysis, as Frederick J. Hoffman pointed out. *Freudianism and the Literary Mind* (2d ed. rev.; Baton Rouge, La., 1957), pp. 293–94. The analyst, Miller believes, seeks to help the patient accept the world as it is, an end Miller cannot accept. Hoffman does not sufficiently recognize Miller's utopian convictions, however; he observes that Miller insists on abandoning the will, "submitting to the flux of experience"

(p. 293) and seeks to live in the world as womb, dwelling in a sort of prenatal security (pp. 294–95). Although much of what Hoffman observed appears true of Miller, these remarks do not sufficiently explain the evidence we have examined which suggests that the emergence (not the containment) of the self is Miller's goal.

21. Miller, *Sunday after the War* (New York, 1944), p. 155.

22. Ibid., pp. 157–58.

23. Frye, *Anatomy of Criticism*, p. 307.

Chapter V

1. Miller, *Capricorn*, p. 121.

2. Jung, *Aion*, p. 28.

3. Fletcher, *Allegory: The Theory of a Symbolic Mode*, p. 109.

4. Neumann, *The Origins of Consciousness*, pp. 417–18.

5. Ibid., p. 416. Jung points out the importance of the stone in alchemy. As a symbol of the self it has body, soul, and spirit. It is a homunculus and a hermaphrodite. See *Aion*, pp. 245–46. Miller's fiction is full of allusions to this inner core; it is usually contrasted with the flux in which the self is found: "There is no fundamental, unalterable difference between things: all is flux, all is perishable. The surface of your being is constantly crumbling; within however you grow hard as a diamond." *Capricorn*, p. 64.

6. *Capricorn*, pp. 206–08.

7. Ibid., p. 208.

8. In an analysis of the archetypal significance of the wheel and stone symbolism in alchemical treatises, Jung discusses a relevant passage from the *Rosarium philosophorum* which describes the significance of imagination (Miller's "illumination" in the next passage we examine) or squaring the circle in the search for the self. This discussion is useful in understanding the significance of the *Capricorn* passage: "The layman may be rather puzzled by the serious attention devoted to this problem. But a little knowledge of yoga and of the medieval philosophy of the *lapis* would help him to understand. As we have already said, the squaring of the circle was one of the methods for producing the *lapis*; another was the use of *imaginatio*, as the following text unmistakably proves: 'And take care that thy door be well and firmly closed, so that he who is within cannot escape, and—God willing—thou wilt reach the goal. Nature carries out her operations gradually; and indeed I would have thee do the same: let thy imagination be guided wholly by nature. And observe according to nature, through whom the substances regenerate themselves in the bowels of the earth. And imagine this with true and not with fantastic imagination.'

"The *vas bene clausum* (well-sealed vessel) is a precautionary rule in alchemy very frequently mentioned, and is the equivalent of the magic circle. In both cases the idea is to protect what is within from the intrusion and admixture of what is without, as well as to prevent it from escaping. The *imaginatio* is to be understood here as the real literal power to create images. . . ." *Psychology and Alchemy*, pp. 159–60.

9. The worm is a traditional theriomorphic symbol of the self. Jung, *The Archetypes and the Collective Unconscious*, p. 187.

10. Miller, *Capricorn*, pp. 331–33.

11. This passage of Neumann's is relevant: "Rather surprisingly, the mill stands side by side with the loom as a symbol of fate and death. Baking, like weaving, is one of the primeval mysteries of the Feminine. The woman is a giver and transformer of nourishment, but at the same time we find the negative meaning of the symbol in the death mill as an attribute of the Terrible Mother. The death of the grain god in the mill was later transferred to Christ, and it still survives in the English ballad 'John Barleycorn.' Thus the mill becomes a goddess of death; its relation to fate has come down to us in the familiar proverb, 'The mills of the gods grind slowly,' whose mythical origin is still discernible in the Germanic sphere.

"In the Eddic poem known as 'The Song of the Mill,' the giant's daughters are at work in the wishing mill, seeking to create peace and riches by magic. 'Playing under the earth, nine winters long, we grew mightily.' But these imprisoned virgins and warrior maidens become powers of fate, who turn the blessing into a curse; and as formerly they magically milled life and happiness, now they mill death and doom. Thus the mill becomes a symbol of the negative wheel of life, the Indian samsara, the aimless cycle. But this aimless cycle is a form of the Great Round, whose positive form, in India as elsewhere, is the great containing World Mother who, like the Boeotian goddess, the Vierge Ouvrante, and the Madonna of Mercy, raised her outstretched arms shelteringly. They too belong to the archetype of the goddesses with upraised arms." *The Great Mother*, p. 234.

12. Jung, *The Archetypes and the Collective Unconscious*, p. 357.

13. Jung, *Psychology and Alchemy*, pp. 138–39.

14. Neumann, *The Origins of Consciousness*, p. 307.

15. Miller, *Capricorn*, pp. 75–77.

16. See Jung's discussion of the eye as a symbol of consciousness in *Mysterium Coniunctionis*, pp. 53–54.

17. Miller, *Capricorn*, p. 78.

18. Neumann, *The Origins of Consciousness*, pp. 338–39.

19. Here the eye is a symbol of the entrance into the "womb" or inner world: "All the basic vital functions occur in this vessel-body schema, whose 'inside' is an unknown. Its entrance and exit zones are of special significance. Food and drink are put into this unknown vessel, while in all creative functions, from the elimination of waste and the emission of seed to the giving forth of breath and the word, something is 'born' out of it. *All* body openings—eyes, ears, nose, mouth (navel), rectum, genital zone—as well as the skin, have, as places of exchange between inside and outside, a

numinous accent for early man. They are therefore distinguished as 'ornamental' and protected zones, and in man's artistic self-representation they play a special role as idols.

"The concrete corporeity of the body-vessel whose inside always remains dark and unknown is the reality in which the individual experiences the whole unconscious world of instinct. This begins with the infant's elementary experience of hunger and thirst, which, like every urge and every pain and every instinct, comes from inside, from the body-vessel, to disturb him. And the ego consciousness is typically situated in the head, by which the foreign effects stemming from the inside of the body-vessel are perceived.

"The archetypal body-vessel equation is of fundamental importance for the understanding of myth and symbolism, and also of early man's world view. Its significance is not limited to the exit zones that make whatever issues from the body into something 'born'—whether it be hair-vegetation or breath-wind. The inside of this vessel-body also has its central symbolism.

"The inside of the body is archetypally identical with the unconscious, the 'seat' of the psychic processes that for man take place 'in' him and 'in the darkness'—which last, like the night, is a typical symbol of the unconscious." Neumann, *The Great Mother*, pp. 39–40.

20. Miller, *Capricorn*, pp. 121–22.

21. Ibid., p. 123.

22. Ibid., pp. 123–24.

23. Jung, *Psychology and Alchemy*, pp. 114–15.

24. Ibid., p. 124.

25. See Miller, *Capricorn*, pp. 127–29, for a description of the "sour rye world" of childhood.

26. See Jung, *Psychology and Alchemy*, p. 61, for an analysis of the significance of the imaginary return to childhood.

27. Miller, *Capricorn*, p. 130.

28. Ibid., p. 149.

29. Ibid., p. 325.

30. Jung, *Psychology and Alchemy*, pp. 73–76.

31. Jung, *Mysterium Coniunctionis*, p. 306.

32. The cross itself is a symbol of the Archetypal Feminine, as is the bed which appears in the passage quoted in the text from *Black Spring*. "Regardless of theological superstructures, the archetypal symbolism of the tree reaches deep down into the mythical world of Christianity and Judaism. Christ, hanging from the tree of death, is the fruit of suffering and hence the pledge of the promised land, the beatitude to come; and at the same time He is the tree of life as the god of the grape. Like Dionysus, He is *endendros*, the life at work in the tree, and fulfills the mysterious twofold and contradictory nature of the tree. And the tree of knowledge is identified with the tree of life and death that is the Cross. According to the Christian myth, the Cross was set upon the site where

the tree of knowledge had stood, and Christ, as 'mystical fruit' of the redeeming tree of life, replaced the fruit of the tree of knowledge, whereby sin came into the world." Neumann, *The Great Mother*, pp. 252–53.

Bed and *cross* are complementary: "'The meaning of the cross as a tree of life and death is further amplified by the symbolism of the cross as bed. 'The Cross has become his marriage bed, the day . . . of his bitter death bears thee to sweet life,' sings Ephraem Syrus. The feminine word, *materia*, the maternal substance of the tree, appears as a symbolic foundation in the marriage bed, the bed of birth and death." Ibid., p. 256.

33. Miller, *Black Spring*, pp. 151–53.

34. C. G. Jung, *The Collected Works*, Vol. XI: *Psychology and Religion: West and East* (New York, 1958), p. 185.

Chapter VI

1. Miller, *Capricorn*, pp. 324–25.

2. Valentius, Jung points out, wrote that Christ was born with a shadow that he later cast off. For this discussion of Christianity, see *Aion*, pp. 109–10.

3. Neumann defines centroversion as "the innate tendency of a whole to create unity within its parts and to synthesize their differences in unified systems. The unity of the whole is maintained by compensatory processes controlled by centroversion, with whose help the whole becomes a self-creative, expanding system. At a later stage centroversion manifests itself as a directive center, with the ego as the center of consciousness and the self as the psychic center." *The Origins of Consciousness*, pp. 286–87.

4. See Kenneth Burke, *A Grammar of Motives* (New York, 1945), p. 300.

5. Such formulas are significant means of organizing the self in the external world. Miller, however, shows us the inadequacy of such familiar formulas for organizing the self.

6. Fletcher, *Allegory: The Theory of a Symbolic Mode*, pp. 343–44. See my comments on negative and positive centers in Miller, Part III.

7. Miller, *Capricorn*, p. 100.

8. Ibid., p. 280.

9. Ibid., p. 206.

10. Ibid., p. 220. The flatness of Miller's sentence is not unusual. His sentences of summary or his attempts to describe his experiences in familiar terms are often cliché-ridden. They are formulas which "control" reality, but they acquire vitality only in context, juxtaposed with the grotesque, the bizarre, the obscene, or the obscure.

11. Frye, *Anatomy of Criticism*, p. 309.

12. Widmer, *Henry Miller*, p. 60.

13. Jung argues that these negative characteristics are for the

most part unconscious. The individual must make an effort to acknowledge and recognize the shadow. *The Archetypes and the Collective Unconscious,* p. 244.

14. Jung, *Psychology and Religion,* pp. 197–98.

15. See Neumann's discussion of self and shadow, *The Origins of Consciousness,* p. 353.

16. This incident is explained in *Plexus,* p. 467.

17. Ibid., p. 438.

18. Ibid., pp. 526–27.

19. The relationship between the anima and shadow as symbols of the unconscious is also important. Jung's remarks on this relationship help explain the pattern which appears in Miller: "The inferior half of the personality is for the greater part unconscious. It does not denote the whole of the unconscious, but only the personal segment of it. The anima, on the other hand, so far as she is distinguished from the shadow, personifies the collective unconscious. If threeness is assigned to her as a riding animal, it means that she 'rides' the shadow, is related to it as the *mar.* In that case she possesses the shadow. But if she herself is the horse, then she has lost her dominating position as a personification of the collective unconscious and is 'ridden'. . . ." *The Archetypes and the Collective Unconscious,* pp. 244–45.

20. Miller, *Sexus,* pp. 257–58.

21. Ibid., p. 260.

22. Ibid., pp. 263–64.

23. Jung occasionally describes the archetypes as fragmented "personalities." See, for example, *The Archetypes and the Collective Unconscious,* p. 283.

24. Miller, *Sexus,* p. 265.

25. Ibid.

26. Miller acknowledges the ritual power of art: "At the root of the art instinct is this desire for power—vicarious power. The artist is situated hierarchically between the hero and the saint. . . . To put it quite simply, art is only a stepping-stone to reality; it is the vestibule in which we undergo the rites of initiation." *Sunday after the War,* p. 155.

27. Miller, *Plexus,* pp. 473–74.

28. Ibid., p. 470.

29. C. G. Jung, *Psychological Types or The Psychology of Individuation,* trans. H. Goodwin Baynes (New York, 1961), p. 268.

30. Jung, *The Archetypes and the Collective Unconscious,* p. 122.

31. Ibid., pp. 122–23.

32. Miller, *Cancer,* p. 102.

33. Ibid., pp. 125–27.

34. Ibid., p. 130.

35. Neumann discusses the motif of the hostile twin brothers as part of the symbolism of the Great Mother. The male reaches

self-consciousness by dividing himself into opposing elements—one destructive, one creative. *The Origins of Consciousness*, pp. 95-96.

36. Miller, *Capricorn*, p. 106.

37. Ibid., p. 271.

38. Miller, *The Rosy Crucifixion*, Vol. III: *Nexus* (New York, 1965), pp. 290-91.

39. Jung, *The Archetypes and the Collective Unconscious*, pp. 21-22.

40. Frye, *Anatomy of Criticism*, pp. 291, 304.

41. Miller, *Nexus*, p. 291.

42. See Jung, *The Archetypes and the Collective Unconscious*, Chapter IV.

43. Ibid., p. 159.

44. Miller, *Plexus*, pp. 558-59.

45. Miller, *Capricorn*, pp. 307-08.

46. Neumann, *The Origins of Consciousness*, p. 30.

47. Miller, *Nexus*, p. 303.

48. Ibid., pp. 307-08.

49. Neumann, *The Origins of Consciousness*, p. 218.

Chapter VII

1. Miller, *Nexus*, p. 308.

2. The following dream episode is an excellent example: "To this period belongs a night dream which I recorded with scrupulous accuracy. I feel it is worth transcribing. . . .

" 'It opened with a nightmarish vertigo which sent me hurtling from a dizzy precipice into the warm waters of the Caribbean. Down, down I swirled, in great spiral curves which had no beginning and promised to end in eternity. During this ceaseless descent a bewildering and enchanting panorama of marine life unrolled before my eyes. Enormous sea dragons wriggled and shimmered in the powdered sunlight which filtered through the green waters; huge cactus plants with hideous roots floated by, followed by spongelike coral growths of curious hues, some sullen as oxblood, some a brilliant vermilion or soft lavender. Out of this teeming aquatic life poured myriads of animalcules, resembling gnomes and pixies; they bubbled up like a gorgeous flux of stardust in the tailsweep of a comet.

" 'The roaring in my ears gave way to plangent, verdant melodies; I became aware of the tremors of the earth, of poplars and birches shrouded in ghostlike vapors, bending gracefully to the caress of fragrant breezes. Stealthily the vapors roll away. I am trudging through a mysterious forest alive with screaming monkeys and birds of tropical plumage. There is a quiver of arrows in my girdle and over my shoulder a golden bow.

" 'Penetrating deeper and deeper into the wood the music becomes more celestial, the light more golden; the earth is carpeted with soft, blood-red leaves. The beauty of it is such that I swoon away. On awakening the forest has vanished. To my befuddled senses it seems that I am standing before a pale, towering canvas on which a pastoral scene of great dignity is depicted: it resembles one of those murals by Puvis de Chavannes in which the grave, seraphic void of dream is materialized. Sedate, somber wraiths move to and fro with a measured, haunting elegance which made our earthly movement appear grotesque. Stepping in the canvas I follow a quiet path which leads towards the retreating line of the horizon. A full-hipped figure in a Grecian robe, balancing an urn, is directing her footsteps toward the turret of a castle dimly visible above the crest of a gentle knoll. I pursue the undulating hips until lost in a dip beyond the crest of the knoll.

" 'The figure with the urn has disappeared. But now my eyes are rewarded by a more mystifying sight. It is as if I had arrived at the very end of this habitable earth, at that magic fringe of the ancient world where all the mysteries and gloom and terror of the universe are concealed. I am hemmed in by a vast enclosure whose limits are only faintly discernible. Ahead of me loom the walls of a hoary castle bristling with spears. Pennants blazoned with incredible emblems flutter ominously above the crenellated battlements. A sickly fungus growth chokes the broad sweeps leading out from the terrifying portals; the gloomy casements are bespattered with the remains of great carrion birds whose foul stench is unbearable.

" 'But what awes and fascinates me most is the color of the castle. It is a red such as my eyes have never beheld. The walls are of a warm bloodlike hue, the tint of rich corpuscles laid bare by the knife. Beyond the frontier walls loom more spectacular parapets and battlements, turrets and spires, each receding rank steeped in a more awesome red. To my terrified eyes the whole spectacle takes on the proportions of a monstrous butchers' orgy dripping with gore and excrement.

" 'In fear and horror I avert my gaze an instant. In that fleeting moment the scene changes. Instead of poisonous fungus and the scabby carcasses of vultures there is spread before me a rich mosaic of ebony and cinnamon, shadowed by deep purple panoplies from which cascades of cherry blossoms slither away in billowy heaps on a checkered court. Within reach, almost, stands a splendid couch festooned with royal drapes and smothered in pillows of gossamer loveliness. On this sumptuous divan, as if languidly anticipating my arrival, reclines my wife Maude. It is not a wholly familiar Maude, though I recognize at once her tiny, birdlike mouth. I wait expectantly for her usual inanities. Instead there issues from her throat a flood of dark music which sends the blood hammering to my temples. It is only at this moment that I realize she is nude, feel the vague, splendid pain of her loins. I bend over to lift her in my arms but recoil immediately in full horror as I perceive a spider slowly crawling over her milky breast. As if possessed, I flee in panic towards the castle walls.

" 'And now a strange thing happens. To the groaning and creaking of rusty hinges the towering gates swing slowly open. Swiftly I race up the narrow path which leads to the foot of the spiral staircase. Frantically I climb the iron steps—higher and higher, without ever seeming to reach the top. Finally, when it seems as if my heart will break from exertion, I find myself at the summit. The ramparts and battlements, the casements and turrets of the mysterious castle, are no longer there beneath me. Before my eyes there unfolds a black, volcanic waste furrowed with innumerable chasms of bottomless depth. Nothing of plant or vegetable life is visible. Petrified limbs of gigantic proportions, carbuncled with glistening mineral crustations, lie sprawled about over the void. Gazing more intently I perceive with horror that there *is* a life down below there—a slimy, crawling life which reveals itself in huge coils that wind and unwind about the crazy, dead limbs.

" 'Suddenly I have a presentiment that the towering steeple up which I had climbed in panic is crumbling at the base, that this immense spire is teetering at the edge of the loathsome abyss, threatening at any moment to hurl me into a shattering annihilation. For just the fraction of a moment there is an eerie stillness, then faintly, so faintly as to be almost inaudible, there comes the sound of a voice—a human voice. Now it rings out boldly, with a weird, moaning accent, only to die out immediately, as if it had been strangled down in the sulphurous depths below. Instantly the tower lurches violently; as it swoops out over the void, like a drunken ship, a babble of voices breaks forth. Human voices, in which there are mingled the laughter of hyenas, the shrill screams of lunatics, the blood-curdling oaths of the damned, the piercing, horror-laden cackles of the possessed.

" 'As the rail gives way I am catapulted into space with meteoric speed. Down, down, down, my frail body stripped of its tender flesh, the entrails clawed by leprous talons, by beaks crusted with verdigris. Down, down, down, stripped and mangled by fang and tusk.

" 'And then it ceases, this hurtling through the void; it gives way to a sliding sensation. I am shooting down a paraffin incline supported by colossal columns of human flesh that bleed from every pore. Awaiting me is the wide, cavernous maw of an ogre champing its teeth with fierce expectancy. In an instant I shall be swallowed alive, shall perish to the hideous accompaniment of bones, my own precious bones, being crunched and splintered. . . . But just as I am about to slide into the gaping red maw the monster sneezes. The explosion is so vast that the whole universe is snuffed out. I awake coughing like a smoking bellows.'

"Was it a coincidence that the very next day I should run into my friend Ulric, that he should inform me stutteringly that Maude had been to see him the day before. . . ." Miller, *Plexus*, pp. 369–72.

3. Fletcher recognizes this movement toward androgyny as a familiar goal in allegory, noting Mircea Eliade's observation that androgyny is a universal and archaic symbol for wholeness. *Alle-*

gory: The Theory of a Symbolic Mode, p. 356, n. 61. The similarity to Jung's observations is obvious. See, for example, *The Archetypes and the Collective Unconscious,* p. 174.

4. Jung borrows the term *enantiodromia* from Paracelsus in whose work it was used to describe what Jung calls "the regulative function of opposites." Jung (like Miller) rejects the identification of the *I* with reason: "The rational attitude of culture necessarily runs into its opposite, namely the irrational devastation of culture. We should never identify ourselves with reason, for man is not and never will be a creature of reason alone, a fact to be noted by all pedantic culture-mongers. The irrational cannot be and must not be extirpated. The gods cannot and must not die. I said just now that there seems to be something, a kind of superior power, in the human psyche, and that if this is not the idea of God, then it is the 'belly.'" C. G. Jung, *The Collected Works,* Vol. VII: *Two Essays on Analytical Psychology* (New York, 1953), p. 71.

Jung relates the experience of *enantiodromia* to the psychic process of transformation, which I have been tracing in Miller's fiction. This passage was cited earlier in another connection: "The symbolic process is an experience *in images and of images.* Its development usually shows an enantiodromian structure . . . and so presents a rhythm of negative and positive, loss and gain, dark and light. Its beginning is almost invariably characterized by one's getting stuck in a blind alley or in some impossible situation and its goal is, broadly speaking, illumination or higher consciousness, by means of which the initial situation is overcome on a higher level." *The Archetypes and the Collective Unconscious,* pp. 38–39.

5. Mircea Eliade, *The Myth of the Eternal Return,* trans. Willard R. Trask (New York, 1954), p. 18.

6. Miller sees an eventual end to the cyclic process, but before "we recognize the angel in man" we must become "full-fledged monsters"; at the moments when he temporarily achieves his personal spiritual triumphs, he is likely to exclaim that he has become an angel. The parallel between the cosmic *enantiodromia* and the personal is clearly outlined in "Of Art and the Future." See *Sunday after the War,* pp. 146–60. Numerous references to the parallel appear in his fiction.

7. Eliade, p. 88.

8. Eliade recognizes the historical significance of similar insistence on the primacy of individual consolation and "salvation" for men living in historical moments when catastrophe is expected: "To bear the burden of being contemporary with a disastrous period by becoming conscious of the position it occupies in the descending trajectory of the cosmic cycle is an attitude that was especially to demonstrate its effectiveness in the twilight of Greco-Oriental civilization." Ibid., p. 118.

9. Henry Miller, "Reflections on Writing," *The Wisdom of the Heart* (New York, 1941), pp. 27–28.

10. Fletcher, p. 192.

11. Ibid., p. 195.

12. Fletcher's study of allegory emphasizes such elements. Ibid., p. 198. Ritual organization is the second major substructure of allegory, according to Fletcher. Miller's confessions (and the later anatomies) demonstrate his point. Ritual organization, moreover, reveals the causal mechanism of contagious magic. Ibid., pp. 195 ff.

13. Ibid., p. 161.

14. Mark Schorer used this term in his courtroom defense of Miller's *Tropic of Cancer* in Massachusetts. *Henry Miller and the Critics*, ed. Wickes, pp. 161–67.

15. Miller, *Capricorn*, pp. 41–42.

16. Ibid., pp. 106–08.

17. Ibid., pp. 97–98.

18. I am tempted to see in Miller's extensive use of such ritual devices an analogy to what Jung has described as "magical procedures" used to induce the transformational experience. This is a "technical" elaboration of the natural process of transformation. See *Archetypes and the Collective Unconscious*, pp. 128 ff.

19. See Jung, *Two Essays on Analytical Psychology*, p. 225.

20. In one passage in *Capricorn* (pp. 190 ff.), Miller discusses a distinction between "personal" and "impersonal" erections. The "impersonal" world into which coitus introduces the narrator is described in the images which Jung insists are those which describe the archetypal world of the transpersonal unconscious.

21. The term *individuation* is defined and described in Jung, *Psychological Types*, pp. 561–63. It is the process of development, integration, and renewal that I have been tracing. See also Jung's remarks on the centering process in *The Structure and Dynamics of the Psyche*, p. 203. Jung considers the centering process the "never-to-be-surpassed climax of the whole development. . . ."

22. Miller, *Capricorn*, p. 190.

23. Ibid., p. 189.

24. The term is from alchemy; the *descensus ad inferos* of literature (*Faust* is Jung's example) is, according to Jung, "consciously or unconsciously" an *opus alchymicum*. *Psychology and Alchemy*, p. 36.

25. Miller's recognition of Boehme's *Aurora* and his attraction to Boehme seems to me inevitable. (He records this interest in *The Red Notebook* and elsewhere.) Miller's symbols greatly resemble those Boehme uses (in similar contexts) to describe his concept of the *Ungrund*. Boehme accepts the negative road to God. Moreover, his description of the "negative God" differs from the usual mystic conception of God as a God beyond contrasts, and is undeniably suited to Miller's visions of absolute reality. In believing that the "element of negativity is essential to any conception of the Absolute," that "mere light is mere darkness," Boehme accepts the regulatory principle of opposites or *enantiodromia* that Miller dramatizes. Boehme, like Miller, insists that this knowledge of the absolute reality or God comes from his experience of himself. See

Howard Haines Brinton, *The Mystic Will* (New York, 1930), pp. 185 ff. When Miller speaks of becoming an angel he often seems to do so in Boehme's terms.

26. My italics. See Miller, *Capricorn*, p. 208.

27. Neumann, *The Great Mother*, pp. 34–35.

28. Miller, *Capricorn*, pp. 220–21.

29. Jung notes that Boehme's mysticism is strongly influenced by alchemy. *Psychology and Alchemy*, p. 158. Elsewhere he argues that the central alchemical project is essentially the discovery of the self: "The old master saw the alchemical *opus* as a kind of apocatastasis, the restoring of an initial state in an 'eschatological' one ('the end looks to the beginning, and contrariwise'). This is exactly what happens in the individuation process, whether it take the form of a Christian transformation ('Except ye become as little children'), or a *satori* experience in Zen ('show me your original face'), or a psychological process of development in which the original propensity to wholeness becomes a conscious happening.

"For the alchemist it was clear that the 'centre,' or what we would call the self, does not lie in the ego but is outside it, 'in us' yet not 'in our mind,' being located rather in that which we unconsciously are, the 'quid' which we still have to recognize. Today we would call it the unconscious, and we distinguish between a personal unconscious which enables us to recognize the shadow and an impersonal unconscious which enables us to recognize the archetypal symbol of the self. Such a point of view was inaccessible to the alchemist, and having no idea of the theory of knowledge, he had to exteriorize his archetype in the traditional way and lodge it in matter, even though he felt . . . that the centre was paradoxically in man and yet at the same time outside him." *Aion*, p. 169.

30. Brinton selected a typical passage from the *Von sechs theosophischen Punkten*: "As the first will is an Ungrund to be regarded as eternal nothing, we recognize it to be like a mirror wherein one sees his own image. It is like a life and yet no life, but an image and a figure of life. It is like an eye which sees, yet the seeing is without substance. Also we recognize that the eternal Ungrund without nature is a will, like an eye wherein nature is hidden, like a hidden fire which burns not, which is and is not. It is not a spirit, but a form of spirit like the reflection in a mirror. For all the form of spirit is seen in the reflection or in the mirror and yet there is nothing which the eye or mirror sees; but its seeing is in itself for there is nothing before it that were deeper there. . . . And so it is to be understood concerning the eternal hidden wisdom of God which resembles an eternal eye without substance. It is the Ungrund and yet sees all, yet without essence. . . . But no seeing is without spirit, so is also no spirit without seeing. Understand then that the seeing shines out of the spirit, which is its eye and mirror, wherein the will is revealed. For the seeing makes a will in which the Ungrund can find no ground nor limit; therefore its mirror goes into itself and makes a ground in itself, that is a will. Thus the mirror

of the eternal eye shines forth in the will and generates to itself another eternal ground, in itself. This is its centre or heart from which the seeing continually takes its rise from eternity and through which the will becomes moving and directive of that which the centre generates. For all consists in will and is a being which in the eternal Ungrund takes its rise in itself, enters into itself, grasps in itself and makes the centre in itself, but with that which is grasped passes out of itself. It is its own self, and yet as compared to nature it is a nothing; that is, as compared to conceivable being. Yet it is all and all arises from it" (pp. 185–86).

The symbol of the uroboros can be clearly identified near the end of the passage. Miller does not mention Brinton or Boehme in his *Books in My Life;* but he quotes Brinton's study in *The Red Notebook* (Highland, N. C., 1958).

31. Norman O. Brown discusses Freud and Boehme in this connection. He also distinguishes between Boehme's mysticism (which he calls body mysticism) and sublimation mysticism such as that described by Evelyn Underhill. Miller's mysticism is body mysticism in Brown's sense. *Life Against Death,* pp. 309 ff.

32. Fletcher, p. 350.

33. Ibid., p. 353.

34. Miller, *Cancer,* p. 287.

35. Ibid., p. 317.

36. Ibid., p. 318.

37. Ibid., pp. 317–18.

38. Ibid., p. 49.

39. Ibid., p. 67.

40. Ibid., p. 68.

41. Neumann, *The Great Mother,* p. 65.

42. Ibid., p. 222.

43. Fletcher, p. 224.

44. Edmund Wilson, "Twilight of the Expatriates (1938)," *Henry Miller and the Critics,* ed. Wickes, pp. 28, 26.

45. He is speaking of the meaning of the alchemical process. *Psychology and Alchemy,* p. 138.

46. Miller, *Capricorn,* pp. 279–80.

47. I have omitted discussing *Black Spring* as part of a first trilogy. I think, however, that it is not as well integrated as the other volumes and does not deserve the same attention, even though patterns of *enantiodromia* and confrontation of the Archetypal Feminine are clearly part of its structure.

48. Miller, *Capricorn,* p. 280.

49. Ibid., p. 311.

50. Fletcher, pp. 63–64.

51. Fletcher recognizes anatomy as one of the genres in which "action" is engulfed and allegory thrives, for allegorical digressions "tend usually to be expository. . . ." Ibid., p. 319.

index

"Aboriginal self," 109, 110; *see also* Self

Abstract symbols, 33-34

Abyss, 24, 31, 37, 40, 58, 82, 100, 173; crater as, 52, 60; Black Hole of Calcutta as, 95

Alchemy, 123, 134, 135, 137, 193 n, 197 n, 205 n, 214 n; anima in, 87; psychological aspect of, 86

Alchemy and Psychology, 86

Algolagnia, 85, 199 n

Alienation, 68, 108, 109, 114, 115; in the grotesque, 199 n

Allegorical agent, 95, 185; characters as, 143

Allegorical image, 59, 63, 64; defined, 76, 121; and "cosmic order," 120

Allegory, ambivalence and, 170, 181; archetypes and, 156, 204; in *Capricorn*, 103, 124, 128; characters in, 74, 77, 83, 150; form in Miller as, 37, 140, 157, 181; fragmentation and, 104; goal of, 212 n; hero of, 182; large scale meanings and, 137; naturalism

and, 198 n; paralleling and, 166; ritual and, 170, 177, 214 n; romance and, 77, 80, 81, 167, 198 n; surrealism and, 63

Alter ego, 148; child as, 157; shadow figure as, 112, 146

Ambivalence, 45, 197 n; allegory and, 170, 181; filthy world and, 69; toward centers, 171, 178

Anastasia, shadow figure for Mona, 104

Anatomy, 21, 109, 112, 148, 163, 187, 214; characters in, 77, 142, 143, 145, 146, 149, 150, 155; defined, 23, 76, 77, 216 n; romance and, 203 n; weakness of Miller's, 156

Androgyny, as center, 38, 39, 40, 41; as goal in allegory, 212 n; as goal of development, 101, 102, 107, 164; human perfection and, 203 n; in hierarchy of psychic contents, 121; self and, 107, 116; significance of, 71; uroboros and, 193 n

Anima, and Archetypal Feminine,

Child, as archetype, 110, 156

Childhood, 72; as center, 164, 180; return to, 134, 207 n

Christ, 138-39, 157, 172, 206 n, 207 n, 208 n; alchemy and, 135; as child archetype, 156; fish and, 193 n; shadow of, 138, 208 n; symbol of self, 109, 110, 113, 136

Christian symbols, 138, 207 n, 208 n; *see also* Anti-Christ, Christ, Cross, Devil, Second Coming

Circe, 81, 82, 87, 89, 94, 175

Circle, 126; magic, 127, 205 n; and mandala, 127; significance of, 200 n; squaring of, 205 n

Circumambulatio, see Centering process

City, 24, 25, 26, 143; as centers, 133, 164; elemental symbolism of, 23, 90, 186, 187; feminine significance of, 50, 57; future of, 116; relation to form, 37; as source of imagery, 27, 94, 128; *see also* Dijon, New York, Paris

Clam, and *vagina dentata*, 195 n

Claude, as child archetype, 156

Cleo, 65, 66, 67; as negative elementary character, 68, 69, 70, 197 n

Clown, 60; as symbol of self, 110

Coitus, symbolic, 57, 96, 107, 109, 167, 171, 184

Collective unconscious, 111, 142, 143, 203 n; and archetype of self, 111; relation to personal unconscious, 134; *see also* Archetypes, Transpersonal unconscious

Compulsion, 55, 58, 100; and allegory, 185

Coney Island, 26; of the mind, 51

Confession, 19-49, 92, 94, 97, 100, 112, 149, 155, 177, 187, 214 n; as allegory, 104; anima and, 90; consciousness in, 75; defined, 26, 35, 46, 117; grotesque and, 86; integration and, 49, 77, 150; role

of hero in, 57; role of women in, 70; romance and, 203 n; stylized figures and, 142; symbolic action in, 70, 95

Coniunctio, 71

Conrad Moricand, and anatomy, 143

Consciousness, 20, 29, 33, 44, 48, 59, 62, 110, 128; enlargement of, 21, 89, 101, 111, 139, 141, 160, 173; evolution of, 122; experience of unconscious and, 23, 27, 28, 34, 38, 43, 47, 48, 62, 90, 98, 102, 122, 131, 200 n, 203 n; failure of, 182; light as, 124; masculine nature of, 71; sun as, 102; uroboric incest and, 130

Contagion, 171, 172, 179

Contamination, 180

Control of repressed tendencies, 81

Correspondence, between microcosm and macrocosm, 166

Corridors, 42, 58, 124, 125; *see also* Labyrinth

Cosmic images, 137

"Cosmic joy," 165

"Cosmic order," and allegorical image, 120

Creative change, and center, 127; and unconscious, 182, 201 n

Creative Evolution, 113, 114

Creative process, as subject, 107

Creativity, 41, 44, 45; won from unconscious, 49, 114

Cross, 136, and bed, 207 n, 208 n

Crucifixion, 135; rosy, 140

Crystallization of the anima, 92

Dark Lady, 19, 80, 104

"Dead center," *see* Center

Death, 36, 43, 82, 91, 101, 130, 152, 200 n; desire for, 48, 88, 131, 133; as dissolution, 55, 57, 69, 141; rebirth and, 165; represented by female figure, 25, 34, 40, 44, 45, 51, 88, 99, 206 n

Demonic, 19, 33, 163, 171, 194 n;

Jane A. Nelson is currently a member of the department of English, Bradford Junior College, Bradford, Massachusetts. She has taught in the department of American thought and language, Michigan State University; the University of Maryland, Munich Branch; and Eastern Michigan University. She received her B.A. from Mount Holyoke College (1948) and M.A. and Ph.D. (1949, 1966) from the University of Michigan.

The manuscript was edited by Elizabeth Pass. The book was designed by Don Ross. The type face for the text is Linotype Janson originally cut by Nicholas Kis about 1690; and the display face is Caslon and Caslon 540 based on designs originally cut by William Caslon in the 18th century. The book is printed on Warren's Olde Style Antique paper and bound in Interlaken's AHS Homespun cloth over boards. Manufactured in the United States of America.

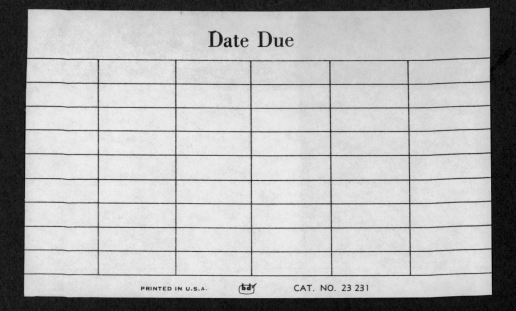